Books in the Series

The Practice of Solidarity

THE PRACTICE
OF SOLIDARITY

American Hat Finishers
in the Nineteenth Century

DAVID BENSMAN

UNIVERSITY OF ILLINOIS PRESS

Urbana and Chicago

*Publication of this work was supported in part
by a grant from the Andrew W. Mellon Foundation.*

LIBRARY OF CONGRESS CATALOGING IN PUBLICATION DATA

Bensman, David, 1949–
  The practice of solidarity.

  (The Working class in American history)
  Bibliography: p.
  Includes index.
    1. Trade-unions — Hat trade — United States — History —
19th century. 2. Hatters — United States — History — 19th
century. 3. Boycott — United States — History — 19th
century. I. Title. II. Series.
  HD6515.H3B46 1984   331.88'18741'0973   83–6592
  ISBN 0-252-01093-0

Contents

Acknowledgments

ONE DAMP DAY day in the spring of 1974, when I was on the verge of abandoning my study of hatters' trade unionism for lack of sources, I wearily trudged across West 42 Street in Manhattan to the storage annex of the New York Public Library. There I discovered old copies of two trade journals previously believed to be missing from the library, their sole depository. I am profoundly grateful to all those who have built up and maintained the library's collections, and to the many librarians who provided access to a vast collection of material about the lives of Americans who so often are invisible. I especially want to thank Dorothy Swanson of New York University's Tamiment Library, which holds the hatters' papers.

Unearthing the hatting journals made it possible for me to write my dissertation, but Professor Kenneth Jackson of Columbia University gave me the guidance and understanding that made writing the thesis more than an academic exercise. At the time, I did not appreciate his careful reading, abundant criticisms, and frequent advice to go back to the library for more information; now that I advise doctoral candidates, I recognize the extraordinary effort and skill Professor Jackson brought to academic advising.

Anyone who reads this book will perceive Herbert Gutman's influence throughout. Professor Gutman's writings and lectures on working class culture and black history sensitized me to the traditional elements of the hatters' work habits; without Gutman's example, the evidence buried in the hatting journals would most likely have remained a cipher to me. Later, as I began to transform my unwieldy dissertation into the present book, Gutman's advice, support, and encouragement were there whenever I needed them.

I was also fortunate to have David Montgomery's severe and thorough criticism at crucial stages in the development of this manuscript. Montgomery insisted that by emphasizing the traditional elements of the hatters' practice, I was missing the way hatters' developed new, more collective forms of social action. After being subjected to repeated doses of his tren-chant criticism, I finally began to see that what was involved in the hatters' turn to the union label boycott was the transformation of craftsmen into class-conscious workers.

When I began my study of the hatters' practice of solidarity, I often re-marked that history remained the bastion of academic individualism, but I am now impressed with the collective nature of our enterprise. Portions of my study of the hatters' trade unionism have been read by a long list of peo-ple, all of whom contributed to the final product. I would like to acknowl-edge the help of Craig Calhoun, Virginia Yans, Milton Cantor, Carol Steinsapir, Michael Merrill, John McClure, Roberta Lynch, Leonard El-lis, Lee Schlesinger, Joseph Bensman, Stuart Bruchey, Luther Carpenter, William Kornblum, Bogdan Denitch, B. J. Widick, John Harper, Jack Metzgar, and Warren Susman.

My understanding of the hatters' changing practice of solidarity was also shaped by political and trade union activists who first taught me what soli-darity was all about. Carl Shier, Bernard Rifkin, Edward Sadlowski, Bren-dan Sexton, and Herman Benson shaped my understanding of the labor movement; Deborah Meier, Michael Harrington, and Irving Howe shaped the way I understand social movements and social change.

There are others whose counsel I wish I had followed. If I had paid closer attention to the advice and example of Joan Scott and Alice Kessler-Harris when I began this study, I would have been more alert to the roles played by working women in communities like Orange and Danbury, and I would have paid more attention to the organization of the hat trimmers, as well as to the hat finishers' mothers, sisters, wives, and daughters. By the time I understood my mistake, it was too late to redress it.

Support for this study was provided by the New Jersey Historical Com-mission, the Graduate School of Education of Rutgers University, and the Rutgers University Research Council.

Shelley Herochek gave of her time and enthusiasm, and she made com-pleting this manuscript not only possible, but fun.

Finally, I would like to thank Joseph and Marilyn Bensman for their pa-tience and understanding, as well as for all they taught me.

This book is dedicated to the memory of the late Gerhard Meyer of the College of the University of Chicago.

Introduction

T HE THIRD OF FEBRUARY, 1908, was a black day for the American labor movement. On that day, the Supreme Court of the United States ruled that organized labor was subject to the Sherman Anti-Trust Act. For the losers in the Court decision, the United Hatters of North America, there was a terrible irony in the fact that a federal law passed under tremendous pressure from antibusiness farmers and workers to control the predatory practices of the robber barons was being applied to a tiny craft union. The Court ruling, known as *Loewe v. Lawlor,* meant that unions were no longer exempt from prosecution for conspiracy to restrain trade; the hatters' chief weapon, the union label boycott, was illegal.

The case began in 1901 when Walter Gordon Merritt, a Harvard undergraduate, returned to his native Danbury, Connecticut, during a school recess and met with two Danbury hat manufacturers who were operating nonunion factories; one was his father, Charles H. Merritt, and the other was Dietrich E. Loewe, a German immigrant who had risen from the ranks of the journeymen to become an employer thirty years before. Loewe told his friend's son that the United Hatters of North America had threatened to call a boycott against his goods and against all retailers who sold them unless Loewe agreed to recognize the union, adhere to its work rules, and hire its members only. The union's threat was not idle; just weeks before, its boycott against Roelofs of Philadelphia had ended in victory.

Walter Gordon Merritt was an idealist, imbued with the laissez-faire ideology he had learned at Harvard, and he was combative. He urged Loewe not to give in to the union's demands; instead, Merritt devised a three-part counteroffensive. To reverse the pro-union tide of public opinion, Merritt wrote a pamphlet, "The Neglected Side of Trade Unionism: The Boycott," which painstakingly argued that union boycotts on behalf of the closed shop were tyrannical violations of the rights of nonunion workers, innocent consumers, and honest businessmen. Merritt's flair for public relations was quickly evident; his pamphlet was reprinted and quoted in newspapers and magazines throughout the country.

The second component of Merritt's strategy was organization. In 1902, he established the American Anti-Boycott Association in New York City. The association's goal was to unite employers in support of businessmen beset by labor boycotts. Loewe was the first recipient of this support. After the United Hatters of North America struck Loewe's factory on 25 July 1902, and declared a nationwide boycott of his goods, Loewe counterattacked. With the support of the American Anti-Boycott Association and its legal adviser, Daniel Davenport, he filed suit with the sheriff of Fairfield County on 12 September 1903, asking that the sheriff attach the homes and bank accounts of 240 Connecticut hatters so that Loewe could seek treble damages from them for conspiring to restrain his trade in hats. Twelve years later, the Supreme Court upheld lower court judgements against the unionists and ordered them to pay $252,130 in damages, even though some of those so ordered had neither approved of the strike and boycott nor participated in them.

Individual members of the United Hatters never had to pay that judgement, however. In a crowning act of solidarity, the American Federation of Labor declared 27 January 1916 as "Hatters' Day" and collected contributions from workers throughout the country to defray the Court-ordered damages.

Nevertheless, the Danbury hatters' case was a terrible blow to organized labor, for it halted labor's massive turn-of-the-century organizing drive which, by means of sympathy strikes and label boycotts, had brought more than 1,500,000 workers into the unions during the recovery from the depression of 1893. Furthermore, the decision marked a fateful step in the growth of the employer counteroffensive against trade unionism. *Loewe v. Lawlor* showed that if employers united, and enlisted the federal courts on their side, the power of skilled workers and their unions could be challenged. American labor tried to defend itself against this threat by engaging in electoral politics more intensely than it ever had before; labor's efforts on behalf of Democrats in the election of 1912 yielded the Clayton Act (1914), which the unions hoped would exempt them from antitrust action, but employers, led by Walter Gordon Merritt, were more successful in their collective approach to labor struggles. On the industrial level, they organized employers' associations; on the community level, they organized citizens' alliances; and on the political level, they not only dominated the post–World War I Democratic and Republican parties, but also enlisted the federal courts in their campaigns against the unions. The open shop drive of 1921–24, buttressed by such Supreme Court decisions as Hitchman Coal and Coke and Coronado Fuel, broke the back of the American labor movement. It would take a breakdown of the American economy, massive organizing campaigns by unskilled workers, a realignment of the American party system, and a revolution in the role of the federal government for organized labor to reestablish its power.

Every standard history of labor recounts the Danbury hatters' case, but none captures the full significance of the hatters' defeat, for none explores why employers had to go to the courts in the first place. Why were the boycotts and sympathy strikes so successful?

For more than a century prior to *Loewe v. Lawlor,* skilled workers had perfected the practice of solidarity. Since 1800, hatters had pursued increasingly collective strategies for controlling the work process and the labor market. They had drawn on their pride as craftsmen to create a militant local unionism in the first half of the nineteenth century, and then they sacrificed local autonomy to build a strong national union. When the hat finishers found that their craft union could not win on its own, they joined with allied workers in 1896 to form the United Hatters of North America. Their new union immediately turned to the AF of L to enlist the entire labor movement on its side.

In the years 1898–1902, the hatters' boycotts brought astonishing success. Alerted by the "We Don't Patronize" list circulated by the American Federation of Labor, American workers shunned hats that lacked the United Hatters' label, and they pressured local retail shops not to carry them. By 1902, workers' solidarity had forced all but 12 of America's 190 hat manufacturers to grant union recognition. The hatters' success at choking the sale of Dietrich Loewe's hats in far-flung places like San Francisco, California, and Richmond, Virginia, spurred Loewe and his supporters in the American Anti-Boycott Association to counterattack in the federal courts.

Thirty years later, the young workers who struck to regain the ground labor had lost in the federal courts knew nothing of "Hatters' Day" or the working class solidarity it symbolized. Recently, however, labor historians have begun to rediscover that past.

In 1977, when I began writing my dissertation on the experiences of

nineteenth-century hat finishers, I wrote, "The discipline of American labor history grew out of the study of economics, and has not yet shaken free
from its origin." Those words are no longer true. The recent appearance of
Herbert Gutman's *Work, Culture and Society,* David Brody's *Workers in Industrial America,* David Montgomery's *Workers' Control in America,* and James
Green's *The World of the Worker* reflect how greatly the field has changed.[1]
This recent literature has uncovered a great many aspects of the historical
experience of American workers that had long been forgotten. Some of the
most interesting literature has shown how workers' solidarity enabled them
to maintain much control of the process of production in the late nineteenth
and early twentieth centuries.[2]

Social relations in the workplace were entirely different then than now.
In 1904, the U.S. commissioner of labor, Carroll Wright, documented the
extent to which American workers throughout the industrial economy restricted their output in order to conserve jobs, resist speedup, and maintain
piece rates.[3] Their practices spurred employers to attempt to force or otherwise induce their employees to work harder and faster. The result was a
fierce struggle in such places as steel mills, machine shops, and foundries, a
conflict which could not be contained in local areas or single industries, but
which spilled over into the national arena, where the bitterness of conflict in
the Los Angeles building trades (1910), the Pennsylvania anthracite fields
(1901), the Colorado mining fields (1914), and the national steel industry
(1919) all elicited great public concern and demands for some sort of collective resolution.

During these struggles, one of the employers' chief weapons for inducing
workers to increase production was some sort of incentive pay system by
which employees would earn substantially higher wages if they boosted output above past levels. Despite the fact that businessmen often went to great
lengths to prove to their employees that both would profit from increased
productivity, in case after case, in union and nonunion shops, American
workers resisted the imposition of the premium pay plans, insisting instead
on maintaining their formal and informal control on the pace of work and
levels of output. Eventually, when employers realized that premium pay
plans were inadequate to the task, they turned to various forms of management reform, including scientific management, welfarism, and personnel
management, to break their employees' resistance.[4]

How were workers able to put up such resistance? First of all, for individual workers to resist the temptations offered by incentive plans, they had to
have a very strong sense of their common interest. They did not think of

themselves simply as individuals. Furthermore, for the campaign to resist incentive pay to be successful, it was necessary not only for workers to organize formal institutions — local and national unions — but it was also necessary for individual craftsmen and operatives to restrict their output. When foremen came round to drive you, when time-study men stood by to clock you, when management experts called you into their offices to cajole you to take advantage of your opportunities, you had to make an individual decision — to stand in solidarity with your workmates or to take advantage of personal opportunity.[5] As Daniel Clawson pointed out in his study of *Bureaucracy and the Labor Process:*

> The best evidence of worker success in enforcing output levels is the simple fact that in most cases, all of the piecework employees earned essentially the same amount, a result that would be practically impossible if each individual worker independently tried to do his or her best. At the Rock Island Arsenal, for example, records showed that during each of four test days spread over six months, each of the twenty-seven polishers earned a minimum of $3.41 and a maximum of $3.52 for eight hours work. . . . The harness makers . . . each produced exactly four hundred (leather) covers in fourteen hours. . . . This uniformity of output did not just happen by chance. Workers collectively decided on production levels. . . .[6]

The campaigns to maintain control of the workplace in the early twentieth century testify to the fact that American workers were joined in tight solidarity in the workplace, that they shared a sense of common interest and commitment to collective work rules that is hard to imagine from the vantage point of a society that has been permeated by a different set of values. Where that sense of solidarity came from, and how it was maintained, is a question central to labor history.

Earlier labor historians did not have a way to explain the solidarity underlying the workers' control struggles. Scholars working in the tradition of John R. Commons analyzed such behavior as simply the workers' rational response to their economic situation: workers resisted premium pay plans because they knew that in the long run, speedup would eliminate jobs and drive down piece rates. That explanation is inadequate because it speculates about why workers behaved as they did, but it does not explain how they were able to put up such resistance, for premium pay plans did offer the individual worker a chance to improve his or her earnings. How were workers able to forge common bonds of solidarity to overcome the individu-

al tugs of opportunity? The economic model provides an incomplete answer to this question.

This economic approach to labor history goes back a long way and is
rooted in the soil of American labor. Richard T. Ely, an economist at Johns
Hopkins University, pioneered in the study of labor history in the 1880s.
His student and chosen successor, John R. Commons of the University of
Wisconsin, established the field in the early years of the twentieth century.
For more than fifty years, scholars followed in their footsteps, writing dozens of books on the development of trade unions and trade union practices.[7]
In the pages of this vast literature, the economic underpinnings and institu-
tional dynamics of labor organizations emerge in sharp focus; this volume
on the hatters' trade unionism is deeply endebted to the work of Commons
and his many disciples.

Nevertheless, the ideological perspective of these institutional labor historians narrowed their vision in important respects. In this literature, workers themselves are rarely discussed or described as people; instead, they are
defined abstractly as economic actors, concerned with improving their market position and thereby their material conditions of life. Indeed, most
workers receive not even such cursory treatment, for labor historians generally ignored the nine-tenths of the labor force that did not belong to trade
unions—almost all blacks, women, and unskilled workers were excluded.

Skilled craftsmen are the subject of this labor history, but only a small
spectrum of their activities is the focus of study. In the Commons model,
the forces of economic change, unleashed by the transportation revolution,
had induced artisans to surrender their concern for control over their work,
for social equality, and for opportunities for entrepreneurship. They had
become a homogeneous mass, forward-looking, job-conscious, and pragmatic. Like most other Americans, their primary goals were materialistic;
they wanted higher pay for shorter work days. To that end, they tried to
limit the labor supply by enforcing apprenticeship restrictions and the
closed shop rule. They had no special group character; such anachronistic
phenomena had been dissolved in the tide of industrialization that swept
over America after the Civil War. Organizations like the Knights of St.
Crispin and the Knights of Labor reflected only the lingering vestiges of
premodern group consciousness.

Radical historians, such as Phillip Foner, disagreed with Commons and
his followers about the relative appropriateness of "reform" versus "business" unionism but shared with the Commons paradigm an "economic" ap-

proach to workers' consciousness. Both mainstream and radical labor historians agreed that differences in trade union behavior could be explained primarily in terms of the differences in the economic conditions in which labor organizations operated; carpenters had more control of their work and stronger business unions than shoemakers had because product markets in the building trades remained narrower than those in the boot and shoe industry.

Thus it happened that although the historical experience of skilled workers has been rich with political action, ethnic conflict and accommodation, and wrenching cultural adaptations to changing economic realities, most studies of craftsmen have focused primarily on the institutional development of their unions, particularly with respect to their efforts to limit the labor supply by maintaining artificially high skill standards and by restricting entrance into the union. The goal underlying this development is defined a priori rather than discerned through careful study; it is simply to secure improvements in "wages, hours, and working conditions."

The phrase "wages, hours, and working conditions" is such a cliché, sounds so natural to our ears, that we rarely stop to think what it means. "Working conditions" can include many things, not simply the dirtiness or cleanliness of a workplace, its temperature, ventilation, noise level, and lighting, though these are important. It can also include authority relations in the workplace; how the work process is designed and who designs it; how work is distributed and who distributes it; how fast work is done and who determines the speed. Nevertheless, most of the studies done in the tradition of Ely and Commons included "working conditions" as an afterthought. Even George Barnett's masterful study of *The Printers* (1909), which did describe the union's attempts to prescribe work rules, did not take these efforts seriously in interpreting the union's history; Barnett, like his fellow scholars, limited himself to searching for "economic" motivations for all workers' behavior and so "wages" became the primary goal of the skilled workers of this historical tradition.[8]

Labor history's narrowness was not simply academic; it was a serious political matter. Such leaders of the American Federation of Labor as Samuel Gompers and Adolph Strasser joined with Commons and Perlman in stressing that their movement's goals were materialistic. They hoped to legitimate trade unionism by defining the unions' goals as being similar to those of all other participants in the capitalist marketplace of classical economics, similar to those of entrepreneurs, of managers, and of consumers.

Legitimating trade unionism was an urgent and continuing goal, for businessmen bitterly denied and contested the right of workers to organize and bargain collectively in their own interests.[9]

These challenges by businessmen and conservatives to trade unionism's very existence were so severe and traumatic at Haymarket, Homestead, Pullman, and Ludlow, during the depression of 1893, and in the open-shop drives of 1904 and 1922 that a terrible irony emerged: in time, everybody forgot that the early claims by labor leaders that their goals were strictly materialistic, just like everybody else's, were polemical claims made for the purposes of legitimation. In sum, trade unionists came to believe their own rhetoric. Today most trade unionists have a very narrow conception of their institutions' proper sphere, even though the American labor movement is, and always has been, a leading force for reform in many arenas.[10]

Finally, the institutional focus of historical writing developed because scholars relied on the unions' documents, usually those at the national level, for most of their information about the skilled workers' experiences. As a result, historical writing has tended to confine itself to the activities therein recorded. Such studies overlook the fact that workers are human beings, with varied and complex motivations. They are members of families, neighborhoods, ethnic groups, and political parties. Moreover, skilled workers belong to a particular community, their craft, which has its own norms, values, and systems of shared meaning.

This study focuses on one such group of skilled workers, the hat finishers. In the late nineteenth century, three thousand union hatters "finished" fur felt hats in factories located in a narrow corridor stretching from Boston, Massachusetts, to Philadelphia, Pennsylvania. Danbury, Connecticut, and Orange, New Jersey, were the leading hat centers. Today, the hat finishers are almost entirely forgotten, even in the towns where they once were dominant. Previous histories of hatters' unionism ignore how journeymen were able to maintain solidarity and control their work. They are primarily accounts of the development of the United Hat, Cap and Millinery Workers International Union. They limit their treatment of the nineteenth century to the early unions' efforts to control the labor supply by closing hat factories to semiskilled workers.[11]

Evidence to chronicle those efforts can be found in the records of the hatters' unions, as well as in the trade journals read by journeymen hatters, union officials, foremen, manufacturers, wholesalers, material suppliers, and retailers. These sources also contain much fascinating information that cannot be fit into the Commons school paradigm of institutional development. There is much data about how hatters interacted with each other and with their employers, about their moral code, their sense of the past, their attitudes toward money and individual advancement. Hundreds of pages of material deal with their work practices, their conflicts with their employers over ways of working, their struggle to maintain control of the work process. Some of the material is startling, according little with our notions about factory labor during the era of industrialization. For example, there were several strikes over the issue of the journeymen's drinking privileges, the end result of which was that finishers retained their ability to leave their factories to drink beer in nearby saloons whenever they wished; alternatively, they could have their apprentices bring in pails of beer.

Analysis of material of this sort led me to the conclusion that while it is true that hatters attempted to maintain relatively high wages by organizing unions to prevent manufacturers from reducing skill standards, it would be a mistake to interpret the workers' actions as being motivated solely by these narrowly materialistic considerations. There was more to it than that. In the late nineteenth century, hat finishers attempted not merely to keep up their wages, but to preserve their culture, their way of life, and their sense of solidarity. Moreover, journeymen valued tradition itself; their union existed, at least in part, to maintain customs whose economic value had since been forgotten, but whose significance for personal and social satisfaction were never subject to doubt.

In the musty pages of a long-forgotten work of labor history, Ethelbert Stewart's "Documentary History of the Early Organization of Printers" (1905), I found a key to the understanding of craft unionism:

> Not only are the economic reasons for some of the things done by the unions to be found in a study of their history; but the gradual transformation of sentiments into customs and the evolution of trade interests into "union principles" [went] on gradually. . . . In the early constitutions and minutes of these organizations will be frequently found stated in terms [sic] those "union principles" which have since become a part of the subconscious thought life of the "union man," and no longer printed or stated because nobody in the union supposes it necessary to state basic principles. . . . So much of this revealed ultimate principle exists; so much depends upon an understanding of this submerged or subconscious, and to the trade unionist axiomatic, hence never expressed, thought life that students of organizations coming from a different mental atmosphere often fail to find in the unions that which is the reason for their existence — the soul of purpose for which

they live. These "fundamental principles of trade unionism" are often the codified experience of former generations under industrial conditions that no longer exist.[12]

When one begins with the assumption that hatters cooperated formally and informally to preserve their traditional values, one can gain a coherent understanding of the endless battles journeymen fought to promote and defend their work rules. Such rules as "going on turn," "piece rates," "no firing," "passing the buck," cannot be understood simply as rational strategies for raising wages; instead, they had a logic of their own. Taken together, they enabled hatters to remain autonomous, "manly," fair-minded, and egalitarian workers.

Hatters practiced solidarity under circumstances not of their own choosing. As manufacturers and commission houses took advantage of improvements in transportation to sell hats in ever wider markets, competition in the hatting trade became intense. This competition bred employer challenges to the hatters' control of the workplace. To protect themselves, journeymen had to develop new practices of solidarity. Their reverence for tradition did not deter them from adapting to altered circumstances but it did shape the way they responded. This book is the story of their struggle. It is dedicated to the memory of those who carried on that struggle, and to those who carry it on today, the hatters' heirs.

NOTES

1. Herbert Gutman, *Work, Culture and Society* (New York: Alfred Knopf, 1976); David Brody, *Workers in Industrial America* (New York: Oxford University Press, 1980); David Montgomery, *Workers' Control in America* (Cambridge: Cambridge University Press, 1979); James R. Green, *The World of the Worker* (New York: Hill and Wang, 1980).

2. See for example, David Montgomery, *Workers' Control in America;* Daniel Clawson, *Bureaucracy and the Labor Process* (New York: Monthly Review Press, 1980); Harry Braverman, *Labor and Monopoly Capital* (New York: Monthly Review Press, 1974); Gregory S. Kealy, "The Honest Workingman and Workers' Control," *Labour/Le travailleur* (1976), pp. 32–68.

3. U.S. Bureau of Labor, *Eleventh Annual Report,* "Regulation and Restriction of Output."

4. David Montgomery, "Whose Standards: Workers and the Reorganization of Production in the United States, 1900–20," in Montgomery, *Worker's Control in America,* pp. 122–23.

5. Clawson, *Bureaucracy and the Labor Process,* p. 174.

6. Ibid., p. 176.

7. Maurice Isserman, "God Bless Our American Institutions: The Labor History of John R. Commons," *Labor History* 17 (Summer 1976): 309-28.

8. George Barnett, *The Printers* (Cambridge, Mass.: Harvard University Press, 1909).

9. Isserman, "God Bless Our American Institutions," pp. 310, 327.

10. The most extensive presentation of this last assertion is "The Invisible Mass Movement" in Michael Harrington's *Socialism* (New York: Saturday Review Press, 1972), pp. 250-70.

11. Charles Green, *The Headwear Workers* (New York: Hat, Cap and Millinery Workers Union, 1944); Donald B. Robinson, *Spotlight on a Union* (New York: Dial Press, 1948).

12. Ethelbert Stewart, "Documentary History of the Early Organizations of Printers," U.S. Bureau of Labor, *Bulletin* 61 (Nov. 1905): 859.

CHAPTER 1

The Hatting Industry

T HE HISTORY OF the hatting industry in the nineteenth century resembles, in broad outline, that of many other skilled trades, such as shoemaking, cooperage, and iron manufacture. Alan Dawley's history of the shoe industry of Lynn, Massachusetts, chronicles how small producers operating in local markets gave way to industrialists who owned large factories manufacturing goods for sale throughout the United States and abroad. Merchant capitalists created and met new market demands by replacing labor-intensive production requiring highly skilled craftsmen with new industrial methods; workshops saw labor divided increasingly fine, and new machines displaced increasingly large proportions of the work force. Consequently, the craftsmen's status declined; the ratio of their wages to the value of their output shrank as the decades passed.[1] The fur felt hatting trade did not undergo as radical a transformation as that experienced by the shoemaking industry; in 1880 the finishing departments of fur felt hat factories still depended on highly skilled journeymen to prepare their products for sale.

The Early Hatting Industry: 1800–1825

At the beginning of the nineteenth century, the limitations of America's overland transportation facilities discouraged the geographical concentration of hat production and limited the division of labor within hat shops. In his 1810 survey of American industry, Tench Coxe found that in the twelve eastern states from Maine to Virginia, and in the District of Columbia, hatting was conducted in 68 percent (161) of the 238 counties. Of course, most shops were small, employing four or fewer men; many were part-time affairs run by farmers who turned to hatting for a few months each winter. Such small enterprises accounted for half the hats manufactured in the young republic. In only 21 counties did hat shops average five or more employees, and of these, three had twenty or fewer men. The remaining coun-

1

ties, ranging from Norfolk, Virginia, in the South, to Rockingham, New Hampshire, in the North, and Berks, Pennsylvania, in the West, produced half the hats made in the United States.[2]

Among the leading hat centers was Danbury, Connecticut, where, as early as 1802, the firm of the brothers Salmon and Seymour Wildman had begun producing hats for export to its own retail outlets in Charleston, South Carolina, and Savannah, Georgia. By 1810 it had nearly fifty employees.[3] The nation's largest hat factory was in Boston, on the Charles River, where 150 men turned out hats for sale in the South and overseas, but the cost of overland freight kept most shops much smaller. Even in Danbury, most of the fifty-six hat shops operating in 1808–10 were jerry-built affairs, set up by farmers who hired 2 to 4 men to work during the winter season.[4]

One of Danbury's early hatters was Ezra Mallory. In 1823, at age thirty-eight, he abandoned farming and cattle-raising to start his own hatting business. With capital borrowed from neighbors, he put up a little wood-shed where he worked at a bench beside his lone employee, a journeyman hatter, and his apprentice, a local boy who boarded out at Mallory's expense. At first, Mallory's sales were confined to the immediate vicinity, as he rode through the countryside, soliciting orders from farmers in the beautiful Housatonic River valley. Most of his products were paid for in kind; with the foodstuffs he received, Mallory paid his assistants and the neighboring Indians, who sold him his pelts, although sometimes he found it necessary to travel as far as Canada to secure an adequate supply of fur.[5]

Despite its primitive beginnings, Mallory's business expanded by 1825, fed by a contract secured from a nearby factory. Soon the young firm had six men working in a "plank-room, small and inconvenient, gathered around one kettle, heated by means of a furnace filled with wood underneath. . . ." Mallory's salesmen rode on horseback throughout New England, in search of customers for the firm's growing output.[6]

The difficulty of transporting completed hats inhibited the development of Danbury's hatting industry. For Ezra Mallory to sell his goods in the great New York market, he had to load his products on the stagecoach which left Danbury for Norwalk every day at 7 A.M., or he could load his own horse and walk it to the port on Long Island Sound. Although the twenty-five-mile trip took most of the day, it was only the first leg of Mallory's journey. Once in port, he had to wait "until the tide suited" the sailing schooner which would carry his hats to New York. In good weather his passage took a full day and during storms could take considerably longer. Of course, there was an alternative to sea travel: during bad weather, Danbury hat manufacturers hired a special stagecoach, but progress on the muddy roads was not very fast either.

One way or another, Mallory reached New York, where he had to visit the various haberdashers to sell them his wares, hat bodies in the rough. Often, by the time he had finished disposing of his goods, sailed back across the Sound, and walked back to Danbury, "more than a week [had] passed."[7]

Cyrus Jones, one of Orange, New Jersey's, pioneer hatters, had a shorter trip to the New York market, but not an easier one, for in the early days of the nineteenth century, he carried his goods on his back the full fifteen miles, crossing the Passaic and Hackensack rivers by flatboat on the way. His return trip was no less arduous, for Jones merely substituted pelts bought in New York for his original burden.[8]

Such transportation blockages shaped the American hatting industry. Because hats were bulky and fragile, manufacturers carrying them to market on horseback, or even on their own backs, found it impossible to transport their finished products overland in sufficient quantities to make the trade profitable. Consequently, the hatting trade divided: outside the large urban markets, hatters like Ezra Mallory and Cyrus Jones made only hat bodies, which could be rolled up two together in a paper and wrapped in a linen bag. "In this manner six to eight dozen could be fit into a leather sack, to be carried into market by stage, or loaded on horseback."[9] In New York, Boston, and Philadelphia, retailers employed journeymen to finish the hats for final sale.

In smaller hat shops outside the trade centers, early artisans made hats from start to finish. Their job consisted of four tasks, each difficult and complex. First, craftsmen made felt from the fur fibers of animal pelts, a process called "forming." Next, they shrank, hardened, and shaped the felt until it was thick and stiff; this was called "making" or "sizing." Third came dyeing, a separate process performed in the larger shops by a specialist.

Finally, the hat was "finished", a task which remained essentially unchanged throughout the century. After drying the hat body over a kettle, the journeymen would rub ("pounce") the outer surface with pumice, seal skin, or emery paper. Then he would stiffen it by applying a mixture of beer grounds to the inside of the crown and cover that mixture with shellac or glue. Since the hat had now lost most of its original shape, the craftsman would soften it with steam and then press it with a hot iron, known as a "shell," in which a heated metal slug was placed. The still-pliable hat would

then be placed over the finishing block, moulded to the block's shape by a
tight string, and ironed again. Now the hat was nearly done. The finisher
had only to cut the brim to proper size and shape it with a guided knife,
known as a rounding-jack; then he would pluck out any remaining surface
hairs with a tweezers. After he had completed these tasks, he would turn the
hat over to a female trimmer, who would sew in the lining and affix a ribbon or hat band.[10]

Hats produced in this manner were expensive. In 1810, fur hats sold for
$3 each; twenty-two years later, "fair quality" headwear was worth $2–2.50,
while finer goods brought as much as $6.15 to $10.[11] Hatters' wages were
also good. Journeymen earned approximately $1.25 per day in the first
quarter of the century; in 1831, labor costs amounted to 42 percent of the
value of the product, a figure which seems very large when one considers
that furs and dyestuffs, the raw materials from which hats were made, were
themselves expensive.[12] As the industry expanded in the following decades,
labor costs would fall.

The Expansion of Markets

In the second quarter of the nineteenth century, the American economy
changed rapidly as businessmen took advantage of opportunities created by
improvements in transportation, overland and on the waters. The building
of turnpikes and canals, and the operation of steamboats, made freight
transportation cheaper and faster. This enabled entrepreneurs to expand
markets for manufactured products as it accelerated population movements, opened new land for agriculture, and stimulated the growth of
cities, particularly in the Ohio and Mississippi River valleys. Such changes
hastened the development of American industry and, at the same time, encouraged the concentration of manufacturing in areas having good access
to labor and raw materials. The hatting trade expanded and concentrated
apace.

Danbury's access to the New York market improved markedly during
Ezra Mallory's lifetime. In 1825, a steamboat began to run regularly between Norwalk and New York, speeding up the voyage and making it less
vulnerable to bad weather. When Commodore Vanderbilt opened a competing line in 1828, the trip became cheaper (twenty-five cents each way) as
well.[13] Such improvements allowed Danbury and the other industry centers
to increase their share of hat production at the expense of small rural shops

making goods for local markets. By 1850, almost 90 percent of all hats made in the United States came from five Northeastern states: New York (43.4 percent of the total market value), New Jersey (15.7 percent), Pennsylvania (11.2 percent), Connecticut (10.5 percent), and Massachusetts (8.3 percent). Elsewhere hat manufacture dwindled.[14]

By the time the Danbury and Norwalk railroad began running in 1852, Danbury hat production had expanded dramatically. In 1856, E. A. Mallory and Company produced 8,640 dozen hats, enjoying annual sales of $155,000 on a capital investment of $20,000. Its work force totaled one hundred hands. Nor was Mallory's the largest firm; Tweedy and White's sales amounted to $400,000.[15]

Long gone were the days when Cyrus Jones and his fellow Orange hat manufacturers grouped together near the town commons, on Parrow Brook, where they shared a flat rock on which they washed their stock. By 1854, the twenty-nine Orange factories employed 947 men and women, producing 3,750 dozen hats each week.[16]

As the hat industry expanded and concentrated geographically, it underwent fundamental transformations. First, the trade subdivided on the basis of two changes in fashion which occurred during the years 1835–45. Silk hats, brought to America in 1835 by Frenchmen who had learned to use silk in China, became so popular as a substitute for the heavier, less graceful beaver top hat, that they engendered their own industry, centered in New York City and later spreading to Philadelphia.[17]

Another change in fashion subdivided the hatting craft in the 1840s. Men's hats began to feature curled brims, and so a new specialty — curling — arose, requiring workers highly skilled with hand and eye. Since not all finishers could do the new work, which was more highly paid than finishing, the craft was faced with a difficult problem of identity: if it allowed the curlers to become a separate, superior group, the solidarity that journeymen valued so highly would be destroyed. In 1845, the journeymen hat finishers of New York tried to resolve this difficulty by declaring "that curling or shaping is, and ever has been, a branch of Hat Finishing. That, hereafter, all curlers will be required to conform to the rules of the trade."[18] Needless to say, this simple declaration did not eliminate friction and jealousy. The new group of craftsmen, though drawn from the larger fraternity, had their own tools, skills, reputations, pride, and wages; not unnaturally they tried to maximize their advantages by limiting the number of journeymen whom they would teach. As late as 1882 this conflict created severe dissension within the finishers' ranks.[19]

Inevitably, technological progress splintered the hatters' craft as well. At first, change was limited to wool hat production, for improvements in the manufacturing of wool cloth spread quickly to the hatting trade. By 1837, machinery could form 300 wool hat bodies per day; at the beginning of the century, journeymen had been able to produce but one hat daily.[20] As a result of this advance, wool and fur hatting became separate industries with distinct locations, unions, and even different consumer markets, for wool hats were cheaper and less durable than those made of fur. Thirty years later, the process of differentiation had gone so far that the journeymen in the two trades had severed relations altogether.[21]

The expansion, concentration, and splintering of the hatting industry intensified competition among hat manufacturers and brought a drop in hat prices. In 1842, a committee of hat manufacturers reported that prices had declined 25–50 percent in the last decade. The value of hats and caps manufactured in the United States in 1840 was 18 percent less than it had been in 1831.[22] Journeymen's wages dropped correspondingly. *The New York Tribune* reported in 1845 that "the business of hat making has been falling off in profitableness for a good many years. In 1832 ten and twelve shillings ($1.25 and $1.50) were the regular prices for making a hat which is now made for seventy-five and even fifty cents. The reduction in the price of finishing hats has been about the same. . . ."[23]

Thus, we see that the fur felt hatting industry had undergone substantial changes in the second quarter of the nineteenth century before any labor-saving machinery had been introduced. Technological advance transformed the trade once more. In 1845, Henry A. Wells patented a machine to felt fur. One of his forming machines, worked by two men and a boy, could produce daily between 400 and 450 hat bodies "all alike in weight, shape and thickness, and better made than they were by the old [manual] process, by which one man could make only 4–5 in a day. The cost of labor for forming and sizing hat bodies [had] been reduced in proportion from 56 cents to 6–10 cents."[24] Within a year a syndicate headed by Henry Burr bought Wells's patent and introduced a strict monopoly, leasing the expensive machines to a limited number of firms in New York, New Jersey, and Connecticut; the syndicate charged each lessee nine to fifteen cents for every body formed. In 1860, one New York firm accounted for the state's entire output of hat bodies.[25]

The Wells fur former rendered the bowers' skill obsolete; this was important because it reduced the journeymen hatters' bargaining power. Moreover, the machine displaced 4,500 craftsmen.[26] Equally important, the introduction of the forming machines split up the hatting craft. After 1846, most hat factories purchased their hat bodies from the Burr company and its lessees to size and finish in their own shops. "Finishing," which had been a distinct craft only in New York, now became distinct throughout the trade. In 1840, most hatters had formed, made, and finished hats. Ten years later, forming was done by machine, and making and finishing were separate jobs. The journeyman's all-round competence had been gravely eroded.

As manufacturers found it easier to divide labor, they expanded their factories. While the number of hat shops declined from 1,048 in 1850 to 622 in 1860, the average capital investment jumped 50 percent, to $6,334 per shop, and the average work crew increased from 14.5 to 17.4.[27]

Before the Civil War broke out in 1861, the hatting industry experienced one more change in fashion that was to have profound, long-term effects. In the early 1850s, American men developed enthusiasm for a new hat style, the soft (unstiffened) hat introduced by the Hungarian freedom fighter Louis Kossuth during his triumphal visit to the United States in 1851. Orange, New Jersey, quickly became the center of the new trade.[28] As its journeymen specialized in soft hat production, the skills involved in stiff and soft hat finishing became distinct; by the 1880s, many craftsmen could not do both kinds of work.[29] William Francis, chronicler of Danbury's hatting industry, wrote a poem describing these changes of fashion in antebellum America:

> The Napped Hat once reigned
> And the Confidence gained
> The Silk Hat came following after.
> The Pug Hat and Soft Hat now carry the day
> We must not forget the old "Castor." . . .[30]

In sum, by 1860, the hatting trade had been divided in response to the transportation revolution, which destroyed local product markets and intensified competition; by repeated changes in style, which popularized silk and soft hats and curled brims; and by technological innovation, which split off the wool branch from the fur felt branch and separated forming from making and finishing. As a result of such changes, hat companies had become larger, more geographically concentrated, and more capital intensive. There was also regional specialization: Orange and Newark specialized in soft hats; Boston and Danbury in wool hats; New York City and

Philadelphia in silk hats. The days when hatting was a single craft, when each journeymen made hats from fur to finish, were long past, yet hat finishing itself was still a handicraft industry, and would remain so for many years.

Early Hatters' Unionism

Journeymen hatters responded collectively to the changes in their industry. Throughout the first half of the nineteenth century, they were among the pioneers in the creation and development of local trade unions to maintain control of their craft, to defend work customs, wages, and working conditions, and to provide aid to the old, sick, widowed, and unemployed.

Trade unionism in the hatting industry began in the early days of the Republic. In Danbury, which had dozens of small shops producing hats in 1800, no single shop crew could govern its affairs on its own, for its efforts would be undermined by the shop's competitors; consequently, Danbury hatters organized a local union in 1800 to coordinate the shop crews' activities. Within a quarter century, journeymen in Philadelphia, Baltimore, Cincinnati, and New York had followed their lead.[31]

The hatters' early unions reflected their industry's local orientation. Since product markets were narrow, journeymen did not concern themselves much with developments outside their town or region. Between the years 1800 and 1840, the hatters' associations merely coordinated the efforts of the shop crews within their jurisdiction to mediate the relations between craftsmen, preserve the craft's high skill standards, and maintain control of the conditions and methods of work. Shop crews met frequently to make sure that all members abided by union rules, which were the codification of hallowed craft traditions.[32] Crews fined any journeyman who did not follow proper procedures to get hired, who bought his own tools, who failed to help a newcomer get a job, or who worked for less than the piece rates established by the shops' bill of prices. Strikebreakers too were subject to union discipline.[33]

At the heart of the locals' concerns was the maintenance of a monopoly of skilled labor. To that end, locals oversaw the training of apprentices, limited their number, and tested boys who had completed their terms. Boys who passed their examinations were fêted at a "maiden garnish," an initiation party where heavy drinking symbolized their acceptance into the ranks of the craftsmen.[34] Furthermore, locals vigilantly enforced the closed shop rule, excluding all job seekers who could not prove that they had been law-fully trained in a union shop and were members in good standing of a hatters' local.[35] This rule got New York hatters in trouble in 1822 when a shop owner filed a criminal complaint against the journeymen's organization for excluding a foul (non-union) hatter from employment in his fair (union) shop, for enforcing the closed shop rule, and for agreeing not to work for any master ignoring craft rules. The union was found guilty of conspiracy in the case known as *The People v. Henry Trequier, James Clausey, and Lewis Chamberlain.*[36]

Such experiences made hatters wary of allowing outsiders to know about their unions' proceedings. The Cincinnati hatters had a rule that "the opinions of the members on any subject that comes before the Association shall not be disclosed."[37] Secrecy was a part of the craft's traditions.

Although these features might seem to demonstrate that hatters' unionism was selfish and restrictive in outlook, mutualism was another dimension of the hatters' collective life. Unemployed hatters who took to the road could be sure they would be welcomed by their craftmates. When a newcomer arrived in a hatting town, he could be sure of finding a hearty welcome. The constitution of the Cincinnati hatters' local, for example, stipulated in 1827 that "any journeymen leaving this city, being clear of the books, shall receive from the secretary a certificate" making him eligible for aid in other cities.[38]

John Hawkins, a hatter who became a temperance advocate, described in his autobiography his life as a young, single, itinerant hatter. In the depression of 1819–22 that followed the Napoleonic wars, Hawkins walked the tramping circuit from Baltimore to Pittsburgh, then down the Ohio River to Cincinnati, then to Madison and Bedford, Indiana, and finally back to Wheeling, Virginia, stopping wherever he could find employment, staying until there was no work to do. Wherever Hawkins traveled, local craftmates helped him find a job; if no work was available, they gave him money to travel on to the next town.[39]

When he arrived in a new town, Hawkins's craftmates welcomed him with a round of liquor, for drinking was a confirmed feature of hatters' conviviality. In his autobiography-cum-temperance tract, Hawkins later described the hat shops of his youth: "stimulating liquors were daily dispensed to journeymen, under the erroneous belief that they tended to increase their vigor and activity. The use of liquors in the shop only led to the continued use of them when the labors of the day were over. Thus, many were led imperceptibly to form habits of inebriety. I was bound out to the hatting business in as perfect a grogshop as ever existed."[40] One would presume that Hawkins's description is exaggerated, for he wrote his autobiography to convert people, not record reality, but there is much supporting evidence for Hawkins's claim; after all, the apprentice's initiation into journeyman status was marked by a ritual of social drinking.[41]

Hawkins's craftmates welcomed him with more than a drink, for they helped him find a job by a process of "going on turn." As early as 1810, the Danbury hatters' union stipulated that "any member going to an employer and asking for work for himself without having a journeyman of that shop with him to ask for him shall be fined two dollars." "Asking for" a newly arrived traveler was a duty of every journeyman: "any journeyman coming into this city who has never been a member of this association, going into a shop for work, shall be helped to get a job by union members if he agrees to join the union."[43] According to the journeyman hat finishers' association of New York (1845), this custom of "going on turn" was that "one great principle which always distinguished [hatters] from other trades."[44] It was a significant principle, for its thrust was to maintain all fair journeymen on an equal footing: if employers had to hire the first available unionist, they could not hire men on the basis of skill or experience. Within the union too, equality prevailed, for seniority did not entitle men to preferential treatment.

European Origins

Traveling, apprenticeship restrictions, the closed shop, going on turn, shop-set price bills, shop discipline, secrecy, mutualism and equality—all these features of early American hatting trade unionism derived from an artisan tradition passed down by English and French hatters. Traces of that tradition can be found as early as the sixteenth century.

The hatters' effort to preserve a unique identity through regulating apprenticeship had its roots deep in the past. As early as 1556, Elizabethan law required boys wishing to enter the trade to serve terms of seven years. Masters could take their sons on as apprentices without limitation, but fathers who worked at other trades had to pay large sums to the journeymen to provide their sons with a trade. Law and tradition combined to produce "virtually a hereditary caste of tradesmen," who had "little solidarity with other crafts."[45] When Parliament repealed the apprenticeship laws in 1777, at the request of employers, the journeymen hatters organized combinations to preserve the old system and generally succeeded in doing so, at least in urban areas.[46]

Apprenticeship regulation came to the American colonies via the Hatters' Statute of 1731, passed by Parliament to discourage colonial hat production. In force until the Revolution, the act followed Elizabethan precedent. After 1783 journeymen hatters organized unions to replace imperial regulation with corporate control of apprenticeship.[47]

Jean Vial's masterly study of French hatting, *La coutume chapeliere,* reports that as early as the seventeenth century, the hatters' guilds enforced a five-year apprenticeship, during which time youngsters were to learn the entire craft. At the end of the learning period, the apprentices were tested by the journeymen to ascertain whether they were good, honest workers, prepared to keep craft secrets. If they passed the test, an initiation ceremony followed, a secret ritual with white decorations, a cross, six candles, a sword, and a plate.[48]

Enforcement of apprenticeship rules enabled European hatters to exclude outsiders — in effect, to maintain a closed shop. From the beginning of hatters' trade unionism, late in the eighteenth century, English journeymen excluded anyone who had not served an apprenticeship and were therefore regarded as "foul men." Moreover, "fair men" could not work in foul shops.[49] French hatters carried out similar rules in their guilds and in their later, quasi-legal trade unions of the early nineteenth century. They insisted that employers hire only men attested to by the shop committee. When an employer refused to follow this or other union rules, he was "blacklisted," as were all those who continued to work for him.[50]

The efforts of French and English hatters to maintain their monopoly of skill by regulating apprenticeship and by enforcing the closed shop frequently brought them into conflict with employers and the government. Consequently, secrecy was an important part of European hatting traditions. In England, during the years 1799–1824, when unions were illegal under the Combination Acts, unionists met clandestinely in pubs or disguised their activities by pretending to be benefit associations. They learned such techniques from Freemasonry, the radical societies, and the Methodist movement.[51]

In the early years of the nineteenth century, when French law was equally hostile to workers' collective action, the hatters of Paris "alone knew how to create, under cover of mutualism, real unions of resistance."[52] Jean Vial, the craft's historian, reports that the hatters kept guard of their rites and

mysteries with such jealous care that the "Hatters' Custom" was quite hard
to study. Indeed, the early French unions left so few documents behind that
Vial had to rely primarily on police reports for his chronicle.[53]

When he analyzed these reports, Vial found that inside the walls of exclusivity and secrecy what the hatters had constructed was a tradition consisting "essentially of practices of solidarity bequeathed by the trade guilds
to open societies and by them to the unions."[54] One dimension of that solidarity was aid to travelers. French hatters, particularly before they were
thirty years old, did a *tour de France,* visiting such hatting towns as Lyons,
Bordeaux, Nantes, and Paris. The guilds facilitated this tour by issuing
traveling books which had to be cleared by one locality before another
would accept it; if a journeyman were out of work, his guild would give him
traveling aid to help him take to the road in search of employment. When
he arrived in a new hatting town, he would go to the home of the "mother
innkeeper" of the craft's inn. His arrival would be celebrated by a round of
drinks, and soon thereafter the guild gave him help in finding a job.

English hatters made tramping a way of life as early as the eighteenth
century. Indeed, hatting was one of the first trades in which the custom appeared. In the 1730s, the hatters had "houses of call," where craftsmen who
were "on the road" could apply for sustenance and work.[56] By the 1770s,
hatters had established a tramping federation which allowed traveling journeymen to collect relief from fellow craftsmen wherever they wandered.[57]
To facilitate mobility, the hat locals began to issue official traveling checks,
which were certificates from the club to which the tramp belonged, attesting
that he was out of work and recommending him to prospective employers.
In short, it was "a kind of passport of good character."[58]

In 1850, an English journeyman told Henry Mayhew how much of the
tramping tradition had survived:

> many a hatter went on tramp, and got to like the life, when he needn't
> have gone, if he'd looked out fairly for work. When I started from Lon-
> don, I needn't have gone if I hadn't like it, if I'd exerted myself; but I
> wanted a change. . . . It was a pleasant life enough. You saw some-
> thing new every day, and the fresh air and exercise made a man as
> strong as a horse. I should be very sorry to see the allowance for
> tramps done away with, for I think it helps to keep a man more inde-
> pendent and prevents many a man from having to work at under
> wages as he might be driven to otherwise.[59]

When the French or English hatter arrived in town, he got himself hired by "going on turn." According to a London manufacturer, George Ravenhill, who testified before a parliamentary select committee in 1824, "If a man is foul, he cannot be asked for by any of the men at the fair shops and therefore he is obliged to confine himself to the foul shops."[60] An oblique reference to the same phenomenon appears in the rules of the Stockport hatters (1818): ". . . when any person comes wishing to be asked for, the person that goes and asks for him [is] to take his ticket. . . ."[61]

Jean Vial described almost exactly the same custom, called in France the "tour de role." When a job aspirant approached the guild or union, he was directed to the oldest member of each shop. That man would approach the employer or foreman and ask, "Y a t'il place pour la camarade?" If the shop were hiring, the first comer got the job, but French hatters enforced one rule unknown among their English and American counterparts: the job seeker was required to take the first place offered him. If he refused, the guild, or later union, would extend no further aid.[62]

For hatters, equality meant more than sharing job opportunities—it meant sharing work as well. In French shops, early in the nineteenth century, "in case of a shortage of work, a slate is put on the wall of each factory; each worker marks the work he does. At the end of the week, the earnings will be shared equally."[63] Contemporary journeymen in Stockport, England, required equal divisions (1808); forty years later, a London finisher explained to Henry Mayhew: "When there's a slack, my employer divides the work among us in preference to discharging hands. We like that plan better than a small number being kept on at full work."[64] As we shall see, American hatters divided up work in the same manner late in the nineteenth century.

Just as European hatters shared opportunities for work, they shared good fortune. Benevolent mutuality was a cornerstone of the French hatting tradition. French hatters not only aided the unemployed with traveling money, but they helped striking workers in distant towns with financial support.[65] Sickness and death benefits and old-age pensions were more regular and even more important. Mutual help for the sick and old always marked hatters' organizations, and, above all, on the death of a journeyman, the craft's mutualism expressed itself. Surviving craftsmen not only paid for the departed's burial, but they had to attend his funeral as well.[66] Within the culture of European hatters, the mutualism embodied in such customs as equal division of work and aid to the sick and unemployed existed in dynamic tension with a different principle—individualism. Jean

Vial notes that for French hatters, "the disciplines of solidarity were reconciled with a lively individualism to which piece work testifies: the latter leaves to the worker, even the factory worker, a certain freedom of pace and behavior."[67]

Piecework, the cornerstone of the hatters' independence, was also an important feature of the hatters' culture on the other side of the English Channel. English shop crews set piece rates as early as 1667 when the London Court of Aldermen, "responding to a complaint by the journeymen hatters against their masters, ordered the craftsmen to make up a piecework list every year."[68] Change occurred in the eighteenth century, when many employers paid their men day wages, but then, "finding it better for their own purpose," they switched back to piece rates.[69] By the early nineteenth century, English shop crews were again setting prices, in shillings per dozen, for finishing different sorts of work.[70] In 1850, Mayhew discovered that the days before the reinstitution of piece work were "beyond the memory of the oldest members of the trade."[71]

One would expect that a tradition that cultivated equality, mutuality, and independence for its adherents would generate a good deal of friction among them, and that was indeed the case.[72] English and French hatters coped with this friction by establishing rituals for shop discipline: John Bowler, an English manufacturer, testified before the Select Committee on Artisans and Machinery in 1824:

Q. Do you happen to know if any journeyman violates the agreement into which he enters with others, what happens to him?
A. He is fined according to the enormity of his crime.
Q. How is it enforced?
A. It is enforced by the committee.
Q. How is the payment of that fine enforced?
A. Up to a guinea he has to pay it immediately, if it is ten guineas, he has to pay it at so much a week.
Q. If he refuses to pay, what is done?
A. The men will not work by him.[73]

As often as not, the fine collected from the offender was used to buy drinks for the shop crew, a custom which made everyone happy, for the English hatters' predilection for alcohol was notorious.[74] In eighteenth- and early nineteenth-century England, journeymen held their meetings in pubs, where drinking served as a disguise for organizational activity.[75] Considering beer necessary for the performance of their hot and dusty work, the men drank in the hat shops as well.[76] A journeyman interviewed by Henry Mayhew in 1850 commented that "there used to be far more drinking among hatters when I was a lad. I have known some of them to be steady and industrious for the week, and on a Saturday night, order a bottle of wine in a white bottle (decanter) just for themselves. A man was almost forced to drink a lot of beer at that time in a workshop, or he would be counted a sneak. Now we do just as we like in that way."[77] Did French hatters drink like their English counterparts? Vial tells us that when a traveler arrived in town, everyone drank to his arrival, but beyond that, he does not say.[78]

Whether or not heavy drinking was a feature of "la coutume chapeliere," it is clear that early nineteenth-century American hatters' unions were operating on the basis of a craft tradition they inherited from English and French journeymen. Furthermore, that tradition had its origins in the guilds of the sixteenth and seventeenth century. The chief features of that tradition were the maintenance of a skill monopoly by regulating apprenticeship and enforcing the closed shop; piecework; the maintenance of solidarity and equality through the hiring process and work sharing; and mutual benevolence through aid to the unemployed, sick, aged, and to widows of deceased craftsmen.

The activities of the early American hatting locals represented the hatters' collective attempt to preserve their cultural tradition by adapting customs developed in European guilds to early capitalist conditions. Because the economic environment was changing rapidly, the hatters' local unions had to change their approach to preserving tradition by increasing the scale of, and by formalizing, their collective action.

Economic Change and Hatters' Early Unions

In the second quarter of the nineteenth century, the expansion of the hatting industry challenged the hatters' ability to preserve their familiar ways of life. First, as markets expanded, hat prices and piece rates dropped as much as 50 percent in the years 1832–45. Second, whenever one local was able to boost wages above the national average, its shops would suffer a price disadvantage, and its employers would clamor for competitive labor costs.[79] Third, employers in nonunion regions began underselling fair employers in the hatting centers. In 1845, the *New York Tribune* complained that "an inevitable law of necessity . . . is gradually though surely taking out of [New York] City all the manipulatory occupations and transferring them to the country."[80] Finally, any local enjoying high piece rates soon found itself flooded with journeymen from less fortunate areas hoping to share their craftmates' prosperity.

In the 1830s, journeymen tried to solve these problems locally, by trying to keep their wage rates up to the national average, and by providing travel subsidies to unemployed members, so they would not be tempted to work for less than the prevailing prices; the hatters soon learned, however, that national action was necessary to ensure that all shops adhered to uniform policies and that no region would be too weak to keep up standards. Consequently, in 1844, "a Convention of Journeymen Hatters . . . especially those of Massachusetts, Rhode Island, Connecticut, New York, New Jersey, Pennsylvania, Delaware, and Maryland [was called] to consider the decline in the trade" in the previous ten years and "the inadequacy of the wages of the journeymen." On 19 July, delegates meeting in New York approved a bill of prices to be presented to employers throughout the hatting regions by 1 October, in the hope of eliminating the ruinous interdistrict competition.[81]

Although the convention marked one of the earliest steps taken by American craftsmen in the direction of national unionism, it was but a tentative gesture.[82] Even though the adoption of a national price bill in theory deprived locals of one of their important prerogatives, in all other respects hatters held to their policy of local self-determination. Their convention established no procedure for enforcing the national price list; indeed, there was no continuations committee. Furthermore, the hatters did not hold another national gathering until nine years had passed.

Left on their own, the locals foundered; by November 1845, Philadelphia, Newark, and Boston finishers once again had been forced to accept substandard piece rates, and New York journeymen, who maintained the fair bill, suffered high rates of unemployment.[83] Matters remained in this unsatisfactory state for a decade until in 1854 the finishers' locals decided to see if organizing a national union would solve their problems.

Conclusion

The history of the hatting industry in the first half of the nineteenth century is the story of ever-intensifying competition. At first, most hats were made at home, or locally, by part-time hatters or by craftsmen working in small shops. Improvements in transportation overland and on the sea made it possible for hat merchants to sell their goods in ever-broader markets; as a result, the number of hatteries declined, and production concentrated in five northeastern states, each with its own specialties.

Technological innovation reinforced the trends toward concentration and specialization. Machinery for producing wool hats revolutionized that branch of the trade, separating it from the fur felt hat market. Then, in mid-century, Wells forming machines made manufacturing of fur hat bodies much cheaper for the seventy-five factory owners able to lease the expensive apparatuses. Outside the forming branch of the fur felt hatting trade, mechanization made little headway, however, and finishing remained almost entirely hand work.

From the very beginning of the century, hatters organized local trade unions to maintain collective control over their craft, thereby preserving the traditional culture of work they had inherited from English and French journeymen. The locals facilitated the movement of hatters from one center to another, but initially they were relatively self-contained bodies concerned with providing aid for the needy, restricting entry into the craft, and maintaining control of work. As hat markets broadened, and production concentrated, the hatters' locals found it increasingly difficult to achieve their goals. In 1844, they made their first attempt to regain control of the trade by coordinating their activities on a national scale, but it would be several decades before they achieved a satisfactory national organization. During these years, changes in the hatting industry provided additional impetus for the development of national unions.

NOTES

1. Alan Dawley, *Class and Community* (Cambridge, Mass., Harvard University Press, 1976), passim.

2. Tench Coxe, *A Statement of the Arts and Manufactures of the United States for the Year 1810* (Elmsford, N.Y.: Maxwell Reprint Co., 1970), passim.

3. William H. Francis, *History of the Hatting Trade in Danbury* (Danbury: H. & L. Osborne, 1860), pp. 4–5. In 1816 Wildman's hats, worth $90 per dozen in Danbury, brought $120 in Charleston.

4. Ibid., pp. 5, 7.

5. Edward Woolley, *A Century of Hats* (Danbury, Conn.: The Mallory Hat Co., 1923), p. 10.

6. Francis, *Hatting in Danbury,* p. 5.

7. Woolley, *A Century of Hats,* pp. 10–16.

8. Stephen Wickes, *History of the Oranges in Essex County, New Jersey* (Orange, N.J.: Ward and Tichenor, 1892), p. 280.

9. Francis, *Hatting in Danbury,* p. 7.

10. The description of finishing presented here is condensed from William B. Sprague, "Early American Manufacture of Felt Hats," *The Chronicle of the Early Amer-*

ican Industry Association (Feb.-June 1934), Feb. pp. 1, 3; Mar., pp. 2, 3; Apr., p. 6; May, p. 6; June, pp. 4, 7.

11. U.S. Census Office, *Census of Manufactures of the United States in 1860,* pp. xlvii–cliv.

12. J. L. Bishop, *A History of American Manufacturing* (New York: Augustus M. Kelly, 1966), 2: 394.

13. Woolley, *A Century of Hats,* p. 16.

14. U.S. Census Office, *Census of Manufactures* (1860), p. cliv.

15. Francis, *Hatting in Danbury,* p. 17.

16. David L. Pierson, *History of the Oranges to 1921* (New York: Lewis Historical Publishing Co., 1922), 2: 310-11.

17. It was not until 1868 that silk hatters severed their connection with the felt hatters' unions; even afterward, many journeymen worked on both kinds of hats. *National Trades' Union,* 17 Jan. 1835; U.S. Census Office, *Census of Manufactures* (1860), pp. clv, clvi.

18. *Rules and Regulations of New York City Hat Finishers Association,* 29 Mar. 1845.

19. HFNTA, *Semi-Annual Report,* Nov. 1882.

20. Bishop, *History of Manufacturing,* 2: 304.

21. HFNTA, "Proceedings of the Special Convention, 1868," passim.

22. *New York Tribune,* 7 Nov. 1845. *Young America* reported that hatters were also suffering increasing joblessness. *Young America,* 29 Nov. 1844; 19 July 1845.

23. *New York Tribune,* 7 Nov. 1845.

24. Bishop, *History of Manufacturing,* 2: 497-98.

25. U.S. Census Office, *Census of Manufactures,* 1860, p. clx.

26. Ibid.

27. Ibid.

28. Pierson, *History of the Oranges,* 3: 637.

29. *Hatter and Furrier,* Feb. 1885, p. 19; Aug. 1885, p. 37; Mar. 1893, p. 23.

30. Francis, *Hatting in Danbury,* p. 12.

31. Norman Ware, *The Industrial Worker 1840-1860* (Boston: Houghton Mifflin Co., 1924), pp. 65-66; William A. Sullivan, *The Industrial Worker in Pennsylvania* (Harrisburg, Penn.: Pennsylvania History and Museum Commission, 1955), pp. 99, 120; John R. Commons, ed., *Documentary History of Industrial Society,* (Cleveland, Ohio: A. H. Clark, 1910-11), 1: 157-62; Cincinnati Hatters Association, *Constitution* (1827).

32. David Montgomery's "Workers' Control and Machine Production," *Labor History* 17 (Fall 1976): 485-509, contains a full analysis of the evolution of craft traditions to union rules.

33. *Constitution of the Danbury Hatters* (1810); Cincinnati Hatters Association, *Constitution,* 1827.

34. Harry B. Weiss and Grace Weiss, *The Early Hatters of New Jersey* (Trenton, N.J.: New Jersey Agricultural Society, 1961), p. 44.

35. Cincinnati Hatters' Association, *Constitution,* 1827; *Constitution of the Danbury Hatters* (1810).

36. J. D. Wheeler, *Criminal Law Cases* (New York: Gould and Banks, 1823-25), 1: 142.

37. Cincinnati Hatters' Association, *Constitution* (1827). Ethelbert Stewart's study of early American printers' unions concludes that printers kept their union activities secret by printing up minutes concerning only benevolent activities while discussing trade unionism in executive session. Ethelbert Stewart, "A Documentary History of the Early Organization of Printers," U.S. Bureau of Labor Statistics, *Bulletin* (Nov. 1905).

38. Cincinnati Hatters' Association, *Constitution*, 1827.

39. William E. Hawkins, *Life of John Hawkins* (New York: Sheldon, Blakeman and Co., 1859), p. 6.

40. Hawkins, *Life of John Hawkins*, p. 6.

41. Weiss and Weiss, *The Hatters of New Jersey*, p. 44.

42. *Constitution of the Danbury Hatters* (1810).

43. Cincinnati Hatters' Association, *Constitution* (1827).

44. *Rules and Regulations of the Journeymen Hat Finishers of New York* (1845).

45. Sidney Webb and Beatrice Webb, *Industrial Democracy* (London: Longmans, Green and Co., 1902), pp. 52–53.

46. Parliamentary Select Committee on Artisans and Machinery, *Second Report* (1824), pp. 64, 82.

47. *New York Tribune*, 7 Nov. 1845; *Mechanics' Free Press*, 29 Nov. 1825, cited in Paul H. Douglas, *American Apprenticeship and Industrial Education* (New York: Columbia University Press, 1921), p. 61.

48. Jean Vial, *La coutume chapeliere*, (Paris: F. Loviton & Cie, 1941), pp. 22–30.

49. Parliamentary Committee on Artisans and Machinery, *Second Report* (1824), p. 81. According to testimony, one in ten London hatters was foul.

50. Vial, *La coutume chapeliere*, pp. 35, 47.

51. Arthur Aspinall, *The Early English Unions* (London: Batchford Press, 1949), pp. xxiii–xxv.

52. Vial, *La coutume chapeliere*, p. 6.

53. Ibid.

54. Ibid., p. iii.

55. Ibid., pp. 32–34.

56. Eric J. Hobsbawm, *Labouring Men* (Garden City, N.Y.: Doubleday and Co., 1967), p. 43; Sidney Webb and Beatrice Webb, *History of Trade Unionism* (London: Longmans, Green & Co., 1894), pp. 32, 48; M. Dorothy George, *London Life in the Eighteenth Century* (New York: Alfred A. Knopf, 1926), p. 293.

57. Hobsbawm, *Labouring Men*, pp. 43–44.

58. Committee on Artisans and Machinery, *Second Report* (1824), p. 91.

59. Aileen Yeo and Edward Thompson, comp., *The Unknown Mayhew* (New York: Pantheon Books, 1971), p. 450.

60. Committee on Artisans and Machinery, *Second Report* (1824), p. 92.

61. Aspinall, *Early English Unions*, p. 100. The Webbs commented: "The Silk Hatters [of London] expressly arrange so that the employer may not even see the man assigned to him before he is engaged. This is, in effect, to maintain a craft monopoly." Webb and Webb, *Industrial Democracy*, 1: 438.

62. Vial, *La coutume chapeliere*, pp. 33–34.

63. Ibid.

64. Aspinall, *Early English Unions,* p. 106; Yeo and Thompson, *The Unknown Mayhew,* p. 447.

65. Vial, *Le coutume chapeliere,* p. 35.

66. Ibid., pp. ii, 30, 39.

67. Ibid., p. iv.

68. Webb and Webb, *History of Trade Unionism,* p. 28.

69. Committee on Artisans and Machinery, *Second Report* (1824), pp. 97, 74, 79–81.

70. Ibid.

71. Yeo and Thompson, *The Unknown Mayhew,* p. 447.

72. Vial, *La coutume chapeliere,* p. 22.

73. Committee on Artisans and Machinery, *Second Report* (1824), p. 29. The Stockport hatters' union could impose fines upon masters and journeymen for a wide variety of abuses, including taking work out of turn, speaking ill of a shop mate, leaving a meeting early, assigning apprentices over to new masters, and failing to go on turn. Aspinall, *Early English Unions,* pp. 106–11.

74. Aspinall, *Early English Unions,* pp. 106–7.

75. George, *London Life,* pp. 291–93; Aspinall, *Early English Unions,* p. 223.

76. Committee on Artisans and Machinery, *Second Report* (1824), pp. 98–99.

77. Yeo and Thompson, *The Unknown Mayhew,* p. 447. Curiously, all accounts of hatters' drinking, no matter when written, allege that consumption was greater in the recent past.

78. Vial, *La coutume chapeliere,* p. 33.

79. In 1833, master hatters in Baltimore complained that "every improvement by which the facilities of commercial communications are increased between Baltimore and our neighboring rival cities brings . . . competition nearer to our doors." Consequently, they formed an employers' association to drive down wages. Commons, *Documentary History,* 4: 106. Philadelphia had twenty-four fair employers and only two foul in 1845, but in ten of the union shops men were working at below standard rates. According to a report of the corresponding secretary of journeymen hatters, made to the trade in July 1844, "These cat gut employers [in Philadelphia] are a great nuisance to the trade. When their regular business fails they go to cutting one another's throats by underselling each other." *New York Tribune,* 7 Nov. 1845; see also John R. Commons, et. al., *History of Labor in the United States* (New York: Macmillan, 1918–35), 1: 154.

80. *New York Tribune,* 7 Nov. 1845.

81. *Rules and Regulations of the Journeymen Hat Finishers of New York,* 20 Mar. 1845; *Workingmen's Advocate,* 8 June 1844; *New York Tribune,* 7 Nov. 1845.

82. Commons notes that unlike other groups of journeymen, hatters did not consider organizing a national union in the 1830s. Commons, *History of Labor,* 1: 414.

83. *New York Tribune,* 7 Nov. 1845.

CHAPTER 2

The Development of the Modern Hatting Industry, 1854–1880

IN THE YEARS 1854–80, the hatting trade changed in ways that shaped the finishers' collective action. Perhaps most important, the industry grew dramatically. Despite the temporarily crippling impact of the Civil War, which deprived the northeastern factories of their southern markets,[1] the number of hatters more than doubled from 10,841 in 1860 to 23,000 in 1880.[2] Moreover, much of the expansion occurred in the fur felt branch, whose product in 1880 ($21,300,000) exceeded the output of the entire hatting industry twenty years before.[3]

Fashion changes during the postwar years significantly affected manufacturing patterns. First, the soft hat, which had caught on in 1851, largely replaced silk toppers in the half-decade after the Civil War. Although New York City and Philadelphia hatters continued producing the fancy dress hats, their output failed to keep pace with the growth of the hatting industry as a whole.[4] Then, in the 1870s, soft hats began to lose ground to a new style, the derby. Brought to America from England in 1860 by Crofut and Knapp, a young South Norwalk, Connecticut, firm, the derby became very popular, eating into sales of the old felt top hats, and silk, soft, and wool hats as well.[5] Crofut and Knapp grew to meet demand, and competitors sprang up to tap the new market. By 1876, South Norwalk had six factories producing derbies, and many Danbury, Bethel, and Brooklyn firms had begun putting them out as well.[6] Production in the soft hatting centers, particularly Newark and Orange, had declined so much that many observers feared for the trade.[7]

At first the growth of the stiff hat industry paralleled the postwar prosperity; the new derbies sold for substantially more than most of the headwear they replaced,[8] but the depression of 1873 brought an end to good times. From 1874 to 1880, hat sales grew, but hat prices and quality fell, causing many firms to fail, among them two giants of the trade, James H. Prentice of Brooklyn and Smith and Palmer of South Norwalk.[9]

The Organization of a National Union

Changes in the hatting industry during the years 1854–80 made it impossible for the hatters' locals to protect the craft effectively. As the industry grew and concentrated, competition between hat manufacturers grew increasingly intense. In response, the hatters created a national trade union in 1854. For the next quarter-century they painfully sought to perfect their union as an instrument for defending their craft interests and values.

On 5 June 1854, in the midst of a business surge, finishers met to devise a means of protecting themselves from the interdistrict competition that was depressing their wages. Twenty-seven delegates, representing twelve locals, met in Philadelphia to organize the Hat Finishers' National Trade Association.[10] In so doing, they were following the lead of the printers, who three years earlier had founded the first American national trade union.

Like the printers', the finishers' association was organized in order to exclude from the trade those journeymen who had not served full apprenticeship terms because such men were thought to depress craft skill and wage standards.[11] To that end, the journeymen adopted a constitution requiring that all applicants for union membership prove that they had served a four-year apprenticeship. Moreover, the convention decided that all members looking for work outside their home local would have to produce a paid-up traveling card issued by the association's national secretary. Such cards would constitute necessary evidence that the applicant had satisfied the training and financial requirements of his home local.[12]

Wishing to preserve, rather than supersede, their traditional ways, the delegates passed no other general rules and decided to hold conventions only once every two years. The new Hat Finishers' National Trade Association (HFNTA) was to employ only one officer, the secretary, and he would receive only $100 per year. National dues — in the form of a per capita tax on the locals — were set at twenty cents per member per year, enough only to pay the secretary's part-time salary and to publish semiannual officers' reports.[13]

In its first six years, the "loose federation of virtually autonomous locals"[14] did not succeed in limiting the labor supply. Particularly in the growing soft hat manufacturing centers, Newark and Orange, New Jersey, the cost advantage of hiring numerous apprentices and low-skilled journeymen was still too great for many employers to pass up.[15] Consequently, the twenty-one delegates to the New York City convention of 1860 decided to enhance national union power as a way to stem the cheap labor tide. By a vote of 15–5, they limited each shop to three apprentices.[16] Their action was hardly radical, inasmuch as three had been the customary limit; nevertheless, because the new law took from the locals discretion to relax the ceiling, it represented a significant precedent.

The Civil War soon undermined the restrictive efforts of the fragile association. War orders stimulated a boom in the soft hat branch of the industry and created a demand for workers that the New Jersey locals, whose ranks were already depleted by the Union Army, could not meet. As employers turned increasingly to nonunion men, the soft hat finishers began making concessions in order to maximize the employment of union members. Their shops and locals first accepted wage cuts and ceased restricting the hiring of apprentices. When these tactics failed to keep their shops fair, the journeymen resorted to whitewashing unqualified men, a basic violation of the craft's principles.[17]

Although the silk hatters were themselves not much affected by wartime conditions, they objected to the felt finishers' relaxation of traditional standards. Conflict between the two groups came out in the open in Philadelphia in 1863 when the soft hat finishers successfully organized all the town's new war-bred shops. Rather than view this campaign as a victory for trade unionism, the silk hatters, who still dominated the Quaker City local, saw it as a threat. Their numerical superiority enabled them to drop from membership the two-score men who had not served regular apprenticeships.[18]

This intralocal conflict became a major focus of the association's national convention in 1864. The Philadelphia soft hatters, whose ranks had dwindled as a result of the previous year's expulsion, appealed to the convention to reinstate their shopmates, but the silk hatters prevailed. Pressing their advantage, delegates from the silk hat shops voted to reestablish a national uniform price bill so that fur finishers could not continue accepting wage cuts. To prove it meant business, the majority faction fined the Bethel, Connecticut, local $100 for allowing its employers to hire more apprentices than they were entitled to.[19]

The fur hatters, however, were not deterred by their convention defeat. Unable to force their employers to boost piece rates, they ignored the uniform price bill, which soon became a dead letter. For the same reason, the

Bethel and Danbury locals kept taking on apprentices in defiance of the three-boy rule. It was the soft hat finishers of Orange and Newark, however, who took the most extreme steps to keep their shops fair under unfavorable conditions; in the winter of 1867–68, when the number of small commission shops was increasing greatly, and neither local controlled half the factories in its jurisdiction, both whitewashed all the foul journeymen and placed their shops under union rules. [20]

Such mass consolidations were new to the finishing trade, a sharp departure from the craft's traditional exclusivity. They not only gave the fur felt finishers a new weapon to use in their struggles with their employers, but they also enabled the minority locals to function independently of the national association. The Connecticut and New Jersey locals, many of whose members had never served union apprenticeships, became the champions of the time-honored principle, local autonomy, while the traditionalistic silk hatters, on the other hand, became champions of a decidedly new principle, strong national discipline, for they saw this as the only way to preserve craft standards and culture.

Believing apprenticeship training to be essential to the preservation of skill standards and craft pride, the silk hatters refused to accept the actions taken by the Danbury, Bethel, Orange, and Newark locals. In a militant frame of mind, E. S. Williams, leader of Philadelphia's silk finishers, challenged delegates to the Newark Convention of 1868 by demanding adherence to the apprenticeship limit and expulsion of all journeymen who had not served full terms. Williams backed his demand by citing the case of Sylvester Cornell, a finisher who came to Philadelphia seeking work after being whitewashed by the Newark local during its consolidation. Philadelphia denied Cornell's application for a local check, Williams averred, because the newcomer had previously worked and gone foul in Prentice's Brooklyn factory. No local had the right to whitewash a man who had gone foul somewhere else.

Unfortunately, Mr. Williams had chosen a bad example, for Newark delegate Charles Costello, who had just been elected HFNTA vice-president, defended his local's honor by pointing out that association officials had approved Sylvester Cornell's whitewash in advance. When Thomas Spinning, who had been the national secretary at the time of the Newark consolidation, confirmed Costello's claim, the sentiment of many delegates switched against the silk hatters. Although the latter comprised a majority of the convention (eleven of the eighteen delegates originally seated), the

Philadelphia motion not to seat the full Newark delegation failed 17–4, with the Quaker City delegates entirely isolated.

Angered by its defeat, the Philadelphia delegation withdrew. When Newark's five representatives were seated, the felt finishers had a clear majority. Although they tried to reach accord on a compromise with the silk hatters of New York, disagreement over the three-boy rule proved an insuperable obstacle. When the fur finishers refused to pledge adherence to the apprenticeship limits, all the silk hatters left.[20] They organized their own union, the Silk and Fur Hat Finishers' National Association, signaling their determination to destroy the rival association by claiming all finishers within their jurisdiction. For a quarter-century thereafter, the two national unions competed for members, going so far as to scab on each others' strikes. But time was against the silk hatters; the declining popularity of top hats in the 1870s eventually rendered the dual union impotent. At the time however, the silk hatters' withdrawal from the convention of 1868 put the inexperienced fur felt hatters on the spot. Now that the silk finishers were no longer present to tell them what they could not do, they would have to discover whether or not they could control their trade and keep their union together.

First indications were not promising. Delegates to the 1868 convention took no decisive actions after the silk hatters left, merely voting to reaffirm the old bylaws, many of which the locals had no intention of honoring. No doubt their inaction can be attributed in part to the delegates' exhaustion — five days of bitter wrangling had already passed, and the journeymen were becoming impatient to get back home — but it was also disorientation that accounted for the delegates' paralysis. They had not come to Boston to take over the association; now that they had control, they did not know what they wanted to do.

At first, the new association made gains, as fur hat finishers in Brooklyn, Philadelphia, and Boston withdrew from their respective silk hat locals to affiliate with the HFNTA, and the Bethel hatters brought themselves into compliance with national rules so they could rejoin.[21] Soon, though, the finishers discovered deep-seated differences among themselves, and the association found itself embroiled in crisis once again.

The trouble started on 29 January 1869 when a "number of foul men" went to Orange from Danbury to fill the benches in "some of the shops." Wishing to organize all the shops in their district, the Orange journeymen asked association president E. D. Cornell what to do. Cornell, the one ex-

perienced national union leader the fur finishers had, advised the Orange
local "to make the shops fair on the best possible terms, but to get them fair
at all costs." After trying without success to force the manufacturers to hire
union men, the local did the next best thing: it gave membership cards to
the foul men from Danbury.

While this solved Orange's dilemma, it precipitated a national crisis for
the association; immediately upon receiving word of the whitewash, the
Danbury, Bethel, and Norwalk locals protested on the grounds that only
the local where a man had gone foul had the right to readmit him to membership. Ironically, the silk hatters had invoked this same principle two
years earlier. If it had been upheld, the Newark and Orange locals would
have had to abandon their consolidation policy, losing the local autonomy
that it made possible. Danbury made clear it was determined to stand firm,
announcing as Philadelphia had the year before that it would no longer recognize the card of any journeyman who had not served a four-year apprenticeship.[22]

Beyond the dispute over policy was an issue even more fundamental—
the association's survival. If Danbury did not withdraw its declaration of
nonrecognition, the young union would have had to disband, for no national organization can exist when its local affiliates ignore the rules with im-
punity. Some way had to be found to deal with the ever-recurring problem
of foul shops. The Orange, Newark, and Brooklyn locals believed that repeated consolidations were the best solution; the Connecticut locals preferred liberalized apprenticeship rules. The association could not go off in
both directions at once.[23]

Hoping to restore unity, President Cornell called the locals to a special
convention in Brooklyn in December 1869, only seventeen months after the
previous conclave had adjourned. He blamed the association's problems on
the fact that "owing to the unhappy condition of things at our last convention we were precluded from making revisions in our laws, adapting them
to our wants as fur hatters, laws which were proven unfit for us, containing
irreconcilable contradictions, so arbitrary as to be unworkable in some localities and working unwell in all."[24]

Cornell proposed a revision of the national laws to make them more flex-
ible, more responsible to local conditions; the majority of delegates con-
curred. First, the convention relaxed the old restrictions on consolidations,
allowing locals to decide whether or not to accept foul men into membership on an individual basis.[25] Moreover, the delegates voted to encourage
whitewashing by ruling that only locals which conducted consolidations

could allow more than three apprentices per shop. Since both decisions were contrary to the wishes of the Connecticut locals, the majority faction passed one rule to placate the Yankee minority: it agreed in principle that each local had the right, "by a judicious expansion and contraction" of the number of apprentices, to control the labor supply and meet the needs of its employers. The journeymen from the Housatonic River valley were not mollified by this concession, but they did not leave.

While the convention majority attempted to compromise between the needs of both factions, it was consistent in enlarging local autonomy; not only did district organizations gain the right to conduct consolidations and control the supply of apprentices, they also gained discretion to give members permission to work in foul shops when that seemed desirable.[26]

Soon the consolidation-local autonomy strategy had a chance to prove its effectiveness. In Orange, the hat manufacturers were alarmed by the success of the finishers' whitewash campaign of 1867–68; consequently, in the winter of 1869–70, they banded together in a trade association to resist what they saw to be the local's newfound power. Their strategy was to weaken the union by refusing to obey the restrictions on apprenticeships and by proscribing (blacklisting) the district's leaders. The manufacturers justified their actions by charging that the journeymen were making "outrageous demands" because they were "under the control of intolerant leaders" who magnified "to them their wrongs" and fostered "a spirit of discontent."[28] For the next twenty-five years, factory owners in every hatting district would repeat this refrain, not realizing that the dynamics of intragroup competition rather than personal irresponsibility impelled the local leaders to be militant.[29]

To halt the blacklistings, 700 Orange hatters, including many men who recently had been whitewashed, went out on a general strike on 15 February 1870. The men were "bitter in their denunciation of the [commission manufacturers] small . . . as they are and not princely dictators, few of them able to live longer or more comfortably without work and wages than the men who stand at the kettle or work at the knife or iron."[30] The journeymen's bitterness must have been softened by the support they received from their townsmen. As happened so often in the early days of America's industrial expansion, community sentiment swung sharply to the strikers who, after all, represented a quarter of the town's population.[31] The Orange *Chronicle*'s coverage of the strike was consistently prounion, and its editorial stance was clear: "To one who looks without prejudice, the manufacturers have little to lose by giving up a persecution of men who demand just treatment and recompense."[32] The reason for the paper's position was very simple. So long as the conflict continued, "the other branches of the trade sicken. One thousand men and women in the town are idle, and $30,000 worth of business weekly, or the amount of wages of those persons, is lost to dealers about town who depend on this class and not upon the 'dwellers on the hills' for substantial patronage and support."[33]

After eight days, the general strike was settled by the mutual concession of both the manufacturers and the journeymen.[34] The union agreed to rescind its law prohibiting the hiring of new apprentices; moreover, it dropped its requirement that apprentices join any strike over wages. Although these concessions were substantial, the factory owners gave up much more. They had to sign a pledge

> that they rescind all motions and resolutions passed by their Association directly or indirectly injurious to any journeyman individually or the Hat Finishers' Association collectively. And they also promise and declare they will . . . not prevent any journeyman from obtaining employment by proscribing him or assist others to do so. And they further declare that they will leave the apprentices in the state they are placed by the . . . laws of the Hat Finishers' Association.[35]

President Cornell believed that "the success of the Orange strike proved that when all of a locality is organized and united, employers can be resisted"; the Orange, Brooklyn, Philadelphia, Newark, and Milburn locals agreed with him.[36] Nevertheless, all through the year 1870, the New England locals, once again led by the Danbury militants, refused to conduct a whitewash campaign despite the convention's instructions to do so. Finally, in January 1871, the members of the Danbury local elected officers favorable to consolidation. Although the organization of the foul men was hampered by the disgruntled minority, who split to defend their sense of craft exclusivity, by May 1871 the district had brought in 75 new men to increase its membership to 155, and Bethel and South Norwalk had added 100 more.[37] Following these gains, Brooklyn, Orange, and Newark finishers whitewashed their shops once again, so that by the end of 1872 a greater proportion of the fur felt finishers was organized than ever before.[38]

With the successful whitewashes of 1869–72, the finishers' policy of local autonomy, bolstered by occasional consolidations, was set for a decade. The hatters had learned, however, that this policy alone was not viable, for whenever one local whitewashed a man who had worked foul elsewhere, as Orange had done in 1869, it provoked strong resentment that threatened the union's integrity.[39] To make local autonomy possible, the national association had to have the power to mediate between the jealous districts.

The Growth of Central Union Authority

The growth of the association's role as mediator began in 1869 when the special convention established the principle that "all local bodies are subject to the national trade and cannot disfranchise each other."[40] It was up to the board of directors to meet and decide on charges brought by one local against another.[41] As the board adopted this role, it became the trade's central authority, though still a weak one, and began legislating trade policy in the periods between conventions. In the process, the directors came to see themselves as national leaders, rather than merely local representatives as they had been originally.

The board's first legislative action came in 1875, and it concerned immigrant hatters whom finishers viewed as a threat. Supporting the national secretary, who in 1874 had begun writing European hatters' unions for information about their trade policies and membership rules, the board, without any formal authority to do so, adopted a rule requiring all hatters who had served apprenticeship abroad to submit proof to the national secretary of their affiliation with a fair European union, along with their membership application. At the same board meeting, the directors also decided to exclude all silk hatters who had worked at the trade after the split of 1868.[42]

By 1876, the board was confident enough in its authority that it voted to forbid locals to charge dues on traveling cards, a move locals resented because the practice had been a convenient way of collecting dues. The board considered its action necessary to diminish jealousy among the districts, however, so it turned a deaf ear to the districts' complaints.[43]

The Persistence of Local Autonomy

Despite such encroachments by the board in the locals' power, the success of the consolidation policy enabled the districts to control work in their shops, thus making it unnecessary for them to cede essential authority to the national association. The locals' self-direction was still so strong in 1877 that when the Philadelphia district, in the course of a whitewash campaign, accepted the applications of some journeymen who had recently worked foul in Newark, the enraged Newark local vowed never to honor cards issued by the Quaker City local. President Cornell complained that the misdeeds of both parties were "a blow at our constitution, which if not speedily and thoroughly discountenanced, will sap the foundations of our whole National organization."[44] Though the issue was compromised, the problem remained; three years later, it was Norwalk refusing to recognize cards issued by the Newark finishers, who were now conducting a consolidation of their own.[45] Twenty-six years after its founding, the association still led an unstable existence, threatened by the centrifugal force of local autonomy.

Conclusion

During the years 1854–80, most hat shops remained small and lightly capitalized. Competition was intense as salesmen, factory superintendents, and journeymen entered the manufacturing field to do a commission business on the smallest of margins. The short-lived postwar boom brought a few years of prosperity for hat factories and their employees, but the depression of 1873 inaugurated an era of declining prices, wages, and quality standards.

While the depression drove many manufacturers from the field, journeymen found their craft threatened as well. Low start-up costs, intense competitive pressures, and declining prices all encouraged manufacturers to cut wages and eliminate their employees' customary work practices. Moreover, deteriorating quality standards induced many employers to dispense with highly skilled labor altogether; they turned to prison inmates, runaway apprentices, and semitrained employees to make the cheaper grades of hats.

Intense competition and decreasing hat prices impelled hatters to attempt to organize a national union, but the hatters' commitment to local control of the trade and to craft exclusivity conflicted with their desire to establish an effective defense organization. Consequently, development of the national association was slow and full of conflict. In these early years, whenever the national union made a decision with which a local strongly disagreed, the national union's authority to make the decision was questioned. As a result, the silk hatters withdrew from the association in 1868, and a portion of the Danbury local split off in 1870.

The problem that gave rise to the most serious local-national disputes was the increasing number of low-skilled men brought into the hatting trade by nonunion employers. Local unions fiercely resisted admitting such men, but the national officers held a broader perspective on the hatting trade. In their eyes, if the locals continued to refuse to admit such men, the entire industry would eventually be nonunion. Over the years from 1854 to 1880, national power did grow, and low-skilled men were "consolidated," but the process was uncertain. Not until the 1880s did the Hat Finishers' National Trade Association develop enough power vis-à-vis the locals for it to formulate a policy to stabilize the hatting industry.

The story of that development will soon be told. Before moving on to that discussion, it is important to look at the hatting industry of 1880 and the hatters' collective approach to conditions in the trade at that time; for to understand why the hatters' national association developed as it did, we need to know three things: first, what economic conditions the hatters were facing; second, the values they were trying to implement; and third, the methods with which they customarily attacked their problems.

NOTES

1. Lynn W. Wilson, *History of Fairfield County, Connecticut* (Chicago: S. J. Clarke Publishing Co., 1929), 1:284.

2. While we lack comparable data on volume and value of output, it is likely that production increased even more rapidly than the work force, inasmuch as mechanization increased.

3. U.S. Census Office, *Census of Manufactures in 1860* (Washington: U.S. Government Printing Office, 1865), p. cliv; (1880), pp. 45–46. The New Jersey hatting industry's work force doubled during the two decades. New York state's work force increased from 2,866 in 1860 to 4,789 in 1870, and capitalization more than doubled. U.S. Census Office, *Census of Manufactures* (1860), p. clv; U.S. Census Office, *Census of the United States* (1870), 3: 612; U.S. Census Office, *Census of Manufactures* (1880), (Washington: U.S. Government Printing Office, 1882), 2: 290.

4. *Clothier and Hatter,* Sept. 1877, p. 14.

5. Elsie Nicholas Danenberg, *The Romance of Norwalk* (New York: The States History Co., 1929), p. 275; Samuel R. Weed, *Norwalk After 250 Years* (South Norwalk, Conn.: C. A. Freeman, 1902), p. 374; Lynn W. Wilson, *History of Fairfield County,* 1: 284; Crofut and Knapp Co., *The C + K Book* (New York: Crofut and Knapp Co., 1924), p. 19; *Hatter and Furrier,* Jan. 1888, p. 44.

6. Danenberg, *The Romance of Norwalk,* p. 289; Weed, *Norwalk After 250 Years,* p. 374; *Hat, Cap and Fur Trade Review,* Aug. 1868, p. 5; *Hatter and Furrier,* Apr. 1886, p. 44; Dec. 1882, p. 13.

7. After 1885 fashions changed, and the soft hat trade revived. *Hatter and Furrier,* Feb. 1885, p. 19; May 1885, p. 30; Aug. 1889, p. 37.

8. Ibid., Apr. 1889, p. 41.

9. Ibid., May 1881, p. 16; U.S. Census Office, *Tenth Census of the United States* (1880), 3: 105; R. G. Dun & Co., "Field Reports, Fairfield County, Connecticut,"

12: 313. Smith and Palmer's liabilities exceeded $100,000 while its assets amounted to only $30,000 in 1880.

10. HFNTA, "Proceedings of the Founding Convention, 1854," p. 4.

11. Lloyd Ulman, *The Rise of the National Union* (Cambridge, Mass.: Harvard University Press, 1955), p. 119.

12. HFNTA, "Proceedings of the Founding Convention, 1854," pp. 16–21.

13. Ibid.

14. Donald Robinson, *Spotlight on a Union* (New York: Dial Press, 1948), p. 48.

15. The HFNTA convention of 1860 noted that the loss of shops to the foul trade "in many cases could be avoided if the local associations but enforce their rules" on apprenticeship and the like. At the 1860 convention, soft hat districts Orange and Newark sent only two and three delegates respectively, while Boston, which had a smaller workforce, had three delegates. HFNTA, "Proceedings of the Regular Convention, 1860," p. 64.

16. Ibid., p. 59.

17. Ibid., 1864, p. 49; 1868, pp. 159–62.

18. Ibid., 1864, p. 89.

19. Ibid., 1864, p. 101. The Bethel local claimed it had to do so because there was a labor shortage and employers would have gone foul had they not been allowed to use apprentices.

20. Ibid., 1868, pp. 159, 160, 162, 168.

21. HFNTA, "Proceedings of the Special Convention, 1869," p. 190.

22. Ibid., p. 192.

23. Neither approach was really a solution, as the association was soon to discover.

24. HFNTA, "Proceedings of the Special Convention, 1869," p. 193.

25. Ibid., p. 194.

26. Ibid., p. 193.

27. The local claimed that "at various times, twenty-two men were singled out." *Orange Chronicle,* 19 Feb. 1870.

28. Ibid., reprinted in *Newark Daily Advertiser,* 21 Feb. 1870, and *Newark Centinel of Freedom,* 22 Feb. 1870.

29. See Chapter 4.

30. *Orange Chronicle,* 19 Feb. 1870.

31. Herbert Gutman noted this phenomenon in his "Class, Status and Community Power in Nineteenth-Century American Industrial Cities," in Frederick C. Jaher, ed., *The Age of Industrialism in America* (New York: The Free Press, 1968), pp. 270–72.

32. *Orange Chronicle,* 18 Feb. 1870.

33. Ibid.

34. Ibid., 21 Feb. 1870.

35. Ibid.

36. HFNTA, *Semi-Annual Report,* May 1870.

37. Ibid., May 1871. *The Danbury News* had not a word on these tumultuous events.

38. Union membership increased from 1,128 in May 1871 to 1,417 in Dec. 1872.

By the latter date, Newark had seventy-five foul men, Orange, twenty, and South Norwalk, twenty-five. No other local had more than ten. See HFNTA, *Semi-Annual Report,* Dec. 1872.

39. Another drawback of the consolidation policy, that it threatened to dilute the craft's skill standard, will be discussed in the following chapter.

40. HFNTA, "Proceedings of the Special Convention, 1869," p. 236; HFNTA, *Semi-Annual Report,* May 1873.

41. HFNTA, "Proceedings of the Special Convention, 1869," p. 198.

42. HFNTA, *Semi-Annual Report,* May 1876.

43. Ibid., May 1877. The same board meeting also voted to exclude silk hatters altogether.

44. Ibid.

45. Ibid., May 1880.

CHAPTER 3

The Hatting Industry
in 1880

T HE SUBSTANTIAL CHANGES undergone by the hatting industry in the years 1860–80 did not change the method of work in the finishing shops. Finishers continued to iron, block, pounce, and lure; curlers still cut the brims, curled their edges, and shaped them. Nevertheless, hatters were under strong economic pressure to surrender prerogatives to their bosses, and low-skilled, nonunion journeymen threatened to undermine the craft. To understand why both these facts are true, we must turn to the structure of the hatting trade.

Hat production in 1880 continued to be concentrated in the Boston-Philadelphia corridor, close to the suppliers of the two primary ingredients of manufacturing — furs and skilled labor. The most important reason for the industry to remain in the old hatting towns of the Northeast was their proximity to the fashion centers of New York and Philadelphia, which set the styles for trade and housed the fur markets and merchant houses that provided manufacturers with credit and distributed their products to retailers throughout the country.

Within this corridor, the hatting industry was divided into two branches: stiff hatting centered in Danbury, South Norwalk, and Brooklyn, and soft hatting concentrated in Orange, Newark, and Philadelphia. Although there were important differences between them, fundamentally both resembled the garment trades with which they were closely allied.[1]

In the stiff hat trade, the fashion leaders, D. D. Youmans, Robert Dunlap, and Edward Knox in New York, and Joseph A. Miller in Philadelphia, unveiled new derby styles in January for the spring season, and in June for the fall. While fashion changes were not radical, each season the hats would vary in the depth of their crown, the cut of their brim, the roll of their curl, and the variation in their color and trimming.[2]

Upon receipt of the proposed styles, the manufacturers would set their most skillful journeymen at work producing a few dozen sample hats, in each of the price ranges, for derbies varied in price according to the quality of the fur mixture, the ribbon, the exactitude of the pouncing, and the grace of the curl. After setting prices for the samples, wholesalers (jobbers) sent their commercial travelers out to the New York City, northeastern, southern, and western markets, drumming up orders from haberdashers wherever they went. Only after the first batch of orders had been placed did the jobbers telegraph their orders to the waiting hat factories, which would finally begin production in earnest.[3]

The soft hat trade was less fashion oriented; consumer demand came mainly from the South and West, and remained relatively consistent from year to year.[4] Consequently, factory owners in Orange, Newark, and Philadelphia could form their fur and size their bodies in advance of the jobbers' orders, waiting for only the distributors' telegram to put the finishing touches and trim on their goods.[5] Even soft hat sales, though, were subject to fluctuations in weather, which might accelerate or retard orders, to changes in color preferences, and to periodic swings of taste. Since manufacturers made up their bodies in advance, such changes often left them with unneeded stock on hand, eating up capital needed elsewhere and generating costly interest charges.[6]

Both stiff and soft hat firms resembled the garment trades in the small size of their shops as well. In 1880, Connecticut's thirty-four stiff hat factories averaged only ninety-two employees, with a capitalization of $24,000, of which tools and machinery accounted for perhaps one-eighth. New Jersey's seventy-nine soft hat shops were, on average, even smaller, employing sixty-eight hands each and requiring $17,000 capital.[7]

Few factories, however, resembled the median type. Far more common were the less substantial "commission shops" which could be established for as little as $300. An enterprising journeyman could rent an old hat shop, buy or rent a few tools, and commence business. A New York or Newark merchant house would furnish him formed hat bodies to make and finish; the commission manufacturer would set his employees to work making and finishing hats. For weeks, the entrepreneur would have to pay the men out of his own pocket; only when the merchant house received orders from wholesalers for finished goods would it begin to pay the shop owner for the hats he had produced.[8]

Because it cost so little to set up a commission shop, competition was intense, as a disillusioned hat manufacturer complained to the *Hatter and Furrier:*

> A cut-throat system that is fatal to every honest man has come into operation in the (commission) shops. . . . A few men in Orange have been accustomed to keep up an incessant bidding for work. If work gets slack in their shops, they will go to New York, bid from one quarter of a cent to two cents less per hat, until business . . . is booming in their shops. Then the next-door and other commission men must follow that example. The result of this is that the coal men, the working men, and the dealers in the raw material must stand the cost when a crash comes. Now this business has taught the "commission" men such ultra economy that they are able to subsist on a crust.[9]

A commission manufacturer who kept his production costs way down might make a profit, but few were able to go into business on their own. Where could they get access to sufficient credit to pay for the fur, dyestuffs, and labor needed to produce hats for sale to the wholesalers? At the height of a busy season, an independent factory owner, whose firm was capitalized at $25,000, might have liabilities of $12,000 for stock on hand alone. Few commission shop owners could ever gain access to that kind of money.[10]

Even if a manufacturer did expand his credit basis and productive capacity, he still had to compete with all the little commission shops for the jobbers' orders. The wholesalers dominated the industry, driving hat prices inexorably downward. Hats that sold for $6.50 in 1860 brought only $3.50 twenty years later.[11]

> Each manufacturer went on, continually and fiercely contesting with each other, who shall cut fastest and deepest, as if the only object in life worthy of man was the gratification of an ambition to be the cheapest and meanest of . . . hat makers. From $18 (per dozen wholesale) to $16.50; from that to $15, then what were termed $15-hats were sold at $14.50 and $14. Then came $13.50 and then began the occupation of selling what are euphemistically termed second hats, which in days of honesty were used to heat up the boilers.[12]

Moreover, although the decline in quality standards in the face of fierce cost-cutting during the depression of the 1870s was a major problem, the higher standards that followed did not improve things, for retailers and jobbers passed on stricter standards without increasing commensurately the price they paid manufacturers.[13]

Often manufacturers would grumble that they could make no profit on the jobbers' orders, but even if they could, they still faced serious difficulties. For example, the fur mixture used to produce the sample might become unavailable, go up in price, or unaccountably become more difficult to work with, in which case the journeymen would demand higher piece rates, nullifying the manufacturers' projected income.[14] Consumer demand might change in midseason, causing jobbers to cancel orders for goods already in the works but not yet shipped and paid for. To forestall the dreaded countermanding telegrams, manufacturers would strain to get out orders as quickly as possible, but since stiff hats took four to five days to complete, factory owners were often left in the lurch.[15] Finally, defects in the hats could kill the manufacturers' hopes:

> Each hat is taken separately (by the jobber), subjected to a critical inspection, the slightest evidence that the fur ever had a dag in it, a missing stitch, a speck of stiffening, the ordure of a fly, no matter how low the quality, back comes these single hats, and away goes the profit on the case; bad as this is, it is not equal to the practice of the jobber in pretending he has no time to examine and ships hats without looking at them, and awaits the retailers' return of them to him (and then to the factory.)[16]

When the jobber finally got around to paying, he did so on terms extremely advantageous to him. He did not pay for the goods he had received from the factories and sold to the hat retailers until six to eight months after he placed his order; when he paid, he deducted a "cash" discount of 10–15 percent of the bill. A factory owner's necessity to obtain credit to buy raw materials in November, when he would not receive payment for his goods until the following August, proved a terrible stumbling block for all but the most ingenious of entrepreneurs.[17]

Because manufacturers were so helpless in the face of the jobbers' price cutting, they constantly had to reduce labor costs. There were many different ways to do so. They could decrease their journeymen's piece rates; they could hire less-skilled men who would work for lower wages; they could further divide up the labor process; they could introduce machinery; and they could sign contracts with prison officials to set convicts to hat making. Manufacturers tried all these means of cutting their labor costs, with what results we shall soon examine, but the general trend for hatters' wages was clearly downward. Piece rates in 1880 were more than 10 percent below those of 1870.[18] In 1888 labor costs had been reduced to 34 percent of the value of the product.[19] Erosion of income was a dominant fact in the life of nineteenth-century artisans.

Given the constant pressure on manufacturers to cut labor costs, one might assume that industrialists would have mechanized their finishing shops in order to reduce their need for skilled labor. Indeed there was some movement in that direction. In the 1870s, manufacturers installed final blocking machines, which when operated by an unskilled laborer, could block from four to six dozen hats per hour; this freed skilled finishers to iron, pounce, and curl.[20] Moreover, American shop owners experimented with ironing machines, pouncing lathes, and hydraulic presses during the 1870s. Brooklyn's largest firm, James H. Prentice and Company, gambled heavily on such apparatuses; in 1877–78 the firm outfitted its entire finishing room with lathes and presses,[21] but machinery did not stick in the finishing departments. Within a year, Prentice had to sell off its machinery to satisfy creditors. The *Hat, Cap and Fur Trade Review* commented, "There is a growing tendency among a number of large manufacturers to return to hand labor. . . ."[22]

The reason for the slow pace of mechanization in the hat industry is not hard to find: manufacturers were short of capital. Most were commission shop owners with at most a few thousand dollars of their own tied up in their plant and land. They lacked the credit basis to buy their own machinery, and whatever profits they made they invested in enlarging their shops. Larger manufacturers, like Prentice of Brooklyn, Tweedy of Danbury, and Stetson of Philadelphia, could afford to buy finishing machinery; they had tens of thousands of dollars invested in their businesses. As Prentice's unfortunate experience demonstrated, however, even for the large firms, investment in finishing machines could be unduly risky because entrepreneurs already needed large amounts of credit each season to buy fur stock and pay wages six to eight months before they would be paid for their output. Even large concerns like Prentice's were vulnerable; if their products did not sell well one season or if one of their jobbers failed, the factory owner might be severely embarrassed.

The manufacturers' reluctance was reinforced by the fact that retailers and buyers had not become accustomed to machine-finished hats, scorning them as low-quality, containing too many imperfections. Perhaps the new products would have caught on in time, but the proposition seemed too risky.[23] Of course, if manufacturers in England, Germany, or elsewhere had been able to flood the American market with cheap hats, American manufacturers would have had to mechanize their finishing departments. In 1880, though, European hatters were even more backward than their counterparts in the United States,[24] and imports posed little threat to domestic hat producers. The value of fur hats imported into the United States in 1880 was only $208,975, less than 2 percent of the output of American manufacturers.[25]

Conclusion

The hatting industry of 1880 was dynamic and static, progressive and tradition-bound. Production had concentrated in six cities of the Northeast, but within these cities small units accounted for the bulk of output. While the industry employed more than 10,000 men and 3,000 women in factories from Danbury to Philadelphia, most factories employed only seventy-five hands and embodied only $20,000 in capital.

Competition among such small units was intense and merciless. Manipulated by the wholesale merchants, manufacturers strove desperately to cut production costs. To do so, they tried to decrease the workers' piece rates and decrease their skill level as well, but the structure of the hatting industry imposed limits on what manufacturers could do to beat the competition. Even the relatively prosperous manufacturers had little fixed capital — most of what resources they had went into fur and labor. Consequently, investment in machinery seemed to most manufacturers overly risky, as it proved to be when James Prentice's experiment with finishing devices brought him straight to bankruptcy court.

There was another reason for the slow pace of the hatting industry's development. Men's fur felt hats were expensive, and they sold on the basis of their style. If manufacturers rushed into mechanization, or employed men of too little skill, their hats would not sell.

Finally, there was a third reason the hatting industry changed slowly — the journeymen finishers organized militantly to resist change. They did so because they were heirs to a long artisan tradition which they wished to preserve and extend through their national union. At the heart of their tradition was a determination to control the work process in the factories. The next two chapters will analyze the hatters' work culture and their strategies for maintaining mastery of the workplace.

NOTES

1. Until 1880, one of the two principal hatting journals was called the *Clothier and Hatter* because it published information on both industries.

2. *The Hatter and Furrier* (Jan. 1882, p. 17) commented that the Miller derby had

a decidedly flat set brim, and was the subject of very favorable comment for its clean and shapely lines. The Youmans' derby was called boldly unconventional, for its brim was very flat set, and so broad at the corners as at first glance to appear out of shape.

3. Ibid., Oct. 1888, p. 13; Feb. 1889, p. 20; Nov. 1892, p. 33; *Hat, Cap and Fur Trade Review,* Mar. 1882, p. 149.

4. *Hat, Cap and Fur Trade Review,* Mar. 1890, p. 19.

5. Ibid., Oct. 1889, p. 11.

6. Ibid., Feb. 1889, p. 19.

7. U.S. Census Office, *Census of Manufactures,* 1880 (Washington: U.S. Government Printing Office, 1882), p. 45. The hatting industry had the lowest ratio of capital invested to value of production of any industry.

8. *Hatter and Furrier,* Oct. 1889, p. 15; *Hat, Cap and Fur Trade Review,* May 1879, p. 178.

9. *Hat, Cap and Fur Trade Review,* Mar. 1882, p. 27. In 1885, twenty-two of twenty-seven hat shops in Orange made hats on commission only. Ibid., Oct. 1885, p. 35; Nov. 1892, p. 26; July 1889, p. 27.

10. The case illustrated is L. H. Johnson and Co. of Danbury. See R. G. Dun & Co., "Field Agent Reports, Connecticut," 12: 184.

11. Parker and Tilton, *American Hat and Fur Exhibit* (New York: Parker and Tilton, 1883), n.p.

12. A disillusioned manufacturer, writing in *Hat, Cap and Fur Trade Review,* Mar. 1882, p. 199.

13. New Jersey Bureau of Labor, *Annual Report* (1881), pp. 154–55. "The general prosperity has created a demand for a better grade of goods." Also see *Hatter and Furrier,* Sept. 1885, p. 18; Oct. 1885, p. 35; Aug. 1888, p. 47.

14. *Hatter and Furrier,* Aug. 1885, p. 13; Aug. 1880, p. 1.

15. Ibid., Mar. 1886, p. 8.

16. *Hat, Cap and Fur Trade Review,* Mar. 1882, p. 149. See also May 1879, pp. 177–79; April 1879, p. 157; June 1879, pp. 198–200.

17. *Hatter and Furrier,* Nov. 1882, pp. 15, 18. In 1893, manufacturers were still suffering disadvantageous terms of sale. Manufacturers' bills to jobbers were commonly dated Mar. 1 to Sept. 1, and jobbers had three months after those dates to pay. Consequently, goods sold to jobbers in Sept. would not be paid for until nine months later. *Orange Chronicle,* 21 Oct. 1892.

18. U.S. Census Office, *Census of 1880,* 3: 105.

19. New Jersey Bureau of Labor, *Annual Report* (1888), pp. 312, 316. Materials cost 55 percent of the value of the product. Profits were less than 7 percent.

20. Edward Henry Knight, *Knight's American Mechanical Dictionary* (Boston: Houghton, Osgood and Co., 1876), pp. 843, 1004.

21. *Clothier and Hatter,* Dec. 1878, p. 33; Feb. 1879, p. 7; *Hatter and Furrier,* Dec. 1882, p. 13.

22. *Hat, Cap and Fur Trade Review,* May 1881, p. 200; *Hatter and Furrier,* Apr. 1880, p. 5.

23. *Hatter and Furrier,* Apr. 1880, p. 5.

24. *Hatters' Gazette* (London), 1 July 1881, p. 334.

25. United States Treasury Department, Bureau of Statistics, *Annual Report on Commerce and Navigation* (1880), p. 98. The tariff on imported hats was 35 percent, but this was lower than the tariff American hat manufacturers paid for raw materials.

CHAPTER 4

An Artisan Culture

THE HATTER'S ATTEMPTS to preserve their traditional culture of work met severe challenges during the years 1825–80. Employers introduced forming machines to eliminate one of the hatters' most difficult tasks, bowing. Improvements in transportation spurred manufacturers to separate the operations of making and finishing. Wholesale merchants gained control of the trade, fostering such intense competition among factory owners that the latter strove desperately to decrease their labor costs by hiring less-skilled and nonunion journeymen. In union hat shops the finishers' insistence on maintaining such craft principles as equality and piecework met with frequent and sustained opposition.

Under these conditions, one would expect that the finishers' culture of work, the customs and principles they had received from their English and French predecessors, would have been extinguished or at least would have been seriously eroded. Indeed, the dominant school of American labor history, the Commons school, leads one to expect that to be the case. The Commons school claimed that in America the economic forces unleashed by the transportation revolution destroyed the old craft traditions and replaced them with "job-consciousness." This was a thoroughly rational, antitraditional approach to collective action, in which workers responded to their economic opportunities on the basis of rational calculations as to how to improve their market position.

In the case of American hat finishers, this was not true. Evidence compiled from two trade journals that commented on the journeymen's actions every month, as well as from trade union documents and local newspapers, indicates that inside the hat factories of the leading trade centers in the 1880s, the traditional craft culture lived on. Of course, there were changes here and there as hatters adapted to adverse circumstances, recognizing the need for increasingly collective action, but overall what is impressive is not

how much the hatters' culture of work changed but how much was preserved. The values and customs of French and English journeymen lived
on in Gilded Age Danbury, Orange, Newark, Brooklyn, South Norwalk,
and Philadelphia.

Craft Identity

Hat finishers defined themselves as a group by marking off the boundaries between their members and others. Their community could be defined
loosely as consisting of everyone working in hat factories, including the
owners; more strictly, it included only journeymen finishers. Both definitions were meaningful because the finishing craft had emerged only recently; fifty years before the Gilded Age, hatting had been a single trade in
which each journeyman formed fur, blocked, pounced, sized, finished, and
curled hats. Finishers in the late nineteenth century still shared common
traditions and customs with craftsmen in what had become the other
branches of their industry. Even their employers shared the craft's traditions, for they too had been apprentice or journeymen hatters.

In all probability, the inhabitants of Danbury, Connecticut, and
Orange, New Jersey, had little difficulty telling hatters apart from other
tradesmen, for they looked distinct. An "old English poem" tells us,

> The next that came in was a hatter,
> Sure no one could be blacker. . . .[1]

The journeyman's color was not a moral quality, as one might suspect;
rather, "jour hatters in the olden times were proud of their vocation, and it
is said that some of them would actually dip their hands into the black dye,
that there might be no doubt about their being hatters."[2]

Apprenticeship rules provided a more precise gauge of membership in
the trade than personal appearance. Ideally, hatters accepted no one into
their fraternity unless he had served a four-year apprenticeship in a union
shop.[3] Immigrant journeymen were not exempt from this rule; they could
not join the HFNTA until they had furnished proof that they had served
their term in a recognized European union.[4] Apprenticeship was more than
an exclusionary device, though; it was also a means of socializing outsiders.[5]
If hatters were a homogeneous group, a hereditary craft, apprenticeship
would have been important enough as the transmitter of skills and customs,
but in the expanding hat industry of Gilded Age America, when hatters
came from a great variety of backgrounds, apprenticeship was crucial. The

Table 1. Birthplaces of Members of the Orange Finishers Union and Their Parents: 1880

Father's Birthplace	Hatter's Birthplace								
	Ireland		Germany		Other Foreign		U.S.		Total	
	N	%	N	%	N	%	N	%	N	%
Ireland	61	16					77	21	138	37
Germany			39	10.5			16	4	55	15
Other European					33	9	25	7	58	16
United States							121	32	121	32
Total	61	16	39	10.5	33	9	238	64.5	372	100

Source: Manuscript Schedule, U.S. Census, 1880

U.S. census for Orange, New Jersey, reveals that one-third of the town's union finishers were immigrants, mostly from Ireland with a few from Germany, and another third were the children of immigrants (see Table 1). The burden placed on hatters to teach old craft customs to such a large group of newcomers was staggering.

During their terms, boys became members of a new community, learning trade customs, union rules, a peculiar language, and even personal habits and modes of thought. To cite an example, when journeymen sent their young helpers out to pick up beer from the nearby saloon, the curious youngsters often took a few sips as they carried the brew back to the factory in a pail. As a result, by the time they were twenty-one, they had usually developed a taste for beer.[6] Although apprentices no longer left their homes to live their adolescence in the home of a master craftsman, their training experience, beginning at age seventeen or eighteen, was a formative one, which forged lasting loyalties to an adult society.

When a young man completed his apprenticeship, his shopmates threw a graduation party, the "maiden garnish" or "blow-out." This centuries-old ritual, marked by heavy drinking, symbolized the apprentice's acceptance into the ranks of the fair men. He had entered an exclusive fellowship and was responsible for maintaining its traditions. As a part of his new role, he looked down on the foul hatters, who lacked both the skill of the union men and their communal way of life.

The hatters' exclusive fellowship was bounded by a wall of silence; hatters were sticklers for secrecy. As late as the 1890s, their national and local unions refrained from detailing controversy or disagreement, lest outsiders seize on such dissension for their own ends. Thus, when Brooklyn journeymen quarreled in 1888 over the election of convention delegates, they promptly burned the minutes of that meeting.[8]

In the ten-year period from 1884 to 1893, the hatters failed only two times to keep their disputes from the public eye. The first lapse occurred when Republican and Democratic journeymen quarreled over the presidential election campaign in 1884. When the Brooklyn local contributed money to the campaign of Grover Cleveland, who as governor of New York had helped the finishers eliminate prison hatting, Republican journeymen protested the donation in the daily papers instead of in association meetings, which was the normal procedure. "It is the first time that the Association proceedings have been published in a newspaper," the *Hatter and Furrier* reported.[9]

That the wall of silence was breached so seldom testifies to how seriously hatters took their secrecy rules. They excluded owners and foremen from their meetings and established elaborate procedures to contain conflicts within the craft circle, lest they spill over to the hostile world beyond. The Danbury local required that all charges preferred by one journeyman against another had to be "signed by the person making the charge, and the person so charging must be present when the charge comes up for trial."[10] If the local president deemed the allegation of "sufficient importance he shall place it in the hands of the vigilance committee, but any person preferring a malicious charge against a journeyman or shop shall be subject to such fine as this association may think proper."[11]

Symbols of a Cultural Community

The hatters' language, studded with terms unique to their trade, sustained the craft's unity and marked off its uniqueness. Even contemporary reporters assigned to cover the industry had difficulty untangling the idiosyncratic terminology, most of which was carried over from the English hat shops of an earlier era.[12]

Some of the hatters' special terms referred to phenomena peculiar to the industry. When a journeyman looked for work, he followed a custom called "going on turn," which involved his obtaining a craftmate's consent to "ask for" him, that is, to ask the foreman if he wanted to hire anybody. Hatters shared their work by "running the buck," or passing a piece of wood from one to another to indicate who was next in turn to receive the "stock," or bodies ready to be finished. The new machines introduced by manufactur-

ers during the 1880s were called "bicycles" and "merry-go-rounds." "Buckeye shops" were factories doing work on commission for a retailer or jobber.
They produced "hammocks," as cheap hats were called. Finally, the last
bench to be set up in finishing shops during very busy seasons was known
as the "fly bench."[13]

Such terms were peculiar to the hatting industry of course, but what really made the finishers' language special were the uncommon terms they used
to describe common phenomena. For example, hatters were not fired, they
were "bagged," and they were "shopped," not hired. Rather than quit work,
they "cried off." When an apprentice was training under a journeyman's
supervision, he was "under teach"; when he completed his term, he "came
out of time." A "fair" man worked in a union shop, while a "foul" man could
not. In the dreaded instance when a foreman claimed a hat was defective,
and refused to pay for it, the journeyman's wages were "knocked down."
The hat was called a "knockdown," or a "kd," or, facetiously, a "Katie," who
was not the finishers' favorite girl.[14]

Lending an especially exotic flavor to the finishers' speech were terms
used despite the fact that the phenomena they described no longer existed
or had substantially changed. For instance, hatters in the 1890s still set
piece rates in terms of shillings, even though shillings were not in use in the
United States after the Civil War.[15] Similarly, finishers in the 1880s used
the phrase "on the road" to mean unemployed, whereas it had once meant
literally that a hatter was tramping on the road in search of a job.[16] Similarly, the journeymen said "weigh out" to mean "divide up work," although by
the 1880s, the actual weight of hatting fur no longer concerned finishers.[17]

Common rituals strengthened the hatters' sense of identity. One was the
party, called the "blow out," celebrating the apprentices' coming out of
time.[18] Another opportunity for convivial drinking was provided by the
custom of sealing each new season's wage bill with a round of drinks for factory owners and journeymen.[19] Brooklyn finishers adopted a new ritual to
bind themselves together and with the past when they began to celebrate St.
Clement's Day in 1888. According to legend, the hatters' patron saint was
the first man to make felt; he did so by putting lambs' wool in his shoes,
where the dampness and warmth of his feet changed the wool to felt. The
hatters of Ireland and other Roman Catholic countries traditionally observed St. Clement's Day every 23 November; not surprisingly, the American hatters followed suit.[20]

Common recreational activities thickened the web of the finishers' culture. Like all groups of people, hatters had particular tastes in leisure; al-

though they played checkers, dominoes, and card games, they preferred outdoor sports, perhaps because the shops in which they worked were poorly ventilated.[21] Baseball, the new popular sport of the Gilded Age, was the journeymen's favorite; they played married men versus single, finishers versus makers, one shop against another.[22] The men also took trips to the seashore, went on picnics, hunted, fished, and played the horses. One thing they did not like was paramilitary drills.[23]

Heavy drinking was another, darker feature of the hatters' culture. The ability to imbibe in the shop was a privilege which in itself set finishers apart from most contemporary craftsmen.[24] "It was the untrammeled right of every journeyman hatter to bring as much beer as he wanted to . . ." in most union finishing shops.[25] Apparently, working in the stifling factories, thick with fur dust, made for large thirsts. Brooklyn journeymen had a regular "mail delivery" three times a day, and at one time Boston hatters were "drinking so much that they were becoming a nuisance to their neighbors."[26] Orange men, not to be outdone, left their shops to drink so often that "within a block of every hat shop in Orange can be found two, three or four saloons, and all day long can men and boys be seen 'rushing the growler.' "[27]

Dependent on drink to get through their work days, hatters made alcohol part of the fabric of their leisure activities as well. The men drank notoriously on social occasions and at union affairs. At the Danbury town fair, for instance, the *Hatter and Furrier* reported in 1889 that "it was (very) evident that the hatters of Danbury do not favor Prohibition."[28] When Brooklyn journeymen helped elect their friend, James P. Graham, to the New York assembly in 1892, he found that the most frequent request of hatters was to get them released from the local jail's drunk tank.[29] Recognizing beer's popularity among the membership, the union used it as an organizing tool. During the Orange local's consolidation campaign in June 1890, the local set up its office in a pub and "used liquor to whitewash" the foul men, and in Brooklyn, union officers dispensed beer freely to win supporters and heal old wounds.[30]

Time and Leisure

Unlike modern American workers, who value steady employment, time to be with their families, and home ownership, the hatters tended to prefer unsteadiness, variety, and adventure. Their preference resembled what Edward Thompson has called a "preindustrial" approach to time, an approach geared originally to the rhythms of agricultural labor. Hard work was followed by hard play and then rest; the factory system, with its continuous use of machinery and labor, where time is subdivided into regular intervals, was the very antithesis of such rural rhythms.[31]

Of course, the hatters' values corresponded to conditions of their industry, which was a "fluctuating and precarious nature, depending largely on changes of fashion. . . . [W]hen the fashion prevails in one branch more than the other, there is a rush to those districts where it is done, giving a nomadic character to the hatter — so like that of the miner, rushing from one bonanza to another, too often, like him to find that he is chasing a will o' the wisp. . . ."[32] Moreover, because the industry was both seasonal and erratic, every year hatters faced two to four months of slow work or complete idleness, and a similar amount of time when work was hot and heavy. Such economic conditions did not determine the hatters' behavior; had they wished, they might have oriented their union activity to maximize steady work so they could stay at home as much as possible and rarely travel.[33] The hatters had other values, as the following statement by President Cornell indicates:

> Now, let us go into a hat shop a week after trade has fairly started. These men we see at work have been idle for weeks, perhaps for months. If they had anything left at the close of last season's trade it is all gone, and for weeks they have lived on a credit stretched to its utmost capacity. And yet who that did not know would suspect that this collection of jolly fellows, cracking their jokes like a set of Merry Andrews, and singing and shouting like so many bobolinks, owed any man a cent? But what of that? The winter of their discontent has changed to a glorious summer, and though hope may tell a flattering tale, they believe her, and give themselves up to the fullness of their joy. . . .[34]

If one gives oneself up to the spirit of another time, it is not hard to understand why these hatters were happy. They were, after all, back in the shops, reunited with old friends whom they had not seen for weeks, months, or even years. They could look forward to a brisk season with high earnings;[35] moreover, they had just finished a period of relaxation and recreation, which had given them a chance to unwind after months of hard work but which had, toward the end, begun to get tedious and touched with financial anxiety.[36] If unemployment went on for too long, or if credit were stretched past the breaking point, journeymen took to the road, traveling to a hat shop in a nearby district, where they would meet old friends, make new ones, and learn a bit about the world outside their own town. The *Hat-*

ter and Furrier treated the matter with amiable flippancy: "This is the season when the [Brooklyn] journeymen hatter feels a twinge of impecuniosity and naturally travels Jerseyward to relieve it. Creditors in some cases anxiously await their return."[37] Robert Robbins's poem, "The Jolly Hatter," treats traveling necessitated by seasonal unemployment in a similarly lighthearted manner:

> When there's no work in one location,
> No matter whether frost or flowers,
> We take the road for a vacation,
> That's the way that we spend ours.
> Summer or Winter makes no matter,
> Soon or late we'll make a hit;
> For well is known a genuine hatter
> From a clod-hopping counterfeit.[38]

The *Hatter and Furrier* was quite sure the hatters enjoyed the seasonal rhythm of their trade: "hatters in general look forward to dull times for part of the year; they're disappointed if there's no dull spell."[39] Indeed, many chose to take vacations during dull times, rather than hang around the shop for a few dozen hats to finish each week; they wanted time off to recuperate from the busy season's work in hot, ill-ventilated shops.[40] Sometimes manufacturers agreed; Danbury manufacturers shut down their plants in the dull summer of 1891 to give everyone a vacation.[41] It is clear that the unsteady rhythm of the hatting trade permeated the journeymen's work life; not only was he wholly or partially idle two to four months each year when orders lagged, but during busy seasons he had to work hard and fast to keep up with incoming orders. As the busy season reached its end, he was pressured by management to get work out before the jobber or retailer had time to cancel.[42]

One wonders, however, if President Cornell's jaunty prose and the trade journal's flippancy suppress a dark side of the journeymen's life. Was heavy drinking more than simply the practice of solidarity? Did married journeymen with young children to feed really enjoy their months of joblessness, their inability to save money, their enforced traveling in search of work? One can only speculate, for the written records do not speak to such questions. It is certain, though, that the finishers were not willing to let their work pace be dictated by others. As much as possible, they arranged their rate of output so they could take time off for an afternoon break, keep Saturday afternoons free, or even have a long July Fourth celebration or Danbury Fair holiday.[43] If they had to work at a killing pace for a few hours or days to earn their leisure, they were used to that; indeed, finishers prided themselves on their ability to get out work fast when they wanted — though quality counted first.

Bonds of Dependence

Common socialization experiences, language, rituals, recreational activities, drinking and leisure patterns, and work rhythms all intensified the hatters' sense of group identification. Moreover, apprenticeship rules, the union shop, and secrecy requirements closed off the craft circle from the outside world. The finisher's relationship to his trade was not simply limited to a sense of belonging; it partook also of dependence, for although hatters were supposed to be autonomous vis-à-vis the outside world, they relied on each other for sustenance, employment, and affirmation. Growing out of English and French tradition, by which the trade guaranteed food, drink, and lodging to unemployed, tramping men, the mutual dependence of American hatters was strongly developed. In the numerous cases where journeymen were incapacitated by consumption, shopmates took up collections among themselves to tide the sick man's family over until better days dawned. Nor did the hatters' sense of obligation end with their craftmate's life; many were the widows who benefitted from the finishers' determination to take care of their own.[44]

Even healthy men were not free from such binding ties, for a finisher could not get a job without putting himself in the hands of his fellows. No matter how skilled or well known a man might be, he could not walk up to a foreman and ask to be taken on; instead, he had to approach someone already working in the shop and ask him to intercede with the foreman. Nor could a man work on his own, unencumbered by the whims and needs of his mates, for he would have to break off from work whenever a shopmate called the crew together to discuss a grievance. In dull times, he could not work at his own pace, for custom dictated that work be divided among the men equally.

Reputation

The accumulated pressure over many generations of such rules and customs produced a breed of men who were extremely group conscious. In this sense, hatters were unlike late nineteenth-century iron and steel workers who "had always been eager to rise"; who read "Horatio Alger-type stories";

whose leaders often entered "politics or business, often with firms dealing with the union"; and of whom Samuel Gompers said that "their eagerness to leave the laboring class" conflicted with their solidarity.[45] For hatters, life's values came from the group; the most important things were to be well liked by one's fellows and to have the reputation of being "manly." Such concern for approval provided the impetus for trade union leadership, for union office was an "honor," a recognition of "merit"; it provided "an opportunity to distinguish" oneself.[46]

Negatively, concern for one's reputation was a key to the hatters' "dozening" system, which curbed gossip and slander with rules requiring all charges preferred by one journeyman against another to be signed, and accusers to be present when their charges were heard. It explains the dynamics of local trade unionism, where majority rule often tyrannized a minority that feared to risk its good name. Thus, in 1883 President Richard Dowdall had to admonish the association membership to "attend meetings, maintain what you consider right, and the man who condemns or insults you for doing so, his good opinion is not worth having and his bad one cannot hurt you."[47]

Such words may have been wise, but they carried little weight against the journeyman's dread of group opinion. Consequently, just two years later Dowdall's successor, Brooklynite Dennis Hagerty, complained in his first presidential report that the "practice of backbiting the officers and committees of national and local organizations [is] not only a source of annoyance to some who have been maligned, but it prevents many good men from taking a more active interest in the welfare of our organization through fear of having their actions unjustly criticized and their motives suspected."[48] Finally, a decade later, another Brooklynite who rose to the presidency attributed the association's collapse during the depression of 1893 to the same excessive concern with prestige: "Local officers are to blame in a great many cases for the unwise actions of their Associations . . . because they have not the sand, or backbone, to stand up against the majority of unthinking, careless, and indifferent members of their Association. They think they should be with the majority right or wrong."[49]

In the Spring of 1886, Reverend Edward Fleming, pastor of Orange's Irish Catholics at St. John's Church, sternly admonished the hatters for allowing themselves to be bullied by irresponsible elements. "There are no leaders, no men who can speak directly and state their grievances logically. The men who can do this prefer to be silent, for to reason directly and to speak to the point is to be a creep."[50] Of course, the worst opprobrium one could earn was to be called "foul" by one's fellows; the threat of being so branded was the ultimate form of the tyranny of group opinion.[51]

Preserving one's good name spilled over into public life. Finishers mounted a moderate and decorous campaign against prison hatting because they had "some character at stake and [did] not wish to bring themselves into disrepute," according to the campaign's organizer, John Phillips.[52] During the South Norwalk strike of 1884–85, association President Dennis Hagerty carried to the scene of conflict strict instructions for picketers to behave courteously and for all strikers to refrain from public drunkenness. Hagerty's concern for the trade's reputation was widely shared, and his advice proved unnecessary.[53] President Dowdall may have been exaggerating when he said, "I was mortified to hear from a boss that some of our men acted in a manner discreditable to themselves and to our Association," but nevertheless, at national conventions, which were never dry affairs, delegates went out of their way to keep breaches of decorum from public view.[54] Even on the most mundane level, the hatters' concern expressed itself in the expensive, well-kept hats and boots they affected whenever they left their shops. It would seem that the craftsmen sensed their respectability was fragile, that their coarser nature might gain the upper hand.

Nevertheless, the hatters' primary concern was for their status within the craft circle, rather than in the larger public. To diminish the tension such preoccupation generated, as well perhaps as to furnish needed distance in situations of unbearable intimacy, finishers were always "cracking their jokes like a set of merry Andrews. . . . The hatters in a shop, like the brothers in a family, will joke and chaff each other to a degree they would not presume with a stranger, and which a stranger would not be wise to imitate."[55] An old journeyman described one such prank:

> The apprentices and some of the men had got into the habit of leaning out of one of the windows and talking with those passing by. "The old man" had given strict orders that it should be stopped, and threatened not only to "bag" the first one that he caught at it, but also to kick him out of the shop. Not long after the boys got together, and with the aid of an old pair of pants, boots, etc., succeeded in getting up a pretty good representation of a man. This they carefully placed at one of the windows, and awaited the result. Shortly after, "the old man" came into the shop, in a very irritable state of mind, and discovering the dummy, and supposing it to be one of the boys, who had disregarded his orders, rushed upon it, and seizing it in the place upon which it was supposed to set, yelled out, "Dash, dash you! didn't I tell you to stop this!!!" and giving the figure a tremendous pull, the seat of the old pan-

taloons came out, leaving to his astonished gaze a bit of the straw and hat shavings. The boys gave a shout that could be heard for a block away. This made "the old man" madder than ever. Maybe he didn't swear. The air was blue with profanity. He wanted to "bag" every man in the shop — he would give fifty dollars to know who put up the job on him, but he never did. . . .[56]

A Man's Culture: Independence

"If a master said a word that wasn't deserved, when I first knew the trade, a journeyman would put on his coat and walk out," an English curler told Henry Mayhew in 1850.[57] A generation later, American hatters considered independence from authority the most important constituent of a man's reputation. The journeyman hat finisher and amateur poet Robert Robbins, of Orange, New Jersey, placed such pride at the very beginning of his song of "The Jovial Hatter":

> We unto no bosses humble
> When our trade begins to flag
> When they begin to growl and grumble
> We resent and give the bag [quit][58]

Finishers went to extreme lengths to preserve their rights. They often risked losing their shops to the nonunion trade in order to retain their privilege of drinking in the shop. "In the past dozen years, one or two concerted efforts have been made by the [Orange] manufacturers to keep out beer, but in each instance," they failed, the *Hatter and Furrier* noted in 1886.[59] Then, when twenty-one manufacturers, led by the Episcopalian minister William Richmond, launched a temperance crusade, their "restriction on beer drinking had to be dropped because of the journeymen's resistance."[60] J. J. Perrine, a Baptist and one of the town's leading factory owners, had the misfortune to learn the extent of the workers' tenacity. On 1 April 1886, he reversed his rule allowing men to drink in the shop but soon found that "too many were going too often" to neighboring saloons, so on 6 June he forbade his men to drink altogether while at work. The shop crew immediately struck, and within a few days forced Perrine to surrender.[61]

To avoid the dreaded evil, subservience, journeymen threw their weight around, often by fining foremen who abused their authority, but when they reached the limits of their power, finishers were willing to make sacrifices as well. To avoid needless temptation during dull times when many men were out of work and deep in debt, in November 1885 the Brooklyn local ruled that henceforth when a factory had no work to do, its crew would leave by noon. Although shops were centers of recreation and fellowship, the finishers decided it was more important to make sure that no one beg the foreman for work in an undignified fashion.[62]

Asserting one's independence enhanced one's status within the group. James Graham, leader of Brooklyn's anti-prison labor forces, won particularly fulsome praise from association president Richard Dowdall:

> To one who has never faltered or weakened in the face of obstacles that were insurmountable; who never hesitated to use the most forcible and convincing arguments when the time or occasion required it; fearlessly denouncing anybody and everybody who tried to belittle the movement, or ridicule its work; I refer to Mr. James Graham, the genial and active President of the Committee of Fifteen, to whose indomitable pluck (yes, I'll say it) and cheek we are indebted for a large measure of our success. . . .[63]

As much as hatters desired to be singled out for such praise, independence was as much a group phenomenon as an individual one. The values in whose name one asserted oneself were group values; it was to one's craftmates that one looked for approval and more often than not, it was with one's shop crew that one went to the foreman or employer with one's grievance.[64] Indeed, the hatters' rules diminished the likelihood that individual workers would have to confront their foreman, for the rules spelled out what journeymen could and could not be made to do, and provided that stewards, shop crews, and locals should enforce such rules.

A Man's Culture:
Prudence, Duty, Generosity, Improvidence

It was precisely because hatters accorded prestige to men and groups who stood up for their rights that the association's national officers so often complained of the tyranny of the majority;[65] the majority was likely to favor the most militant, intransigent posture. The story of the growth of national unionism is in large part the story of how association officers convinced the locals to temper their independence with discretion, but we must note that the officers succeeded, at least in part, because in the hatters' culture a real man was supposed to be prudent as well as independent. When President Dowdall exhorted his membership to be "firm in resisting oppression and injustice," he bore down equally emphatically on the need for prudence: "No imaginary or sentimental grievances should be allowed to endanger the trade. . . . Give all business slow and careful consideration, and never allow the prospect of a temporary improvement to govern your judgment."[66]

Being "conservative" was a duty, for a mistake made by one crew or local could endanger the interests of the trade as a whole. President Graham severely criticized the Orange finishers for demanding a twenty-five-cent pay hike during the depression of 1893: "The people in that district did not seem to have the slightest idea of what their duty was to organized labor."[67]

It was around the concept of duty that the hatters' local rules pivoted. It was a journeyman's duty to "ask for" a job hunter, to report infractions of the rules, and to attend local meetings.[68] The finishers had obligations to their bosses as well: "the Association is duty bound to furnish employers with enough men."[69]

Failure to perform one's duties was a most unmanly attribute. President Thomas O'Rourke, of Danbury, harshly scolded the manner in which some finishers were illegally working on machines to make maximum wages: "Their greed and desire to get that almighty dollar seems to make them forget the very first principles of our Association, and the duty that they owe to their fellowmen."[70]

Generosity and self-sacrifice, indeed, were important characteristics of manliness, resolving at least partially the tension between assertive independence and the fulfillment of social duty. Big-hearted did not mean independent alone; it meant generous as well. "Hatters as a class — especially the old school — are a generous-hearted set of men, and are ever ready to assist the needy. I have now in my mind's eye an old boss hatter, still living, who, to those who do not understand what lies beneath his brusque exterior, would think him about as hard a hearted man as ever lived; and yet he has a heart in him as big as an ox, and never refuses any appeal made by those who need assistance."[71] The *Bethel Ledger* put it as simply as could be: "To be a hatter is to be generous."[72]

Generosity was only one facet of a man's view of money. Finishers were also "free hearted," caring "little for money," except, of course, when it was scarce.[73] An old English poem about a meeting of six tradesmen, where the hatter "threw his hat upon the ground and swore each man should spend his pound,"[74] provides a hint about why finishers rarely saved any money: they were more interested in drinking with their fellows, matching round for round. Although the *Hatter and Furrier* spoke for employers when it hoped that the hard times following the depression of 1873 would "teach the boys — old and young boys — to hoard their shekels more snugly than in the high times," within two years, Norwalk's weekly *Hour* reported that "hatters as a class spend money freely when they have it, and at the end of the trade, few have funds sufficient to last until business resumes."[75]

A Man's Culture: Justice

Finally, a hatter was supposed to be fair-minded. In the case of a dispute with his craftmates or his employers, he was supposed to place justice above personal self-interest. The finishers' writings not only employed the rhetoric of fairness, but the men also carried out their responsibilities. When arbitration between Brooklyn employers and journeymen broke down in 1887, and the unionists continued to conduct hearings on grievances advanced by the membership, the manufacturers testified to the finishers' character, pronouncing themselves satisfied with the rulings of the union committee, and declining to rejoin the arbitration process.[76]

An Artisan Republic

The finishers' group character is perhaps best summarized by Fred Willis, a former journeyman silk hatter, who describes craftsmen in London hat shops at the end of the nineteenth century in terms thoroughly applicable to their American counterparts:

I think it is worth considering what effect such a life had on a man's character. First, it gave him a sense of freedom. He had no man with any power over him and he met all men on terms of equality. Toadyism was anathema to him. Realism was instilled into him by the ups and downs of seasonal trade and the conditions of his employment. He got nothing but what he worked for, dodging or slacking was impossible, and a fair price for a good job prevented scamping the work and encouraged interest in it. He had no fear that a big week's wages would give the master a hint to reduce the rate, prices were too secure for that. The *camaraderie* and traditions of his union gave him a sense of community, and stability, and the freedom of discussion during work sharpened his wits and expanded his mind beyond the limits of his life. When he "got the word off" he blamed nobody; he knew the "old man" had no alternative. He had to exercise his wits as to the best way of getting over the slack periods without advice or help from anyone. . . . The collective influence of all this, I think, make a man a good citizen and one that any country should be proud of. Looking back to my days with the journeyman hatters, I think I had a peep into a justice that was as near justice, honour, and fair play as mortals can ever hope to get.[77]

A Practical Craft

The finishers' artisan culture was traditional and coherent; it marked off the boundaries between itself and the outside world, established a unique identity for its adherents, provided them a set of values to give their lives meaning, contained rituals and symbols to bind journeymen together, and furnished a code of conduct for all to follow, yet, the coherence of the finishers' culture came at a price, and that was narrowness. In a turbulent period of American history, when violent strikes on the railroads, in the mining towns, and in the streets of the big cities called into question the viability of American democracy amidst industrial capitalism's explosive growth, the finishers' culture shielded them, allowed them to ignore in important ways the changes going on all around them.[78]

In the possibly exaggerated words of John Phillips, national secretary of the HFNTA for much of the 1880s, we can get a sense of the limited nature of the finishers' world view. Asked by a member of the Massachusetts Commission on Contract Convict Labor what alternative to that system he would propose, a perfectly reasonable question since Phillips was testifying for the abolition of prison hatting, the journeyman replied as follows:

> I am sorry you asked the question, sir. I have never thought of it, and I have never asked a workingman such a question. I think it is a horrible question to ask of a workingman who is compelled to work at a bench all his life. You cannot expect us to be up in political economy. . . . I never could see how people could expect a man that has been working for 25 years at a bench, and has very little or no time to read or study any more than the daily paper, to answer such a question. It is hardly fair to expect us to supply a remedy when the greatest political economists in the world are puzzled over it. I see the trouble very plainly but certainly my mind is not equal to the occasion so far as a remedy is concerned.[79]

Clearly, Phillips's problem was not really lack of time for reading political economy; shoemakers, who worked just as long hours were avid students of political, religious, and economic developments, discussing new ideas in their shops and reading about them at home. Nor can the hatters' intellectual indifference be attributed to conditions at work, for unlike the coopers, whose workshops were far too noisy to permit discussion and disputation, and unlike the carpenters, who worked alone, the hatters — and shoemakers as well — labored at repetitive tasks which left minds free to speculate, in quiet surroundings, close enough to their craftmates to sing and discuss whatever they wished.[80]

The hatters were practical, not theoretical men, for the same reason most people are: they had a firm world view which left them no need to question its presuppositions. The finishers' literature reveals no discussion of such popular contemporary radical writers as Edward Kellog, Henry George, Edward Bellamy, or Daniel DeLeon, men who concerned themselves with changing the organization of society as a whole. Impervious to radical currents, the hatters could be pragmatic because they believed they could achieve their narrow goals by following traditional, well-worn paths.

If the hatters were uninterested in economic theory or political radicalism, social or religious reform was no more to their liking. The finishers' writings were free of any strong religious feeling or concern for the moral condition of society. A brief flare-up of revivalist temperance agitation in Danbury, during the depths of the depression of 1873, stands out as a lonely exception. The manly, proud, dutiful, and prudent journeymen had their feet firmly planted in their small corner of the earth.

Finishers remained aloof from the social and political reform movements of their day because they thought of themselves primarily as craftsmen.[81] As craftsmen, finishers were concerned with the conditions of labor in the hat shops, conditions they believed they could control by their own efforts. External forces that did affect their status as journeymen, such as economic downturns, or changes in fashion, they believed to be beyond human control.

Perhaps the hatters' conservatism was linked to their industry's character. Hatting was a fashion-conscious industry, oriented to style, status, and respectability. It would not be surprising if hatters absorbed some of their industry's spirit, internalizing the social values embodied in the hats they furnished with their own hands.

As a tight-knit, self-sufficient group, hatters tended to stick together when it came to political action. There were Democratic and Republican finishers, but among both, the craft identification provided the basis for political coherence. As a result, in towns like Danbury and Orange, where hatters made up a majority of the population, leadership in the trade union local often served as a vehicle for political advancement.[82]

When finishers did see themselves as impinged on by controllable political and economic developments, they acted as members of the hatting industry. Their two major national political efforts in the years 1878–93 were for the abolition of prison hatting and for the passage of a protective tariff on imported hats. In both cases, the journeymen joined with their employers, whose interests coincided exactly with theirs. Such joint activity reinforced the union's traditional motto, "the interests of journeymen and employers are inseparable," a belief that certainly militated against class consciousness.

The journeymen's identification with their employers and their industry was dramatically manifested in their political activity. Finishers often supported their employers for elected office; indeed, in 1886, when Orange workingmen, led by the hatters, nominated a labor slate for municipal government, their mayoral candidate was Christopher McCulloch, a hat manufacturer who had recently failed in his business and gone to work as a superintendent in Newark.[83] More revealing still was the decision of Orange journeymen to rally behind the candidacy of Lawrence T. Fell, the manufacturer, for the post of New Jersey state labor inspector, in the spring of 1885. Their support for Fell betrayed strong local feeling, as well as an extreme lack of class antagonism, for Fell's rival was John C. Craigie, a journeyman hatter from Newark.[84]

When the finishers did reach out to other workers for support, they did so in a limited way. For example, in 1878–83 the hatters asked for aid from workers in other trades in order to overturn the pro-prison-hatting rural majority in the New Jersey and New York State legislatures.[85] Even more revealing was the hatters' relationship with the dynamic Knights of Labor. For many workers throughout the United States, the Knights expressed a radical protest against the evils of industrial capitalism, but for the hatters, the Holy Order was merely an instrument for pursuing narrow craft interests. During the South Norwalk strike of 1884–85, they asked the Knights of Labor to support their boycott.[86] Finding the Knights' support helpful, the finishers' association joined the Holy Order as District 128 in 1885, not because they viewed this as a step towards industrial democracy but because they wished to launch a union label and viewed membership in the Knights as a way to make the label potent.[87]

While it is true that the hatters' contact with the Knights affected the way they viewed the world, the impact was limited. In 1885 and 1886, Orange and Danbury journeymen organized their own independent labor parties, as workers were doing in cities throughout the country. The hatters' plunge into workingmen's politics gained fair success at the polls but was soon abandoned.[88]

There were more lasting signs that the hatters' traditional craft consciousness was slowly becoming overlaid with a new sense of class. In Brooklyn, the hatters dominated the local Central Labor Union, which opposed independent political action, but backed candidates who supported legislation favorable to the interests of organized labor.[89] To further that strategy, Brooklyn hatters mounted campaigns that delivered hundreds of their craftmates' votes.[90] Moreover, Orange and Newark finishers were prime movers in the Essex County Trades Assembly and the New Jersey Federation of Trade Unions, two bodies that pushed the state government to adopt significant protective labor legislation.[91]

Nevertheless, despite such important forays into class politics and organized labor action on the local and national level, the hat finishers expressed little class feeling. Phrases such as "capitalist" or "capitalism," "the working class," "exploitation," "the economic system," or "monopoly" seldom appear. The hatters' social consciousness was still in transition during the years 1878–93. Traditional craft consciousness remained strong but was slowly giving way to a new sense of class.

Conclusion

The notion that the hatters attempted to preserve a unique tradition may appear sentimental, but John B. Stetson, who owned and ran a large non-union hat factory in Philadelphia, knew very well that the hatters possessed a unique culture; he himself came from a hatting family and had served an apprenticeship in a union shop. Moreover, Stetson knew that the hatters' traditionalism, independence, mobility, and irregular work rhythms had economic consequences; rapid labor turnover, frequent absences from the shop, and hostility to new work methods all cost him money. Undeterred by the sentimental traditionalism which governed the management policy of most manufacturers, and indeed most industrialists of the time, Stetson determined to break the finishers' culture, to improve the efficiency of his plant. To that end, he set up a cafeteria in his factory so the journeymen would not go out to the saloons to eat and drink, and he gave a Christmas bonus to all men who stayed with him year round. To enable his journeymen to buy their own homes and abandon their transient ways, he set up a mortgage fund. Stetson was a successful manufacturer, a pioneer in industrial management — and a great threat to the hatters' culture.[92]

Nevertheless, until the depression of 1893 and the simultaneous introduction of improved finishing machines, hat finishers were able to preserve their accustomed way of life. They limited the labor supply, excluded outsiders, maintained trade secrets, spoke a unique language, and practiced hallowed rituals to preserve their sense of distinctiveness and solidarity. They remained independent, dutiful, generous, big-hearted men, extremely conscious of their standing among the fellows. They preserved their mobile way of life, valuing adventure, rest, and recreation, and enjoying their hard work among friends as well. Finally, they remained a practical sort, little prone to speculation or experimentation, conscious primarily of their status as an exclusive craft but ever more conscious of their membership in the working class and the world of organized labor.

The American hat finishers' culture of work resembled in broad outlines the craft tradition handed down from French and English journeymen. Continuity was expressed in language, in phrases like "going on turn" that hatters had used for many generations. It was expressed in customs like the "maiden garnish," the celebration of the apprentice's "coming out of time," in the traveling system, in the maintenance of shop-set piece rates, in hard drinking. Most importantly, the hatters continued to live by hallowed principles of solidarity, equality, and benevolent mutuality, the cornerstones of the French and English craft tradition.

Though the hatters' success in preserving their tradition was remarkable, it was not complete. The craft was divided into several branches of which finishing was only one; consequently, journeymen no longer could make hats from start to finish. The term of apprenticeship had been shortened, and some less-skilled men, some who had never served full terms of apprenticeship, had been allowed to enter the trade.

The change in the hatters' culture of work was not simply declension; a transition was taking place toward greater collective consciousness. "Going on turn," for instance, was no longer a transaction between one craftsman and another; it had become a rule governing the behavior of a journeyman and his union. Benevolent mutuality was no longer a craftsman's generous act; it had become a union duty, paid for in union dues. On the broadest scale, finishers were learning to think of themselves not simply as proud craftsmen but as proud craftsmen who needed the help of fellow workers, and as the years passed by, the hatters came to recognize that interdependence was based on common needs, interests, and values. While it is true to say that American hat finishers preserved a traditional subculture of work during the Gilded Age, it is necessary to add that their culture was changing in response to the changing world.

NOTES

1. *Hatter and Furrier,* Sept. 1880, p. 7.

2. Ibid., Mar. 1881, p. 7. When a New Jersey gubernatorial candidate campaigned at an Orange hat factory in Oct. 1889, he found the hands he had to shake were black. Ibid., Oct. 1889, p. 16. Coopers could be similarly distinguished by the deep furrows formed in the palms of their hands in the course of arduous labor. Bob Gilding, *The Journeymen Coopers of East London,* History Workshop Pamphlets, no. 4 (Oxford: Ruskin College, 1971), p. 67.

3. In reality, the association had to make many exceptions to its apprenticeship rule. In 1888, it had to shorten the apprenticeship term to three years.

4. The HFNTA stood virtually alone among American unions in corresponding with its European counterparts. F. E. Wolfe, *Admission to American Trade Unions,* Johns Hopkins University Studies in Historical and Political Sciences, series 30, no. 3 (Baltimore: Johns Hopkins University Press, 1912), p. 108.

5. M. Dorothy George, *London Life in the Eighteenth Century* (New York: Alfred A. Knopf, 1926), p. 157. "Apprenticeship tended to make trades hereditary — trades had their own customs, their own localities, often a distinctive dress, and much corporate spirit."

6. William E. Hawkins, *Life of John Hawkins* (New York: Sheldon, Blakeman and Co., 1859), p. 6; *Hatter and Furrier,* Apr. 1886, p. 23; Mar. 1886, p. 50.

7. *Hatter and Furrier,* Sept. 1884, p. 28; Mar. 1891, p. 38; Dec. 1890, p. 52; Harry B. Weiss and Grace N. Weiss, *The Early Hatters of New Jersey* (Trenton, N.J.: New Jersey Agricultural Society, 1961), p. 44.

8. *Hatter and Furrier,* June 1888, p. 33: "Hatters don't like their dirty linen out in public." See also ibid., July 1888, p. 39.

9. Ibid., Nov. 1884, p. 27. Partisan loyalties proved strong enough to open the hatters' normally closed mouths, a reason why the finishers generally avoided committing their organizations to partisan causes. The other exception to the tight-lips policy was the controversy between the Brooklyn hat makers and the hat finishers, which appeared in the columns of two Brooklyn daily newspapers. See the *Brooklyn Eagle,* 26 Nov. 1888; 16, 18 Dec. 1888; *Brooklyn Citizen,* 27 Nov. 1888.

10. Danbury Hat Finishers' Association, *Constitution and By-Laws,* bylaw 21, sections 2–4, reprinted in Connecticut Bureau of Labor, *Annual Report* (1890), p. 276.

11. Ibid.

12. The following terms were of English origin: go on turn, ask for, come out of time, to shop, shilling, fair, and foul. Late in the nineteenth century, London silk hatters also spoke a "queer slang" based mainly on trade terms. Frederick Willis, *101 Jubilee Road* (London: Phoenix House, 1948) p. 94.

13. In addition to these terms, there were other technical terms denoting tools and machinery used only in the hatting industry. Since all industries have their own technical terms, these have been omitted here.

14. *Hatter and Furrier,* Dec. 1890, p. 52.

15. Ibid., Oct. 1893, p. 19; June 1887, p. 23. While American craftsmen used the term before 1850, by 1880 only hatters did. A shilling was twelve and one-half cents.

16. Ibid., Dec. 1884, p. 30.

17. Ibid., Dec. 1890, p. 52. Dockers also had their language. Bob Gilding, a bench cooper, understood it, but only because his father had been a docker. Coopers had their own language as well. They called the steward a "collector." Shop meetings were "roll-ups." To make themselves a drink, or "waxer," they "bulled" a cask that had recently contained rum by pouring hot water into it. Their apprenticeship initiation was called a "trusso," and payday was "hog day." When they did overtime, they "worked a dark 'un." The extra wages earned on piecework by dock coopers was known as the "plus." Gilding, *Journeymen Coopers,* pp. 10, 24, 43, 49, 54, 81.

18. *Hatter and Furrier,* Mar. 1891, p. 38.

19. Ibid., Dec. 1890, p. 51; Aug. 1885, p. 13.

20. Ibid., Aug. 1887, p. 52; Nov. 1888, p. 37; Dec. 1888, p. 21.

21. Ibid., Apr. 1885, p. 30; Mar. 1888, p. 34; June 1889, p. 33.

22. Ibid., Apr. 1885, p. 14; Sept. 1885, p. 12; Oct. 1885, p. 35; June 1887, p. 23; Aug. 1886, p. 30; Mar. 1887, p. 15; June 1892, p. 27. Orange finishers at McGall, Allen and Company, and Cummings and Matthews, had such an intense rivalry in their baseball competition that both shop crews "hunted up" good baseball players and got them hired. They then argued over eligibility and ended up not playing. Ibid., July 1882, p. 20.

23. Ibid., Oct. 1885, p. 35; Aug. 1886, p. 30; May 1889, p. 27; Feb. 1887, p. 25; Oct. 1889, p. 15; April 1886, p. 31; June 1890, p. 40; Sept. 1886, p. 32; Aug. 1890, p. 23; Aug. 1891, p. 29.

24. In England, an "old compositor" wrote in 1859, "I always observed that those trades who had settled wages, such as masons, wrights, painters, etc. and who were obliged to attend regularly at stated hours, were not so much addicted to day drinking as printers, bookbinders, tailors, and those tradesmen who were generally on piecework, and not so much restricted in regard to their attendance at work except when it was particularly wanted." Cited in Sidney Webb and Beatrice Webb, *Industrial Democracy* (London: Longmans, Green and Co., 1902), pp. 326–27.

25. *Hatter and Furrier,* Apr. 1886, p. 23.

26. Ibid., Sept. 1886, p. 18.

27. Ibid., Apr. 1886, p. 23.

28. Ibid., Oct. 1889, p. 20. Boston hatters drank heavily to celebrate Independence Day in 1886. Ibid., July 1886, p. 21.

29. Ibid., Dec. 1892, p. 35.

30. Ibid., Jan. 1890, p. 23. In June 1891, after the Brooklyn local elected new officers, the winning candidates provided many rounds of drinks for the men. Ibid., July 1891, p. 27.

31. Edward P. Thompson, "Time, Work-Discipline, and Industrial Capitalism," *Past and Present,* 28 (Dec. 1967): 56–97.

32. *Hatter and Furrier,* Sept. 1880, p. 7. Lloyd Ulman has noted that the work forces in seasonal industries "were characterized by relatively high proportions of 'floaters,' " or itinerants. Lloyd Ulman, *The Rise of the National Union* (Cambridge, Mass.: Harvard University Press, 1955), p. 62.

33. If the hatters had accepted weekly wages, rather than insisted on piece rates, it would have made it more likely that manufacturers would even out their production schedules.

34. *Hatter and Furrier,* Sept. 1880, p. 7.

35. In 1884, most journeymen got four months steady work each year in two, two-month seasons. The rest of the year there was only partial work. *Hatter and Furrier,* Dec. 1884, p. 31. Four years later, New Jersey hatters averaged eight and three-quarters hours work per day, and were idle sixty-three days per year. New Jersey Bureau of Statistics of Labor and Industries, *Annual Report* (1888), pp. 372–73.

36. The *Hatter and Furrier* predicted that when the journeymen started their idle period, they would spend their time fishing and taking walks. *Hatter and Furrier,* Apr. 1885, p. 12. Bethel hatters used their leisure to plant flowers, go fishing, and tend their lawns. Ibid., May 1890, p. 38.

37. Ibid., Dec. 1880, p. 4.

38. *Clothier and Hatter,* Sept. 1878, p. 7.

39. *Hatter and Furrier,* July 1886, p. 21. London dockers shared the hatters' aversion for steady work in the 1940s. "Many [casual] men likely to make reliable permanent workers had been interviewed but few had jumped at the chance of a regular job. Pressed for their reason for refusing . . . it was explained that they had no objection to work as such but enough was enough. In the boom conditions that then prevailed, a good worker could pick his own job. When one job came to an end, he might take two or three days off, or wait until he could snare a well-paid job at the same or at another department . . . Colonel R. B. Oram, *The Dockers' Tragedy* (London: Hutchinson and Co., 1970), pp. 46–47. Printers also enjoyed itineracy. According to the professional strikebreaker, Allan Pinkerton: "Printers are not all tramps, but . . . there is scarcely a printer who has not at some time been upon the road. The fraternity are quite proud of their accomplishments in this direction. Half the chatting among the employees of an office is upon the adventures of certain of their number. . . ." Allan Pinkerton, *Strikers, Communists, Tramps and Detectives* (New York: G. W. Carleton and Co., 1882), pp. 52–53, cited in Ulman, *Rise of the National Union,* p. 64.

40. *Hatter and Furrier,* Aug. 1888, p. 26; Oct. 1889, p. 39; Aug. 1890, p. 2.

41. Ibid., July 1891, p. 33; Nov. 1892, p. 33.

42. Ibid., Oct. 1885, p. 11; Mar. 1886, p. 15; Oct. 1888, p. 33; Feb. 1889, p. 23; Dec. 1892, p. 33.

43. Ibid., July 1886, p. 21; Nov. 1888, p. 57; Oct. 1887, p. 19; Aug. 1889, p. 25; Dec. 1890, p. 29; July 1890, p. 33.

44. Ibid., Mar. 1881, p. 12. The journeymen had both formal and informal relief systems. Each local administered a benefit plan of some kind; in addition, shop crews took care of their members' families.

45. David Brody, *Steelworkers in America* (Cambridge, Mass.: Harvard University Press, 1960), p. 86.

46. Association conventions followed an etiquette by which victorious candidates for national office were accorded unanimous approval and defeated candidates were awarded lesser posts. Invidious comments on officers or candidates were discouraged and not recorded in convention proceedings. HFNTA, *Semi-Annual Report,* Nov. 1880; Nov. 1886; Nov. 1887; The *Hatter and Furrier* commented, "It is an honor to be elected to union office." *Hatter and Furrier,* Feb. 1888, p. 15.

47. HFNTA, *Semi-Annual Report,* Nov. 1883.

48. Ibid., May 1885.

49. Ibid., May 1895.

50. *Orange Journal,* 20 Mar. 1886.

51. The hatters' concern for their reputations had its origin in English shops, which had fining systems and distinctions between fair and foul, where a "man was almost forced to drink a lot of beer or he would be counted a sneak." Aileen Yeo and Edward P. Thompson, comp., *The Unknown Mayhew* (New York: Pantheon Books, 1971), p. 447.

52. Massachusetts Commission on Prison Labor, *Report* (1880), p. 302.

53. *Hatter and Furrier,* Dec. 1884, p. 11.

54. HFNTA, *Semi-Annual Report,* Nov. 1885.

55. *Hatter and Furrier,* Sept. 1880, p. 7. English silk hatters also loved to joke at each other's expense. ". . . Humor, repartee, and practical jokes were indulged in to such an extent that the men became past masters in all kinds of wisecracks . . . if any man had an idiosyncrasy or became a bore on one subject, he was mercilessly caricatured." Willis, *101 Jubilee Road,* p. 95.

56. *Hatter and Furrier,* Mar. 1881, p. 43.

57. Yeo and Thompson, *The Unknown Mayhew,* p. 450.

58. The song was to be sung to the tune of "One-Eyed Reilly." *Clothier and Hatter,* Sept. 1878, p. 7. E. D. Cornell, who served as an officer of the HFNTA through its first quarter century, related this facet of the journeymen's character to the sobriquet by which they were known, "mad as a hatter." "The absence of all those outgrowths of petty tyranny called 'factory rules' gives to the manner of the hatter that freedom from restraints, easy independence, and in some cases perfect abandon, by which he is so generally known." *Hatter and Furrier,* Sept. 1880, p. 7. Above all, hatters were determined not to put up with domineering management, as the following statement by President Richard Dowdall indicates: "The association is duty bound to furnish employers with enough men, provided men do not have to work over again to suit the whim of the superintendant or foreman who forgets his antecedents, and rules as if by 'a right divine' over those who work under him." HFNTA, *Semi-Annual Report,* Nov. 1882. English hatters were also free from all "toadyism." Willis, *101 Jubilee Road,* pp. 92–93.

59. *Hatter and Furrier,* Apr. 1886, p. 23.

60. Ibid., Sept. 1886, p. 18.

61. Ibid., July 1886, p. 18.

62. Ibid., Nov. 1885, p. 20; Dec. 1885, p. 19.

63. HFNTA, *Semi-Annual Report,* Nov. 1881; see May 1883 for an example of praise heaped on individuals.

64. English silk hatters were not allowed to confront their foremen unless accompanied by their stewards. Willis, *101 Jubilee Road,* p. 93.

65. Ibid., p. 67.

66. HFNTA, *Semi-Annual Report,* Nov. 1880.

67. Ibid., Nov. 1895.

68. Danbury Hat Finishers' Association, *Constitution and By-Laws,* reprinted in Connecticut Bureau of Labor, *Annual Report* (1890), pp. 274, 276.

69. HFNTA, *Semi-Annual Report,* Nov. 1879; Nov. 1878.

70. Ibid., May 1891.

71. An old journeyman hatter, quoted in *Hatter and Furrier,* Mar. 1881, p. 43.

72. *Bethel Ledger,* n.d., cited in *Hatter and Furrier,* Sept. 1882, p. 43.

73. *Clothier and Hatter,* Oct. 1878, p. 13. As early as the first quarter of the nineteenth century, hatters were "loose," "shiftless," "migratory," and "spent their high wages freely." William T. Brigham, *Baltimore Hats, Past and Present* (Baltimore: Press of I. Friedenwald, 1890), p. 39.

74. *Hatter and Furrier,* Sept. 1880, p. 7.

75. Ibid., Nov. 1882, p. 11; *Norwalk Hour,* 29 Nov. 1884.

76. The all-journeyman arbitration system worked "because members of the committee were all good, sensible, fair-minded men who weren't prejudiced." *Hatter and Furrier,* Mar. 1889, p. 23. Though "justice" was never defined in the union literature, it is doubtful that the journeymen used the term abstractly. It meant adherence to accepted tradition, conformity to past practice.

77. Willis, *101 Jubilee Road,* p. 95. The major difference between English and American hatters is that the English trade had become much less irregular than the American trade, and journeymen consequently traveled much less by 1890.

78. Indeed, providing such protection is perhaps part of the function of any culture.

79. Massachusetts Commission on Prison Labor, *Report* (1880), p. 32.

80. Robert A. Christie, *Empire in Wood* (Ithaca, N.Y.: Cornell University Press, 1956), p. 16; Thomas Wright, *The Romance of the Shoe* (London: C. J. Farncombe and Sons, 1922), pp. 218–19; John R. Commons, "American Shoemakers," *Quarterly Journal of Economics* 24 (Nov. 1909): 39; David N. Johnson, *Sketches of Lynn* (Westport, Conn.: Greenwood Press, 1970), pp. 4–7; Horace Davis, *Shoes, The Workers and the Industry* (New York: International Publishers, 1940), p. 245. The shoemakers' curiosity and intelligence appear to have been a craft tradition originating in England. See also Blanche Evans Hazard, *The Origins of the Boot and Shoe Industry* (Cambridge, Mass.: Harvard University Press, 1921), pp. 127–29, 131.

81. Secondarily, the finishers regarded themselves as members of the hatting industry, along with other workers, their employers, wholesalers, and retailers.

82. In Orange, journeyman hatters comprised one-quarter of the electorate, and in town elections a similar proportion of the candidates came from the hatting industry. Gossip had it that once one was an officer of the Orange finishers' local, one was eligible for office in the city government. *Hatter and Furrier,* Mar. 1890, p. 29. Although two-thirds of the Orange journeyman hatters were Democrats, at least half voted for an officer of the finishers' local who ran for office as a Republican in 1890. Ibid., Nov. 1890, p. 21. The finishers' involvement in local elections will be dealt with more fully in Chapter 8.

83. *Hatter and Furrier,* Mar. 1886, p. 49. In 1888, John Gill, another Orange hat manufacturer, won election to the assembly as a Republican with the support of many Democratic journeymen. Ibid., Nov. 1888, p. 25. Similarly, Danbury's workingmen's ticket included the manufacturer C. W. Murphy for borough treasurer. Ibid., Mar. 1886, p. 46. See also ibid., Nov. 1889, p. 22.

84. Ibid., Mar. 1886, p. 49. When a journeyman and employer ran against one another in town elections, there was no carry-over into labor relations. Ibid., Feb. 1891, p. 21.

85. See Chapter 7.

86. See Chapter 8.

87. See Chapter 9.

88. *Hatter and Furrier,* Nov. 1885, p. 23; Mar. 1886, pp. 46, 49; Nov. 1886, p. 23. See also Chapter 6.

89. When delegates of Brooklyn labor clubs voted in September 1886 to endorse independent political action, the finishers' representatives withdrew. *Hat, Cap and Fur Trade Review,* Oct. 1886, p. 223.

90. *Hatter and Furrier,* Oct. 1886, p. 11. In Brooklyn's Eleventh Assembly District, where many hatters lived, they worked hard for a Democratic candidate in November 1886. On election day, two journeymen stood at every polling place. The hatters carried their candidate to victory. Ibid., Nov. 1886, p. 27. See also Nov. 1887, p. 25; Aug. 1888, p. 29; Nov. 1889, p. 41; Oct. 1891, p. 51. As a reward for the Brooklyn hatters' political activity, in 1888 President Cleveland appointed D. J. Hagerty a special agent of the U.S. Bureau of Labor, and, in the following year, Hagerty got a Brooklyn city job paying the princely sum of $2000 per year. Ibid., June 1888, p. 16; May 1889, p. 27.

91. See Chapter 6.

92. Ethelbert Hubbard, *A Little Journey to the Home of John B. Stetson* (East Aurora, N.Y.: The Roycrofters, 1916), passim. The Carnegie Steel corporation followed a policy similar to Stetson's. In 1892, it offered low interest loans to employees wishing to buy property. The company also bought land near Homestead and erected houses there for sale to employees. Futhermore, it introduced a bonus plan for continuous service, provided cheap rental housing, sold stock to the skilled men, and gave them jobs in dull times so they would not move away. Brody, *Steelworkers in America,* pp. 88–89.

CHAPTER 5

To Preserve a Man's Culture

IF THE HATTERS were to preserve their unique culture, with its rigid distinction between insider and outsider, its independence from management control, and its preindustrial work rhythm, they would have to maintain that fundamental quality that marked them off from others, their skill. If they could keep the skill requirements high, they could exclude outsiders who lacked not only the ability to produce good work, but, more important, lacked compatible values and codes of behavior. Similarly, as long as hatters were versatile craftsmen, able to finish all sorts of hats, they would be free to move from shop to shop as they pleased and never become dependent on any one employer for a job. Preserving the traveling system contributed to the journeymen's autonomy, for a mobile craftsman could take fullest advantage of any opportunity to better his lot, or escape an overly exacting boss. Thus, the hatters' shop crews, locals, and national association fostered a web of rules and customs designed to actualize their autonomy.

Apprenticeship

For centuries English hatters had required apprentices to serve seven-year terms; in the late nineteenth century, American finishers reduced this to four years, during which time employers were to teach the boys all aspects of the craft. Had the journeymen not required full training of apprentices, factory owners could have subdivided finishing into simple tasks and used the aspirants as a source of cheap labor. Apprentices would have completed their terms with few skills and limited prospects for employment, a situation which in fact prevailed among printers and shoemakers during the last quarter of the nineteenth century.[1]

We may take the rules of the Danbury, Connecticut, local (1885) as typical of the finishers' efforts at enforcing their ideal of apprenticeship training:

1. Apprentices were to serve four consecutive years, beginning at age eighteen.

2. Employers had to teach their apprentices to "finish hats all through" and make them practical workmen at their trade.

3. Apprentices were "under the control of the employer and foremen in the shops where they worked."

4. Journeymen instructing apprentices did so for at least three months, and were to receive "the full benefit of the apprentice's work."

5. If apprentices had grievances, they could report to the local officers. The local vigilance committee adjusted complaints, subject to appeals by the manufacturers for arbitration.[2]

Following such rules, the finishers' locals had little trouble with runaway apprentices and few disagreements with their employers over control of the boys' work or training.

Subdividing Work

In the late nineteenth century, the finishers' craft was divided into two branches, finishing and curling, each made up of several jobs: finishers had to block, iron, pounce, and finish off hats; curlers had to edge up and set off brims, pack, and flange. In order to prevent the erosion of their versatility, the hatters insisted that their work not be divided into separate jobs. Instead, each journeyman was to take a dozen hats and perform all the operations necessary to finish or curl them.

The curlers' job involved edging up a dozen hats, turning them over to women for trimming, and, when the hats were returned, setting off the brims. Until 1886, journeymen received a voucher for each dozen hats they turned over to the trimmer. On payday the curlers received a sum for each voucher they turned in, even if some of the hats they had edged up had not yet been set off. When Brooklyn employers proposed paying for the two operations separately, so as to avoid paying for labor not yet performed, the journeymen vetoed the idea firmly, fearing that it would lead to the division of curling into two distinct specialties.[3]

Regulating Machinery

Hatters were not fond of machinery. As early as the 1840s, English journeymen fought the introduction of ironing machines so fiercely that their employers had to crush the hatters' trade unions before they could fully utilize their machinery.[4] In the 1860s and 1870s, American hat finishers followed a similar course, led by the Knights of St. Clement, a secret association of Brooklyn journeymen. In 1875, the Knights' attempt to sabotage a new blocking machine touched off a major strike. Exasperated Brooklyn manufacturers brought in strikebreakers and obtained police protection for them; eventually, the union men had to concede defeat, and the Knights of St. Clement collapsed.[5]

After this disastrous defeat, hat finishers abandoned the policy of overt obstruction of machinery. Instead, they tried to diminish its impact on the amount and quality of their work. In Danbury, individual shops determined how work would be done, but elsewhere the locals enforced their own restrictions.[6] To discourage employers from installing machines, the hat finishers insisted that the machine operatives earn higher wages than hand workers. If that were not enough to render the competition unprofitable, hatters required that skilled journeymen run the new apparatuses, even though a boy or unskilled helper would have done just as well. Nor was the operative's labor unrestricted; in 1890, when a Brooklyn manufacturer proposed to subdivide the labor of his machine tenders, so one would block, the second iron, and the third finish off, his crew vetoed the suggestion and suggested alternate means to speed up production. Finally, the finishers practiced a legal form of sabotage; they required their employer to specify what his machine was supposed to do, then refused to perform that job by hand, even if the apparatus broke down, hoping by this means to discourage their employers from trying out new technology.[7] These tactics worked well, as long as the manufacturers did not retaliate by going foul. Of course, that is just what many did.

Limiting the Supply of Labor

The hatters could only preserve their autonomy by maintaining high skill standards if they could prevent less-skilled men from entering their trade. To limit the labor supply, hatters relied on apprenticeship regulation as the first line of defense. Between 1860 and 1892 the national association set a maximum of three apprentices per shop; locals could reduce but not raise the figure.[8] Moreover, the association prohibited untrained men from joining the union and insisted upon the union shop as a cardinal rule. Foul men could not work in fair shops; neither could union men work in foul. As the Danbury hatters' constitution specified, "No man shall be considered a fair journeyman who works in any shop that is not under the jurisdiction of the local, except by the consent of the trade or vigilance committee."[9]

Locals could deviate from the closed shop rule only for good reasons. Thus, in 1888, the Orange local "opened" all the nonunion shops in town to its members, in order to organize the entire local trade.[10] Similarly, foul men could join the union at the local's discretion, usually on payment of a fine or high initiation fee. Applicants could appeal to the national board of directors any fines they considered excessive; indeed, they did so often enough that the board devoted much of its time to hearing appeals.[11] On the other hand, locals were inclined to leniency when an organizing campaign was going on; they might even let foul men in for free, a process called "whitewashing," or facetiously, "calcomining."

The operation of the system can be illustrated by analyzing the experience of the Orange, New Jersey, local with nonunion men during the years 1886–93. Trouble began in February 1886 when the local, hoping to unionize F. Berg and Company, turned down the application of Berg's foul men to join the association. Their plan succeeded in April when Mr. Berg agreed to the local's terms, but the journeymen's subsequent harshness toward the foul men at McGall and Allen's alienated him. The local decided that since the men at McGall and Allen's "had thrown so many fair men out of work for so long, they merited" being unemployed. Consequently, it awarded one of McGall and Allen's men a card for free, refused one a card altogether, fined four $300, a half-year's earnings, four others $150, four more $100, and one $75. When the applicants refused to pay, both firms resumed working foul.[12] Within a year, the local regretted its actions but was unable to make the shops fair until 1889, when it took in all the foul men in town, fining some moderately and whitewashing the rest.[13] The resulting dilution in skill standards threatened to undermine the union and the culture it had been established to defend. The finishers' efforts to limit the labor supply were doomed to failure, but that failure was exceedingly gradual.

The Traveling System

> With a groat in each pocket,
> And a coat to keep me dry,
> To travel I'm no stranger
> I'm a roving Hatter Boy.[14]

In the last half of the twentieth century, workers have tended to place a great value on homeownership and a stable family life. Although American workers tend to move once in five years on the average, they usually stay within the same metropolitan areas. Consequently, the geographical mobility of the nineteenth-century artisan is hard to grasp. When journeymen traveled their regular circuits in the nineteenth century, looking for work and good fellowship, they did not resent this as a disruption of their lives. For the "tramp" printer or carpenter, "traveling" was a way of life which allowed for satisfying freedom, frequent adventures, and change of routines. As long as there was a fraternal circle of craftsmen waiting to greet him in each town, the mobile artisan valued his itinerancy.[15] Nor was traveling limited to building tradesmen or printers alone. Highly skilled French glass blowers of the late nineteenth century moved frequently from factory to factory, criss-crossing France in the process.[16]

Even after hatting became factory work in America, finishers continued their mobile ways.[17] In the late nineteenth century the Hat Finishers' National Trade Association protected the right of every member to secure employment in any union shop. When a finisher wanted to leave a particular community, he had to pay his union dues in full in order to secure a traveling card from the secretary of his local. Before he could get work elsewhere, he had to exchange his card for a check from the secretary of the union in whatever town he had stopped. In the words of the Danbury hatters' constitution, "All journeymen coming to work in this district shall deposit their traveling card with the financial secretary, receiving in exchange a local check and said card to be returned upon a strict compliance with trade rules on his desire to leave the district."[18]

Traveling was a regular part of most journeymen's lives. Late every summer, finishers from Orange, Brooklyn, Newark, and Bloomfield went to work in the New York City shops about the time when work in their own shops was slow.[19] Orange men, whose fall season ended late in August, were the mainstays. "It is said that there are so many Orange hatters in New York City's hat shops that you need to be from Orange to get a job there," the *Hatter and Furrier* joked in October 1885.[20] The best evidence we have about how often the hatters moved comes from the minute-book of the Brooklyn finishers' association. During the years 1879–83, every three months an average of 78 men joined the 300-member association, and 72 men left it. Turnover ranged from 11 percent to 52 percent. Clearly, the traveling system was no mere dying relic of times past.[21]

Hatters followed regular traveling patterns when jobs were scarce in their hometowns. Danbury and Orange men traveled back and forth to Brooklyn;[22] indeed, the pattern was so regular that Danbury finishers, working in Brooklyn in the fall, made a habit of returning home each October for the fabled Danbury Fair. Orange and Danbury journeymen visited each others' shops as well.[23] Plant shutdowns were another cause of traveling. For example, when Brooklyn factories closed in March 1889, some of their former employees left for Orange, Newark, and Connecticut.[24] During the five-month South Norwalk strike in the winter of 1884–85, many of the jobless men came to Brooklyn to work.[25]

Thus, the hatters' traveling system both preserved an old craft tradition and enhanced job opportunities. It played an important role in preserving the finishers' autonomy.

Controlling the Shop

The finishers' rules limiting apprenticeship, prohibiting the division of labor, regulating the use of machinery, and requiring the closed shop helped the journeymen retain control of their industry. In the hat shops around the United States, with but a few exceptions, only union men could do the work and only they could be hired. Because the craftsmen insisted on a pay system and a traveling system that gave them flexibility to work when and where they wanted, the hatters were able to control the finishing trade. All their efforts to preserve autonomy would have been unavailing if the finishers could not control the processes and conditions of work in each hat shop. To do so, the hatters enforced rules on such matters as work methods, hiring and firing procedures, and payment plans. Such rules made work in hat factories quite different from present-day industrial production.

Today, factories are places of repetitive work and tight discipline, where employees are subservient to the rhythms of the machines they tend. Naturally, we imagine that factories were, if anything, even more brutal during the initial period of industrialization. Historians have reinforced such conceptions with their descriptions of conditions in the textile mills of Lowell, Massachusetts, and Manchester, England. As Frederich Engels remarked in his *Conditions of the Working Class in England in 1844:*

> Inside the factory . . . the employer is absolute law-giver; he makes regulations at will, changes and adds to his codex at pleasure . . . even if he inserts the craziest stuff. . . . And such rules as these usually are! For instance: 1. The doors are closed ten minutes after work begins, and thereafter no one is admitted until the breakfast hour; whoever is

absent during this time forfeits 3d. per loom. . . . 5. No weaver to stop work without giving a week's notice. The manufacturer may dismiss any employee without notice for bad work or improper behavior. 6. Every operative detected speaking to another, singing or whistling, will be fined 6d.; for leaving his place during work hours, 6d.[26]

The evolution of such a highly disciplined work system is brilliantly sketched in Harry Braverman's *Labor and Monopoly Capital.* According to Braverman, in early industrial capitalism, manufacturers tried "to buy labor as a definite body of work, completed and embodied in the product." To do so they used the putting-out and contract systems, which provided for little supervision of their employees.[27] To increase production, they gathered workers under a single roof, called a factory. At first, "guild and apprenticeship rules and the legal restraints common to feudal and guild modes of production all persisted," but "as the manufacturer consolidated his powers in society and demolished the juridical features of precapitalist social formations," such rules were stripped away. Thus, regular work hours replaced the traditional self-imposed pace which involved interruptions, short days, and holidays.

Braverman argues that through coercion and at other times through skillful manipulation, the capitalists gained control over the work process, thus ensuring that "tradition, sentiment and pride in workmanship played an ever weaker and more erratic role." They brought about a situation by 1850 in which "every step in the labor process [was] divorced from special knowledge and training and reduced to simple labor."[28] The process was completed about 1900 when Frederick Taylor introduced scientific management, which took control over work away from the operative and largely eliminated the skill element in factory labor.[29]

Braverman's description of industrial development is generally sound,[30] but like Engels, he overgeneralizes from the history of the textile industries. In other manufacturing sectors, the degradation of skill and the imposition of tight management control occurred gradually, reaching completion only in the twentieth century. Thus, the Carmaux glass works of France, which employed 250 people in 1880, was run by highly skilled journeymen "souffleurs," who maintained the pace and quality of work, who trained, hired, and fired apprentices, and who even determined whether their trainees would be promoted or given raises.[31] In the Pittsburgh steel mills of the late nineteenth century, industrialists contracted with skilled workers, tying their piece wages to the market price of steel. As Kathy Stone has observed: "The employers had relatively little control over the skilled workers' incomes. Nor could they use wages as an incentive to insure them a desired level of output. Employers could only contract for a job. The price was determined by the market, and the division of labor and the pace of work decided by the workers themselves. . . ."[32] Or, in the words of a company historian of the Carnegie Homestead mill, "The methods of apportioning the work, of regulating the turns, of altering the machinery, in short, every detail of working the great plant, was subject to the interference of some busybody representing the Amalgamated Association."[33]

In a recent study of the mechanization of British industry, Raphael Samuel found evidence indicating that conditions in the French glass works and in American steel mills were not anomalous but were in fact characteristic of the uneven development of industrial capitalism in the nineteenth century. Samuel argues:

> [Mechanization and overall capitalist growth] are in no sense one and the same. Not only is the tempo of change different in different trades, but its character is polyglot. Increased investment was by no means synonymous with the growth of large capitalist firms or the installation of elaborate plant. In some trades—classically in the building industry—it was accompanied by a proliferation of small producers. The response to market competition was also exceedingly various, and impossible to account for simply in terms of economic rationality. The conservatism of the Sheffield employers, which in the 1870s and 1880s exposed them to heavy competition from Germany and America, cannot be separated from the extraordinary power of the workers' trade societies, in mid-Victorian times, and the very special claim of their skills.[34]

American hat factories in the late nineteenth century were also very different from Engels's Manchester mills, for in Danbury and other hatting centers, the journeymen, not the employers and their machines, controlled the process and conditions of work. Rules on such matters as work procedures, methods of payment, and hiring and firing practices enabled the finishers to follow hallowed traditions, to maintain their proud independence in the face of management, and to preserve their favored work rhythms, as the following composite sketch indicates.

Unlike the weavers of Manchester, American hat finishers were not tied to their places, nor were they under the constant supervision of their foremen. They considered it oppressive to work without breaks. When Brooklyn journeymen went to work in the nonunion bonnet shops of New York, they complained about having to work from 7:10 to 12:30 and from 1:00 to 6:00 without stop and without leaving the shop.[35] Since the piece rates were very high in such seasonal ladies' shops, they put up with the obnoxious rules, but in the union's men's hat factories, journeymen insisted upon controlling their work.

We have considered how the men jealously guarded their right to drink; they also interrupted their work for play. When times were dull, they turned their shops into recreation rooms, and played card games, checkers, or quoits; indeed, "no finishing room would be complete without a checker board and a deck of cards."[36] Even in busy times, hatters broke up their work with frequent diversions. Salesmen regularly went through the shops selling jewelry or other wares, while job-hunters from outside wandered about renewing old acquaintances.[37] Meanwhile, the finishers themselves walked through the factories, from department to department, visiting with neighbors and friends.

Funerals and celebrations sometimes brought production to a halt. For example, in September 1885 Newark finishers went out for a picnic to honor Richard Dowdall, a former union officer, on his retirement. Two months later all the factories shut down when Dowdall died. St. Patrick's Day, fair week, Columbus Day, Independence Day, even the week before elections occasioned shop closings.[38]

When work was not piled up too high, hatters left their shops to play baseball or to go on a clambake. Danbury finishers found the lure of the great outdoors to be so strong that they left for picnics even without their bosses' permission during the summer of 1886. So passionate was the Orange men's love for baseball that they played even when they had ample work to do.[39] Even when their employers were rushing out orders, journeymen would break off from their work to go out and tell their friends that the shops were hiring.[40]

Finishers even broke off from work to help journeymen from another trade. They insisted that they would work only on hat bodies that had been "sized" by members of the makers' union. When Orange makers were conducting an organizing campaign in 1886, the finishers' local enforced a system by which each dozen hats sized in a fair shop received a voucher, and only hats with vouchers would be finished. Despite their bosses' complaints that the practice impeded production,[41] the journeymen insisted on asserting their power to aid their fellows.

In all of American industry, perhaps only coopers had equal freedom, at least until machinery destroyed the skilled basis of their trade in the 1880s:

Usually Saturday of each week was payday and of course the temptation to lounge around the shops and chat with one another was most often too great to be overcome by the average cooper, so that day was considered lost so far as production in barrel making was concerned. Furthermore, the old-time cooper had the reputation of being a strong and lusty beer drinker and naturally he couldn't let that reputation lapse. . . .

Saturday night was a big night for the old-time cooper. It meant going out, strolling around the town, meeting friends, usually at the favorite saloon, and having a good time generally, after a week of hard work. Usually the good time continued over into Sunday, so that on the following day he usually was not in the best condition to settle down to the regular day's work.

Many coopers used to spend this day sharpening up their tools, carrying in stock, discussing current events and in getting things in shape for the big day of work on the morrow. Thus, "Blue Monday" was something of a tradition with the coopers, and the day was also more or less lost as far as production was concerned.

"Can't do much today, but I'll give her hell tomorrow" seemed to be the Monday slogan. But bright and early Tuesday morning, "Give her hell," they would, banging away lustily for the rest of the week. . . .[42]

London high-skilled, pieceworking coopers had similar habits: "They strolled in at whatever time of the morning they cared to arrive; they left when they chose; and their lunchtime was spent in the pub across the High Street, wandering over any hour of the morning, and perhaps not returning till half way through the afternoon. When attempts were made to reprimand them, the biggest George would always answer it was his birthday."[43]

If few journeymen could match the hatters' and coopers' freedom, other groups of craftsmen did exert at least some control over their work pace and hours of labor. Not only could each pieceworking union printer decide how rapidly he wanted to set type, he could also determine how much of his share of the job he wanted to delegate to others.[44] Journeymen who were paid by the day or week, on the other hand, had less freedom. Thus, while skilled carpenters were generally free from supervision, they accepted the responsibility for working steadily, without social intercourse, all day long at a rapid pace.[45]

The Structure of Union Power

Neither the individual finisher nor his employer controlled work in the hat finishing shops of the late nineteenth century. Instead, shop crews and the local trade union to which they belonged shared responsibility. The members of each shop elected a steward to collect union dues, to protect the interests of both the journeymen and their employer, and to supervise the hiring of new hands. Stewards had "great power."[46]

To make decisions about work rules and prices, nineteenth-century journeymen broke off from work to discuss the matter. Was the foreman behaving too rudely? Was the current batch of hat bodies harder to finish than previous ones? Was this a good time to ask for a wage increase?

Employers naturally resented their employees interrupting work to discuss such matters, so to placate the manufacturers, in 1882 the HFNTA passed an amendment to the national bylaws requiring shop crews to elect committees to handle grievances, so that the entire work force would not have to stop working.[47] Although many shops disregarded the bylaw,[48] resenting it as an unwarranted expropriation of their rights, shop committees came to bear the primary responsibility for resolving problems in the work place.

Nevertheless, the shop committee was not the key institution in the finishing trade. For one thing, many hatters changed jobs so often they could not form tight ties to their shopmates.[49] More important, shop committees could not determine many of their own work rules, for no employer would long operate under stricter conditions than his competitors faced. To ensure uniformity among the factories within its district, the local became the legislator of work rules on such issues as how apprentices were taught, how many journeymen could work by the week, or what kind of machinery could be used.

In addition to setting policy, the local mediated disputes between shopmates and between shop crews; decided under what conditions men who had quit the union to work in unfair shops could rejoin; and made sure that owners, foremen, and craftsmen in all the shops obeyed local rules. Generally, the local established a vigilance committee, composed of representatives of each shop crew, to handle such matters in the interim between local meetings,[50] but the local remained the hatters' primary institution for control of the trade.

Hiring and Firing

Throughout the late nineteenth century, shop committees and union locals enforced trade rules whose collective impact was to make the finishers, rather than their bosses and foremen, masters of the work environment. Such control contravened the very spirit of the factory system.

Rules limiting management's ability to hire and fire were of crucial importance. The custom of "going on turn" never required a foreman to hire anyone he considered incompetent, but usually employers did not know job applicants anyway because labor turnover was so high in hatting shops.[51] In practice, "going on turn" usually ensured journeymen that they would be hired in the order they appeared at the factory.

If foremen did not have full power to hire, neither could they fire people at will, for firing (or "bagging") was considered antithetical to the spirit of the hatting trade. Foremen occasioned comment whenever they laid anyone off. "I've heard in the last two or three days that some factories are discharging several employees. This is somewhat unusual," the *Hatter and Furrier*'s Brooklyn reporter observed in June 1887.[52] Ordinarily, once a man was shopped, he stayed on until he wanted to leave.

There was an exception to the no firing custom: in Orange, New Jersey, in 1890, manufacturers took advantage of a large labor surplus by discharging their least proficient workers and replacing them with better ones whenever possible.[53] Even in Orange, though, foremen did not fire anyone because of personality conflicts or trade union militancy. Had they done so, they would have met strikes and demands for their resignations. Management's right to hire and fire was severely circumscribed.

While the hatters' customs of "going on turn" and "no firing" were unique, craftsmen in other trades regulated hiring and discharging in their own fashion. Among printers, "the discharging of one man merely because a better one can be had is looked upon as one of the forms of industrial oppression which it is the duty of the union to overthrow."[54] To do so, the International Typographers Union (ITU) allowed foremen to fire men only for incompetence or violating office rules, except during periods of excess, when layoffs in order of seniority were the norm.[55] The foreman's right to hire whomever he wanted was only theoretical, for printers maintained a seniority system which gave first claim on vacant positions to the substitutes who hung around newspaper offices hoping for a bit of work.[56] In many other trades hiring and firing was a management prerogative. Carpenters, for instance, believed that foremen had every right to employ only the best men and to discharge anyone who could not keep up with the pace of the fastest.[57]

Dividing the Work

The finishers limited the foreman's power further by requiring that he give all his crew an equal amount of piecework to do. Equality protected the finishers' independence by denying the foremen the means with which to reward pliable workers and to punish intransigents. Since finishers were often deeply in debt in dull times, favoritism was a major problem. To strip the foremen of such power, the journeymen in Brooklyn and Orange devised a new system, called "running the buck." "In dull times a piece of wood or paper [was] passed from one bench to another" to mark who was next in line to receive his batch of hat bodies to finish.[58]

Hatters were the only craftsmen who ran the buck, but worksharing was known to other crafts, though by no means to all. According to the Webbs, "in [English] trades where work is irregular, the Trade Union objection to its being arbitrarily distributed by the employer—leading as this does, to the extreme dependence of the wageearner—has led to regulations for 'sharing work.' If the workmen know that, however scanty may be the work to be done, it will be fairly distributed among them all, there is much less temptation for the poorer or more grasping members to seek to secure themselves by offering to accept worse conditions of employment."[59]

In American newspaper offices, each regularly employed printer had, by custom, a "sit," a right to an equal amount of work, which he could perform if he wished; if not, he could take off from work and assign a substitute in his place. Although each journeyman could choose whichever substitute he wanted, "there was a strong feeling that each substitute should have at least some work, and public opinion was hostile to undue favoritism."[60] Moreover, printers' rules on overtime work furthered equality, for although newspapers published seven days each week, no journeyman could work more than six days; substitutes received at least one day's work and often more. After 1902, the ITU made equal distribution of overtime compulsory.[61]

On the London docks, each pieceworking cooper received a basic weekly wage, regardless of the amount of work he did. In addition, he received an equal share of the money earned by his shop crew in excess of the guaranteed minimum. American carpenters and London dock laborers, on the other hand, believed that differences within their ranks made equality inequitable. Highly skilled carpenters might "carry"—do some of the work for —younger craftmates, but foremen hired the fastest, generally most experienced men first and summarily fired anyone who could not keep pace. The union locals reinforced such discrimination; their business agents gave out work assignments on the basis of friendship, or family and political connections, rather than in turn.[62] Among London dockers, inequality was formalized. The Port Authority maintained four lists: permanent staff, "A" men, "B" men, and casual workers; men from the first two lists were hired first, for at least a week, while those from the latter two received a day's work or less before returning to the ranks of the unemployed.[63]

Controlling the Work Pace

Labor economist David McCabe found that 65 percent of American trade unionists worked for time wages in 1910, and eight more unions with a membership of more than 60,000 wished to eliminate piecework but could not. Only 314,000 workers, 20 percent of the total organized, preferred and received piece wages; among them were boot and shoe workers, cigar makers, coopers, iron and steel workers, textile workers, miners, some of the longshoremen, moulders, lathers and printers, and finally, the hatters. McCabe believed it was not difficult to explain the varying preferences of different groups of journeymen; in some trades piecework was not feasible because the labor was too varied; in others, it inevitably meant speedups and wage-cuts. Workers desired piece rates only in those cases where they could ensure that manufacturers could not continually cut the rate to increase output.[64]

The hatters knew that matters were not that simple. They maintained piece rates because they wanted the power to set their pace of work and to break off from their labor whenever they wished. Finishers knew they bought that freedom at a price — in forfeited wages, impaired relations with employers, and time lost in disputes.[65] Retaining piece rates required considerable effort on the finishers' part, for in the seasonal and unsteady hatting trade, employers preferred to hire men by the week. Not wanting to get caught short in periods of peak demand, they preferred the security of time contracts.

Moreover, preservation of piece rates in the finishing industry was difficult, for the operation of the system was extremely complicated. At the beginning of each season, the journeymen would draw up a "bill of prices," setting a remuneration schedule for finishing each style, shape, and grade of hat. Fixing piece rates was also frustrating, for new styles appeared frequently, requiring new determinations of what prices would allow journeymen to earn a "fair" wage, approximately $2-2.50 per day. Moreover, whenever a manufacturer changed his fur mixture, he would change the amount of time required to finish the hat, thereby raising the question whether or not the price should be changed. At Dickerson and Brown's factory in Brooklyn, a dispute over a new hat style proved particularly troublesome. The firm gave its finishers' crew a new derby pattern, calling it a square crown. The men objected, insisting the hat was a round crown, and therefore would pay twenty-five cents more per dozen. Unable to resolve the dispute in the shop, the antagonists referred the matter to an arbitration committee, but the employers remained unsatisfied; they appealed the case to the local manufacturers' association, which finally decided in the firm's favor.[66]

Journeymen and their employers spent countless hours arguing over what a fair price would be, and strikes ensued frequently. Indeed, many an employer went "foul" because he could not tolerate his crews' constant requests for adjustments. Since work methods, quality standards, and fur mixtures varied so much from factory to factory, comparability of prices was hard to achieve. Manufacturers often believed that their competitors were paying lower rates than themselves, and it was difficult for the union men to prove them wrong.[67] Moreover, if shop crews set piece rates, there was always the danger that a particularly powerful or crafty employer could obtain lower rates than his competitors, who would themselves soon call for a price cut. When locals tried to meet this threat by adopting uniform price lists, they found it impossible to satisfy their bosses that the prices were truly comparable. In the 1880s, both the Brooklyn and Orange locals adopted uniform bills, and both had to abandon them because the manufacturers' production methods varied so much. Shop-set price bills remained the norm.[68]

By the late nineteenth century, hatters had modified the piecework system to meet their employers' needs for a steady labor force. Like American printers' and English coopers' unions, each finishers' local allowed the manufacturers to employ a limited number of men by the week, primarily to operate machinery. Doing so helped the journeymen resist speeding up of new machines, but the hatters disliked the arrangement, fearing that week workers would become attached to their bosses and act subservient to them.[69]

Their fear was not chimerical; among London coopers, the less-skilled "dry" workers, who were paid by the week, were under much stricter discipline than their pieceworking confreres. At shop meetings held during work hours, they were so "apprehensive of the inevitable reprimand from the foreman cooper for being away from their benches," that they hovered "restlessly, eager to bring the matter to a vote in order to escape to their shop."[70] It was precisely to prevent the development of such dependency that finishers had preserved piece rates, along with the problems they generated, late into the nineteenth century.

Discipline

In order to make sure that journeymen did not break union rules to curry favor with the employer and foremen, the finishers' locals maintained their own disciplinary system. If a finisher took work out of turn, insulted a fellow, or failed to train his apprentice, one of his shopmates, usually the steward, would call a shop meeting or convene the shop committee to discuss the infraction and fine the guilty party.[71] When shops could not resolve such charges, or if an entire crew violated the rules, by allowing too much week work, for example, the union local or its vigilance committee could hear the case and impose fines on the guilty parties.[72] The 1885 bylaws of Danbury's finishers' local made it the "duty of every journeyman who shall be cognizant of a palpable violation of these rules or the common rules of the trade by a member of this association to report the same to the president."[73] While we may doubt that every finisher leapt to tell tales on his brother, it seems clear nonetheless that hatters preferred to police themselves, rather than have management enforce discipline.

Locals had authority over former members as well. A journeyman who had belonged to the HFNTA and then gone foul, wherever he might be, had to apply for reinstatement to the local where he had committed his violation. Naturally, finishers who had seen their bread taken away by a former craftmate were not always quick to forgive. Fines levied against offenders often exceeded $100, two months earnings, and could go as high as $500, although usually provisions were made for installment payments. In the mid-1870s the HFNTA's board of directors began to hear appeals from heavily fined journeymen for reductions in their penalties; the board often granted such requests, but locals always had the first right to punish.[74]

Perhaps there is no better measure of the finishers' dominance in the shops than that foremen were not allowed to attend union meetings, because they were viewed as agents of management, but were required to be union members, subject to punishment by their local's vigilance committee for any violation of union rules.[75] Such power over the foremen greatly enhanced the finishers' control over work in the shops. For example, in October 1887, the Brooklyn local fined a foreman and saw that he was fired because he had taken a $50 bribe from a journeyman who wanted help getting a job.[76] Foremen who abused their power by showing favoritism in dividing the work, a constant temptation, were similarly subject to the union's wrath.[77]

Conclusion

By enforcing shop and local rules, many of which had their origin in earlier periods of English and American hatting, American hat finishers in the late nineteenth century successfully resisted the imposition of industrial factory discipline. They supervised hiring and firing, determined when and how much they worked, controlled the pace of production, and made sure that everyone would share in whatever orders were on hand. In order to maintain their power, they made significant sacrifices in money and involved themselves in bitter disputes with their employers. The rewards, however, were commensurate: hatters were able to remain masters in their shops and thereby to preserve their traditional culture.

The hatters' efforts to retain control of their work were not unique. David Montgomery has demonstrated that throughout American industry in the last quarter of the nineteenth century, skilled workers struggled to preserve mastery of the work process in order to defend their "culture of manliness," in which independence from management authority and generosity toward one's fellows were key features.

Some of the methods the hatters used in their struggle were unique — "going on turn" and "running the buck," for example. Most were shared by some crafts, but no craft shared all. Carpenters, for example, maintained a union-regulated traveling system, but did not practice equality. Printers shared work, but not equally. Thus, we may say that the finishers' culture of work represented a unique constellation of values and customs drawn from a larger cultural pool — the world of American skilled workers in the Gilded Age.

Like their contemporaries, the hatters were finding that maintaining control of the work place required increasingly collective action. Shop meetings became less frequent and less important; local rules, and occasionally national union legislation governed the journeymen's behavior in the shops. The years 1878–93 were a period of transition, during which time hatters joined with allied craftsmen and with employers to fight prison labor; experimented with conciliatory labor relations policies; and developed the union label boycott as a new weapon of struggle. It would not be until after the depression of 1893 had run its course that hat finishers would decide that concerted action by their national union in conjunction with the whole American labor movement was necessary; the prison labor fight of 1878–93 was the first step in the finishers' long journey toward a new practice of solidarity.

NOTES

1. In 1891, only fourteen national unions, representing 14 percent of the organized labor force, successfully regulated apprenticeship, and another ten national unions, representing 39 percent of the organized labor force, left the regulation of apprenticeship to their locals. The fourteen were: American flint glass blowers; hat finishers; eastern bottle blowers; table knife grinders; German-American typographia; pattern makers; iron moulders; hat makers, Philadelphia; amalgamated elastic web finishers; tack makers; and journeymen tailors. See Edward W. Bemis, "The Relations of Trade Unions to Apprentices," *Quarterly Journal of Economics* 6 (1891): 76–93; David H. Bensman, "The Experience of American Apprenticeship" (M.A. thesis, Columbia University, 1972).

2. Danbury Hat Finishers' Association, *Constitution and By-Laws,* Article 23, reprinted in Connecticut Bureau of Labor, *Annual Report* (1890), pp. 277–78.

3. *Hatter and Furrier,* Dec. 1886, p. 23.

4. Andrew Ure, *A Dictionary of Arts, Manufactures and Mines* (New York: D. Appleton and Co., 1850), p. 944; Edward Henry Knight, *Knight's American Mechanical Dictionary* (Boston: Houghton, Osgood and Co., 1876), pp. 1077–78; *Hatter and Furrier,* Aug. 1885, p. 10.

5. Michael Greene, "Supplementary Data on Hatters' Unions," United Hatters Records Collection, Tamiment Library, New York University.

6. *Hatter and Furrier,* Nov. 1886, p. 11; Oct. 1885, p. 11; Mar. 1887, p. 39; Nov. 1889, p. 42; June 1892, p. 27; Nov. 1891, p. 69; Apr. 1890, p. 27.

7. Ibid., Oct. 1885, p. 11; June 1892, p. 27; Nov. 1891, p. 69; Mar. 1889, p. 39; Apr. 1890, p. 27.

8. HFNTA, "Proceedings of Third Convention, May 1860," p. 59.

9. Danbury Hat Finishers' Association, *Constitution and By-Laws,* Article 6, reprinted in Connecticut Bureau of Labor, *Annual Report* (1890), p. 267.

10. *Hatter and Furrier,* Oct. 1888, p. 21.

11. HFNTA, *Semi-Annual Reports,* 1884–93, passim.

12. *Hatter and Furrier,* Feb. 1886, p. 23. During the years 1884–93, the Orange local had more trouble with foul men than any other local save Philadelphia.

13. Ibid., Apr. 1887, p. 15; Dec. 1889, p. 17. This was the largest consolidation undertaken in this period.

14. William H. Francis, *History of the Hatting Trade in Danbury* (Danbury: H. & L. Osborne, 1860), p. 32. Francis reported hearing Danbury hatters singing these words in their shops in 1860.

15. In 1885, when there were 16,183 members of the International Typographical Union, 7,000 men gained employment on their traveling cards. George Barnett, *The Printers* (Cambridge, Mass.: Harvard University Press, 1909), p. 30. Lloyd Ulman, *The Rise of the National Union* (Cambridge, Mass.: Harvard University Press, 1955), p. 65.

16. Joan Scott, *The Glassworkers of Carmaux* (Cambridge, Mass.: Harvard University Press, 1974), p. 54.

17. Steelworking had become so specialized a craft by the late nineteenth century that its members lost their mobility. "The nature of the steelworkers' skill . . . lim-

ited his independence. Unlike a machinist, or bricklayer, his training was only valuable in a steel mill, frequently only those turning out the same product. Moreover, steel plants were largely isolated. . . . Home ownership compounded the problem." David Brody, *Steelworkers in America* (Cambridge, Mass.: Harvard University Press, 1960), p. 87. London coopers were another nonmobile group. They circulated among London shops, but did not travel throughout England. As a result, their unions were "small exclusive societies, each specializing in a particular branch of the trade. . . ." Bob Gilding, *The Journeymen Coopers,* History Workshop Pamphlets, no. 4 (Oxford: Ruskin College, 1971), p. 82. The miners of western Maryland gave little thought to leaving their homes, families and communities. Katherine Harvey, *The Best Dressed Miners* (Ithaca, N.Y.: Cornell University Press, 1969), passim.

18. Danbury Hat Finishers' Association, *Constitution and By-Laws,* bylaw 16, sections 2 and 17, reprinted in Connecticut Bureau of Labor, *Annual Report* (1890), pp. 274–75.

19. *Hatter and Furrier,* Aug. 1886, p. 23; Sept. 1886, pp. 21, 28; Sept. 1885, p. 32; Dec. 1887, p. 32; Nov. 1889, p. 41.

20. Ibid., Oct. 1885, p. 11.

21. Brooklyn Finishers' Association, "Minute-Book," pp. 347, 360, 367, 387, 401, 414, 423, 431, 438, 449, 459, 471, 497, 508, 516, 528, 538. United Hatters Record Collection, Tamiment Library, New York University.

22. *Hatter and Furrier,* Sept. 1885, p. 11; Oct. 1890, p. 47; Nov. 1889, pp. 41, 47; May 1890, p. 33; Aug. 1886, p. 23; Aug. 1889, p. 25.

23. Ibid., Sept. 1886, p. 21; Oct. 1888, p. 33; Sept. 1887, p. 15.

24. Ibid., Sept. 1886, p. 21; Oct. 1888, p. 33; Sept. 1887, p. 15; Sept. 1886, p. 24.

25. Ibid., Jan. 1885, p. 11.

26. Frederick Engels, *Conditions of the Working Class* (Oxford: Blackwell, 1958), p. 179.

27. Harry Braverman, *Labor and Monopoly Capital* (New York: Monthly Review Press, 1975), p. 60.

28. Ibid., pp. 60, 65, 68, 82.

29. Ibid., p. 85.

30. Its biggest flaw is that it does not demonstrate that such developments were inherently capitalist, rather than simply technological.

31. Scott, *The Glassworkers of Carmaux,* p. 22.

32. Katherine Stone, "The Origins of Job Structure in the Steel Industry," *Radical America* 7(Nov.-Dec. 1976): 64.

33. Ibid.

34. Raphael Samuel, "London: Workshop of the World." *History Workshop* 3 (1977): 13.

35. *Hatter and Furrier,* July 1889, p. 36.

36. Ibid., Apr. 1885, p. 30; Mar. 1886, p. 15.

37. Ibid., Sept. 1886, p. 20; Jan. 1888, p. 36; Aug. 1886, p. 24.

38. Ibid., Nov. 1885, p. 35; Sept. 1885, p. 11; Feb. 1886, p. 15; Sept. 1886, p. 21; Oct. 1887, p. 19; July 1890, p. 43; April 1886, p. 32; Nov. 1886, p. 57.

39. Ibid., Aug. 1886, p. 30; Sept. 1886, pp. 28, 32; Oct. 1885, p. 35.

40. Ibid., Dec. 1887, p. 31.

41. Ibid., May 1891, p. 31.

42. Franklin E. Coyne, *The Development of the Cooperage Industry* (Chicago: Lumber Buyers Publishing Co., 1940), p. 21. English wet coopers enjoyed similar freedom well into the twentieth century. See Gilding, *Journeymen Coopers,* pp. 49–51.

43. Gilding, *Journeymen Coopers,* pp. 9–10.

44. Barnett, *The Printers,* p. 213.

45. Robert A. Christie, *Empire in Wood* (Ithaca, N.Y.: Cornell University Press, 1956), pp. 15–16.

46. Danbury Hat Finishers' Association, *Constitution and By-Laws,* Article 14, section 12, reprinted in Connecticut Bureau of Labor, *Annual Report* (1890), p. 273. Stewards kept 5 percent of the dues as compensation.

47. HFNTA, "Proceedings of Special Convention, May 1882," p. 431.

48. This was an issue in the South Norwalk strike. See HFNTA, *Semi-Annual Report,* Nov. 1885. London coopers held shop meetings, called "roll-ups," during work hours as well. The steward, known as the "collector," would stand up in the shop and call "roll-up." All would drop work to discuss piece rates, new materials, the cleanliness of the shops, victimization by the foreman, or employer treatment of "bad" work. Only journeymen could attend. After the meeting was over, the collector would discuss the crew's decision with the employer. The men stayed away from work until after that discussion had been satisfactorily concluded. Gilding, *Journeymen Coopers,* pp. 84–85.

49. *Hatter and Furrier,* July 1881, p. 4.

50. Ibid., June 1892, p. 27; Dec. 1891, p. 48; Mar. 1891, p. 38; Oct. 1885, p. 11; Jan. 1887, p. 15.

51. Ibid., July 1881, p. 4.

52. Ibid., June 1887, p. 27.

53. Ibid., Sept. 1890, p. 25. The local had created the oversupply by signing up low-skilled men.

54. Barnett, *The Printers,* p. 241.

55. Ibid.

56. Ibid., p. 230.

57. Christie, *Empire in Wood,* pp. 14–16.

58. *Hatter and Furrier,* Apr. 1886, p. 31; Aug. 1886, p. 20; Apr. 1889, p. 29. Dividing work equally also helped maintain the finishers' solidarity. If the better or faster men had been given more work to do than the others, the craft could have become divided into high- and low-skill divisions. Also see Ulman, *Rise of the National Union,* p. 553.

59. Sidney Webb and Beatrice Webb, *Industrial Democracy* (London: Longmans, Green and Co., 1902), p. 437.

60. Barnett, *The Printers,* p. 213.

61. Ibid., pp. 221–22.

62. Christie, *Empire in Wood,* pp. 15–16.

63. R. B. Oram, *The Dockers' Tragedy* (London: Hutchinson and Co., 1970), pp. 45–46.

64. David McCabe, *The Standard Rate in American Trade Unions,* Johns Hopkins

University Studies in Historical and Political Science, series 30, no. 2 (Baltimore: Johns Hopkins University Press, 1912): 187–99.

65. In his essay, "Custom, Wages, and Work-Load," Eric Hobsbawm notes that skilled workers in the nineteenth century were often paid at below their market cost, but "demanded some of their extra price in terms of non-economic satisfactions, such as independence of supervision, dignified treatment, and solidarity." Hobsbawm, *Labouring Men* (Garden City, N.Y.: Doubleday and Co., 1967), p. 409.

66. *Hatter and Furrier,* Aug. 1885, p. 14. London coopers had price lists carefully tabulated "to allow no latitude to the employer, and to ensure complete control by the coopers over every element and material of their craft. Because of this they were a constant source of contention between masters and men." Gilding, *Journeymen Coopers,* p. 62.

67. Such was the case in Orange, New Jersey, on 21 March 1887, when manufacturer John J. Perrine asked his finishers to accept a price cut on some grades of hats, claiming he was paying more for them than his competitors were. The journeymen turned down Perrine's request, but called in an arbitration committee, composed of three manufacturers and three finishers, to effect a settlement. The committee proposed a compromise wage cut, but Perrine, believing he was entitled to a larger one, began negotiating with the town's foul men. Alarmed, the Orange finishers' association agreed to take a substantial wage cut. The matter did not end there; because Perrine had antagonized the foul men, they determined not to work for him in future. Emboldened by the foul men's action, the fair hatters struck Perrine twice to regain their old prices. In this case, both sides lost: Perrine production, his men work. *Hatter and Furrier,* Apr. 1887, p. 8; July 1887, p. 19.

68. Ibid., June 1886, p. 43; Apr. 1888, p. 31; Dec. 1884, p. 30; May 1885, p. 8; Apr. 1891, p. 27; Apr. 1893, p. 25.

69. Ibid., Oct. 1885, p. 11; Ulman, *Rise of the National Union,* p. 549.

70. Gilding, *Journeymen Coopers,* p. 10.

71. Danbury Hat Finishers' Association, *Constitution and By-Laws,* reprinted in Connecticut Bureau of Labor, *Annual Report* (1890), p. 276. American printers practiced a similar fining system to prevent infringement on the piece scale and other infractions. Barnett, *The Printers,* pp. 292–95.

72. *Hatter and Furrier,* Jan. 1886, p. 15; Jan. 1886, p. 29; July 1887, p. 31.

73. Danbury Hat Finishers' Association, *Constitution and By-Laws,* reprinted in Connecticut Bureau of Labor, *Annual Report* (1890), p. 274.

74. HFNTA, "Proceedings of the Board of Directors," 1875–85, passim.

75. *Hatter and Furrier,* Sept. 1892, p. 36; Apr. 1886, p. 23.

76. Ibid., Nov. 1887, p. 26; Mar. 1886, p. 50.

77. Ibid., Apr. 1886, pp. 23, 31.

CHAPTER 6

The Prison Labor Fight: 1878–1883

SINCE THE BEGINNING of trade unionism in the American hat finishing industry, early in the nineteenth century, the finishers' locals had borne the lion's share of the responsibility for preserving the hatters' traditional work culture. To maintain the craft's high standards, the locals had severely limited the number of apprentices entering the trade each year, and had enforced strict work rules to prohibit the division of labor.

Such local rules had served as a constant irritant to the hat manufacturers, who found themselves ever more pressed by the stiff competition in their industry to cut costs, particularly the cost of labor. As a result, there were frequent strikes and less frequent, but numerous, decisions by manufacturers to run their shops on a nonunion basis.

Ever since the silk hat finishers had split from the Hat Finishers' National Trade Association in 1868, the remaining fur hatting locals had coped with the proliferation of foul finishing shops by organizing the nonunion work crews wherever possible, a policy known as consolidation. For the decade 1868–78, the consolidation policy had enabled locals to enforce their work rules; consequently, the locals had managed to preserve a high degree of autonomy and to curb the growth of their national organization's power. With each consolidation, low-skilled men came into the trade, diminishing its reputation and standards. In the short run, the effects were minimal, but in the long run, they threatened the very basis of the finishers' craft. The unionists' autonomy and exclusivity could hardly survive when members were no more highly skilled than nonmembers.

Before the finishers could devise a new approach to the problem of declining craft standards, a new problem arose which threatened their craft with a more immediate demise. In 1878, the states of New Jersey and New York announced plans for a significant expansion in their prison hat manufacturing operations. Believing themselves faced with imminent disaster, the finishers made the elimination of prison hatting their chief priority for the next five years.

The Problem of Prison Labor

The contract system, under which businesses paid the state for the privilege of employing convicts in prison workshops, originated in Massachusetts in 1807.[1] The plan not only reduced taxes but also satisfied popular desire to keep inmates busy at productive labor.[2] Although craftsmen frequently complained that prison competition undercut law-abiding workers, the system grew steadily as one way to finance the costs of America's burgeoning penal systems.[3] By 1850, "contractors dominated the scene in all but 3 or 4 of the [state] prisons."[4]

By the 1850s, the original purpose of incarceration had largely been forgotten: "the objective point of . . . penitentiary plans [was] pecuniary gains to the State. . . ."[5] Contracting had become big business; nearly half of America's 30,000 prison inmates worked under contract.[6] It was also good politics; superintendants who collected large revenues from prison labor were an asset to the governors who appointed them and, consequently, could hope to survive changes in their party's fortunes.[7]

Although the HFNTA had opposed prison labor ever since its founding convention in 1854, it was not until 1878, "the most disastrous year ever experienced by the trade," that the union made concerted efforts to bring the practice to an end.[8] The immediate spur was rumors that the superintendent of New Jersey's Trenton State Prison was soliciting bids on a contract for hat manufacturing.[9] Orange and Newark finishers, already suffering long periods of idleness for which they blamed William Carroll and Company's hatting contract at New York's Sing Sing Prison, began a protest campaign in January 1878.[10] To alert political leaders to the opposition, a prison labor committee, headed by Edward Stopford, organized rallies and circulated petitions. Most important, two members of the state legislature, Captain William Pierson, an Orange hat manufacturer, and William H. Fiedler, a Newark hat retailer, agreed to sponsor the anti-contract labor bill. After two months of rallies and lobbying, the legislature voted overwhelmingly on 7 March 1878 to prohibit convict hatting.[11]

One month later, the struggle moved across the Hudson River, when New York State's superintendent of prisons, Louis Pilsbury, announced the transfer of his hat manufacturing contract with William Carroll and Com-

pany to Clinton Prison in Dannemora, New York, where a large, new prison workshop was to be erected to accommodate 500 convicts. The prisoners' labor to finish cheap felt hats would earn the state twenty-five cents per
day, one-eighth the rate of union finishers; prison hatters could not be expected to possess the skill requisite to finish the higher grades.

The Brooklyn hatters hastily established a prison labor committee, and
asked their local representatives, Assemblyman John H. Bergen and Senator John C. Jacobs, to introduce a bill prohibiting prison hatting.[12]
Brooklyn hat manufacturers added their protests to the journeymen's, sending a petition up to Albany "calling for relief from the competition of prison
labor."[13] Lending further respectability to the hatters' protest, Brooklyn's
board of supervisors passed a resolution asking the legislature to heed the
finishers' complaints, but the rural-dominated, economy-minded New
York state legislature did not respond to the appeals of the Brooklyn journeymen. The finishers' lobbyist, John Phillips, found that "the workingmen's representatives were his best friends," but "all the others seemed to be
shy of him."[14] In May 1878, the state senate defeated the abolition bill
14–4; the four favorable urban Democrats were overwhelmed by twelve
Republicans and two rural Democrats.[15] When, just weeks later, prison officials began to install "a large quantity of hatting machinery" in the Clinton
workshop at the state's expense, it became clear that the struggle to halt
convict labor would be a long one.[16]

The hatters' trouble worsened when the Waring Hat Manufacturing
Company of Yonkers secured contracts to employ 200 convicts at Massachusetts' Concord State Prison and 50 more in two penitentiaries in Rhode
Island. By April 1879, nearly 600 prisoners in New York, Massachusetts,
and Rhode Island were making and finishing cheap men's and ladies' fur
hats.[17] The workers and most of the manufacturers agreed that this was an
intolerable burden, for although only 600 convicts worked at hatting, compared to 6,000 in shoemaking, the proportional burden was heavier on hatters than on any other trade. Prison workers worked ten hours a day, six
days a week, all year round, whereas free journeymen suffered unsteady
work and four months seasonal unemployment in every twelve.[18]

When it came to proposing solutions to the prison labor problem, the
hatters were far from consistent. At times they accepted the legitimacy of
for-profit contracting, simply arguing for the diversification of prison industry into many branches of trade. HFNTA President Cornell argued
reasonably, "I have no doubt that the general sentiment of skilled laborers
in this country is in favor of the employment of convicts at some business by

which they can maintain themselves when they regain their liberty provided the amount of labor done in any branch is regulated by a maximum standard to bear equally on all branches of trade carried on in prisons and other institutions." He suggested that the number of prisoners engaged on contract should never exceed between 3–10 percent of the number of free journeymen working at the same trade.[19] The hatters often made a different argument, that the contract convict labor system was itself evil, a source of corruption and a spur to abuse of prison inmates. Following the argument to its logical conclusion, the journeymen often called for the elimination of the contract system altogether, particularly in the years 1881–83.[20]

Goaded by a sense of injustice, the finishers' attacks on prison labor were often false, even hysterical. Captain Julius Ellendorf, German-American leader of the South Norwalk hatters, told the Connecticut Special Committee on Contract Convict Labor, "As in the earliest days of the anti-slavery agitation, men were called traitors for advocating universal freedom, and fools for predicting its final triumph, so we are today content to be opposed and denounced for advocating the abolition of a system that is but little better in its results and in its works than slavery itself."[21] Understandably, men carried away with such passion frequently overestimated the number and productivity of convict hatters; understated the size of the free work force; spread false charges that contractors were practicing ruthless brutality against inmates; and falsely accused contractors of making windfall profits at the state's expense.[22] To give but one example, at the beginning of the prison labor campaign, President Cornell estimated that exploited prison hatters produced twice the daily output of free journeymen; later, the Massachusetts Special Committee on Contract Convict Labor estimated the true proportion to be two-thirds.[23]

Several manufacturers corroborated the journeymen's complaints that prison labor was harming the hatting trade. Testifying before the New Jersey Commission on Prison Labor in 1879, W. D. Yocum, of the Newark firm of Yates, Wharton and Company, was most specific in his complaints:

> From the first of November, 1875, to the first of May, 1876, I made 5039 dozens of hats, similar to those now made in the State Prisons. Last year, under the State Prison system, I did not produce one hat of that description. The lowest priced hats I made last season was the $13.50 a dozen. . . . On the first of May, the contractor of the [New York] State Prison brought some of my hats and put them on sample, and agreed to duplicate them for consumers at $10.50 a dozen.[24]

Twenty-five Connecticut manufacturers agreed. In testimony before their legislature's investigating commission in 1879, they charged that "already prison ladies' hat production [in New York and Massachusetts] has driven most of those engaged in business [in Connecticut] out. . . . The prison-made men's hats sell cheaper than free manufacturers can make them."[25] Danbury's leading hat manufacturer, who was a member of the commission, testified that prison labor had "almost destroyed" his company's ladies' hat trade, impelling a switch to cheap men's hat production.[26]

The National Campaign Against Prison Labor

In the summer of 1878, the finishers decided to mount a nationwide campaign to halt the erosion of their trade. The HFNTA convened a "Convention of Hatters" in Orange, New Jersey, on 10 September 1878, in order to organize an alliance of workers from all the different branches of the hatting industry. Forty-seven delegates attended, representing most of the principal finishers' locals, most of the locals affiliated with the hat makers' national association, and, in addition, several locals of independent makers. Resolving to put an end to the employment of all skilled labor by prisoners, the delegates agreed to establish a continuing organization separate from the two national associations. They elected John Phillips, secretary of the Brooklyn finishers' local, as secretary and authorized him to impose a levy of twenty-five cents per member per year on all the hatters' locals.[27]

Convention delegates designated political activity as their chief weapon. Lobbyists would press the various state legislatures to abolish contracting; they would be backed up by electoral campaigns urging hatters "regardless of Party affiliation" to vote for candidates opposed to prison labor. In addition, locals were to forbid their members to work for employers who contracted for prison work. Finally, the journeymen invited the cooperation of dealers, jobbers, and manufacturers.[28]

For the next five years, similar gatherings were held in the principal hatting districts. They were largely ritualistic and inspirational; the only innovation came in 1879, when delegates approved a campaign to "boycott any wholesale or retail merchant who deals with articles manufactured by prison labor,"[29] but there is no evidence that the locals implemented this decision. Political action was of paramount importance.

Determined to demonstrate their political potency, the hatters of New York, Connecticut, and New Jersey entered the electoral campaigns in the fall of 1878. Danbury finishers elected their former local president, Charles H. Hoyt, to the state assembly, and Judge Lyman Brewster went to the state senate, firmly committed to abolition as well. In neighboring Bethel, the journeymen elected William H. Judson, another former union official, to the legislature on the same plank.[30]

Brooklyn hatters, who had less political experience than their Yankee colleagues, won respect but no victories. Dissatisfied with the way their assemblyman, Mr. Bergen, had marshaled their bill in the previous legislative session, they nominated John P. Egan, a union activist, for assembly in the Ninth District on an anti-prison labor ticket. On election day, the journeymen "voted solid for their ticket," "breaking the old party line in the District, a thing that was never done before."[31] Though Egan ran third, his 1800 votes were enough to boost the Republican nominee to victory over the Democratic incumbent. The hatters had made their point; they wouldn't be "overlooked in the future."[32]

It was in New Jersey's Essex County that the hatters achieved their greatest political success in the fall of 1878. So impressed were the politicians with the journeymen's anti-prison labor campaign of the previous spring that every candidate of both major parties pledged his opposition to the contract system, obviating any need for a third-party slate.[33]

By the following year, the hatters' political campaign, together with protests by stove moulders, shoemakers, and other craftsmen, and agitation by prison reformers, succeeded in inducing the legislatures of Connecticut, New Jersey, and Massachusetts to appoint commissions to investigate the contract labor system.[34] When a number of hatting journeymen and manufacturers were appointed to the commissions, the finishers, and their president E. D. Cornell, were confident that the investigations would lead to the abolition of prison hatting.[35]

The finishers' confidence was soon dashed. After visiting state prisons and holding individual and joint hearings, all three commissions agreed that contracting as a means of making prisons self-sustaining was desirable; moreover, the commissions did not confirm the workingmen's complaint about the impact of prison industry on free labor.

The Massachusetts Commission was blunt:

> The testimony . . . stripped of its verbiage . . . has brought your Committee to the opinion that the effect of prison contracts upon the State is not appreciable. Public sentiment is prone to jump at conclusions, and it is but natural that a mechanic who finds it difficult to earn his bread in times of depression should look with hostile eyes at prison competition. . . . The hat manufacturers . . . whose testimony could

be secured did not . . . show that their business was injured by prison labor to an extent that would call for legislative interference.[36]

New Jersey's investigatory commission, which had been subjected to intensive lobbying by local hatters and shoemakers, was no more impressed by the workers' testimony, concluding "it is only in periods of financial and industrial depression that the competitive labor of convicts can be injurious or sensibly felt."[37]

Most sympathetic to the finishers' plight was the Connecticut commission, whose members included three representatives of the hatting trade. While agreeing with its counterparts that the harm done by convict labor had been exaggerated, Connecticut's commission singled out the hatting industry as an exceptional case. In this, it agreed with the testimony of Massachusetts State Commissioner of Labor Carroll D. Wright who, on the basis of a full-scale study conducted the year before,[38] concluded that "convict labor is not especially injurious to labor except in special cases. In regard to the hat making industry, for instance, the fur hatters number 5 or 6,000 in the United States outside the prison. In the prisons of the United States there are 593 working at the same branch; and I cannot blame the hatters for finding fault, the number is so great against them."[39] To prevent further discrimination, it recommended that future legislatures hold hearings before awarding any contract to employ more than seventy-five prisoners in one industry. Finishers and manufacturers were "disappointed" with such a weak proposal.[40]

Instead of bringing about a regional agreement to abolish prison hatting, the joint committees' recommendation was only that prison industries be diversified, preferably through interstate action, to avoid unduly harming any one trade.[41] Only the state of Connecticut acted on the proposal when, in March 1880, the legislature passed a bill requiring public hearings whenever contracts were proposed to employ more than fifty convicts in any one trade.[42] Frustrated, the journeymen turned once more to political action.

The hatters' electoral efforts were particularly impressive in 1880, when Brooklyn makers and finishers united to push the candidacy of the Reverend J. Hyatt Smith for U.S. Congress from the Third District. Smith, the son of a "Yankee Schoolmaster," was the minister at the Lee Avenue Baptist Church in Brooklyn, when, by chance, his sermon in opposition to prison labor attracted the workers' attention in 1879.[43] Reverend Smith's opposition to convict hatting managed to combine religious piety, conservative political principles, and solicitude for the dignity of labor. In accepting the hatters' support, in 1880, he said:

> God has dignified labor. . . . Industry is insulted by Mongolian labor and I believe God will rebuke it. Free industry is today insulted by prison labor. A man who has his board and lodging free because he is a scoundrel, can throw his goods before the honest mechanics' door, twenty-five per cent less than that citizen can produce these goods. That is an insult to God. . . . I am jealous of the encroachments of government, state or national, in entering the lists as a competitor with the honest toil of the citizen. That exceeds the boundary and just prerogative of a republican government.[44]

Though he was a conservative Republican, Reverend Smith's popularity among the hatters induced Brooklyn Democratic boss McLaughlin to force the regular Democratic nominee to withdraw in the clergyman's favor.[45] The journeymen worked "systematically and without cessation for their favorite"; on election day they had six men at all the polling places, each man wearing a blue badge upon which was printed in ink, "For Congress, Third District, J. Hyatt Smith."[46] Matched against the highly favored incumbent, the millionaire Simeon B. Chittenden, Reverend Smith pulled "one of the surprises of the campaign," "laying out his opponent in a cruel manner" in an election that was otherwise "a sweeping Republican victory."[47] The hatters' votes provided a large part of Smith's margin of victory. In the Eleventh Ward, which included in its population "a very large number of hatters," the clergymen compiled his largest majority, over 1500 votes.[48]

The finishers' dramatic election victory brought stalemate, not success. The problem was that outside the Brooklyn, lower Manhattan, and Yonkers hatting districts, the hatters lacked the political resources with which to induce legislators, whose main desire was to keep taxes down, to oppose a moneymaking prison industry. Nor did it help that the Republican governor, Robinson, supported contract labor for the same reason.[49] In the 1881 session of the New York state legislature, the hatters' bill went down to defeat for the fourth time, despite the fact that all but one of Brooklyn's representatives and most of the states' urban Democrats were favorable.[50]

Even the first significant outbreak of protest by workers in other New York industries failed to bring the hatters victory in 1882. In the spring, when the Buffalo trades' assembly began to pressure local legislators to vote against the contract system, and when Yonkers shoemakers and moulders joined the protest campaign, the hatters' hopes soared, for these were just the sorts of allies the finishers had previously lacked.[51] As if to underscore the importance of the new allies, in May 1882 the state senate passed the hatters' bill for the first time, but the finishers' hopes were dashed once again in the assembly by Republicans and rural Democrats.[52]

Finally, in November 1882, the tide changed when Grover Cleveland, the Democratic mayor of Buffalo, won election as governor of New York. Although Cleveland's stand on the contract convict labor system had not been an issue in the campaign, he revealed his moderate outlook soon after the election: "It is very questionable whether the state should . . . seek to realize a profit from convict labor. In my judgment it should not; especially if the danger of competition between convicts and those who honestly toil is increased."[53]

The hatters' carefully cultivated relationship with the Brooklyn Democratic party leadership paid off in the winter of 1883, when A. C. Chapin won election as speaker of the New York assembly. Chapin, a Brooklynite long associated with the hatters' cause, appointed their lobbyist, Dennis J. Hagerty, as postmaster of the house, and then shepherded the bill abolishing prison hatting through the assembly, where it passed by a vote of 78–28 on 21 February 1883. A week later the senate followed, and Governor Cleveland signed the bill on 8 March.[54]

New York finishers had one final flourish. Their efforts induced the New York legislature to authorize a referendum on the question of abolishing all convict labor in the state, to be held in November 1883. To show their unselfishness, Brooklyn's finishers campaigned hard and with great success. Despite the opposition of most of the state's newspapers, the proposition passed by a wide margin, 405,882 to 266,950, in the heaviest vote ever recorded in a referendum up to that time. In fashioning their victory, the hatters and their allies had convinced an overwhelming majority of the state's urban workers that the protection of free labor was more important than low taxes. The vote in seventeen cities was 279,223 favorable to only 27,406 negative. Kings County voters supported their own by an astonishing 73,395 to 6,188.[55]

Meanwhile, the abolition campaign had slow going in Massachusetts. Largely because there were few free hatters in the Bay State, and complaints from journeymen elsewhere carried little weight, three consecutive sessions of the state legislature ignored the 1880 prison commission's recommendation that the number of convicts under contract in any one trade be limited. Prospects brightened in November 1882, when General Ben Butler, a "workingman's candidate," won election as governor of Massachu-

setts, pledged to the abolition of prison labor,[56] but Governor Butler reneged on his promise, renewing the Concord Prison hatting contract in
May 1883. For two more years, prison hatting continued in Massachusetts,
but in July 1883 the governor did sign legislation limiting the number of
convicts employed in any trade to 150.[57] The fight was almost won; by
1886, hats were no longer made in American prisons.[58]

Conclusion

The prison labor fight had little impact on the internal structure of the
HFNTA. Newark finishers had initiated the campaign on their own, and
thereafter, while the locals attempted to secure state legislation prohibiting
convict hatting, the HFNTA's role was limited to exhortation. Moreover,
despite the fact that association officers placed high priority on the struggle,
their calls to action proved ineffective, for several of the locals declined to
participate in the annual convention of hatters or to pay their assessments
to the campaign funds.[59]

Although the prison labor fight did not change the HFNTA's internal
structure, it did alter the finishers' relationships with other groups. For instance, makers and finishers had previously operated independently, each
group content to control work in its own department, but because convicts
both made and finished hats, journeymen from the two branches united on
the local level to lobby for state legislation and to round up votes in election
campaigns. Such cooperation paved the way for future joint action on a
union label.

In addition, because prison-made fur hats were underselling wool hats,
the prison labor fight also brought the fur finishers into alliance with the
wool hatters, who previously had been bitter foes.[60] The silk finishers, once
the worst of enemies, joined the prison labor fight as well, apparently from
altruistic motives.[61] The HFNTA would need such allies in the near future.

Furthermore, the prison labor fight broadened the hatters' political contacts with politicians and other groups of organized workers. In the ensuing
decade, the finishers' activities in local labor parties and in Democratic party organizations would benefit from the experience gained in the fight for
abolition; moreover, the hatters' efforts to gain protective tariff legislation
in the latter part of the decade would be another outgrowth of the prison
labor campaign.

Finally, the hatters' not-always-successful attempts to coordinate their
opposition to prison labor with the activities of other groups of workmen,

such as stove moulders and shoemakers, facilitated later cooperation in local and national labor organizations, such as the Brooklyn Central Labor Union, the New York State Workingmen's Organization, and the Knights of Labor.[62] The prison labor fight was a bridge enabling the finishers to move from being a self-contained craft organization to being members of a labor movement.

In the long run, the most significant feature of the prison labor controversy was the way it brought journeymen and their employers together in common struggle. As it became clear how much union interests were bound with those of its customary foe, the officers of the HFNTA moved to develop a policy of conciliatory trade relations. From the very beginning of the anti-convict hatting campaign in New Jersey in the winter of 1878, the finishers had joined with manufacturers to lobby in the state legislature. Their cooperation extended to politics in November 1878, when Orange hatters elected hat manufacturer John Gill to lead their fight in Trenton as an assemblyman.[63] Two New Jersey manufacturers were particularly active, George J. Ferry and W. D. Yocum; they lobbied not only in Trenton but in Albany as well.[64]

Empire State hat manufacturers supported the finishers' electoral efforts. New York City's leading hatter, Edward Knox, gave Reverend Smith $500 seed money for his triumphant campaign, for example, and Brooklynite Hosea O. Pearce contributed by giving his men five days off to campaign for Pearce's friend and neighbor, the popular Reverend Smith.[65] Then, in February 1883, in the crucial days when the hatters' bill looked like it might finally have a chance to pass the Albany legislature, Hosea's son, Henry O. Pearce, and James H. Prentice traveled up to the capitol to testify for the abolition of prison labor.[66]

Connecticut manufacturers participated in the campaign as well, particularly when a group of twenty-five of them submitted joint testimony before the State Commission on Prison Labor in 1879, complaining that convict hatting was cutting into their trade.[67] Journeymen in both Bethel and Danbury expressed their appreciation by helping to elect industrialists to represent their anti-prison labor views in Hartford.[68]

Although such cooperation was important, the manufacturers continually failed to meet the journeymen's expectations.[69] Brooklyn manufacturers, for instance, did not once travel to Albany to testify during the years 1878–82.[70] The short-lived Fur and Wool Hat Manufacturers' Association, headed by two ardent foes of prison hatting, George J. Ferry and Edmund Tweedy, did not go on record in opposition; indeed, it accepted prison hat

contractor William C. Carroll into membership. At an association ban-
quet, Massachusetts contractor William Waring even had the audacity to
offer the toast "to prison hatting."[71]

Despite the manufacturers' decision not to embrace the journeymen's
cause wholeheartedly, the leaders of the HFNTA considered anti-prison
labor cooperation significant as an indication of the potential benefits of
labor-management harmony. At the end of his long career as president of
the HFNTA, E. D. Cornell made this point with much feeling:

> I am happy to congratulate you on the growing evidence of a return in
> great measure to our former prosperity; also on the general harmony
> and peace which prevails in the trade at large. I think that this state of
> things is owing in a measure to the existence of large hat contracts in
> the State prisons, the effect of which has been to awaken the bosses and
> journeymen to the fact that they have a mutual interest at stake and
> that the threatening of that interest has called for a unity of sentiment
> and action between them, which has laid to rest all minor questions,
> and given proof that the legend on our Traveling Card, "The Interests
> of Employers and Journeymen are inseparable" is no unmeaning as-
> sertion. If this is the case, as appears to me, then prison labor is not the
> unmixed evil we thought it.[72]

President Cornell's successor, Richard P. Dowdall, shared these sentiments.[73] In the years to come, conciliation was to be a keynote of the finishers' national trade policies.

NOTES

1. E. T. Hiller, "The Development of the System of Control of Convict Labor
in the United States," in *The Journal of the American Institute of Criminal Law and Criminology* 5 (1914–15): 251.

2. Blake McKelvey, *American Prisons* (Montclair, N.J.: Smith, Patterson Publishing Corp., 1968), p. 13.

3. Prison reformers also opposed prison labor, charging that contractors ignored
their employees' moral condition; see ibid., pp. 13, 40, 59.

4. Ibid., p. 40.

5. Eastern Penitentiary of Pennsylvania, *Annual Report* (1875), p. 38.

6. Massachusetts Bureau of Statistics of Labor, *Annual Report* (1880), pp. 10–23;
Hat, Cap and Fur Trade Review, Apr. 1879, p. 163.

7. McKelvey, *American Prisons,* p. 59.

8. HFNTA, "Proceedings of the First Convention, 1854," pp. 53–54.

9. John S. Perry, "Prison Labor" (Albany, N.Y.: 1882–83), n.p.

10. *Hat, Cap and Fur Trade Review,* Jan. 1878, p. 114; *Clothier and Hatter,* Apr.

1878, p. 25; May 1878, p. 23. Later, Dennis J. Hagerty, a Brooklyn union leader, said: "Hatting was first introduced [in prison] in 1876 through a contract given by Mr. Pilsbury to Carroll and Co. It attracted no special notice from the trade as it was generally considered that it would not amount to much. That the competition had both weight and influence was realized in the year 1878 which was the most disastrous year ever experienced in the trade." *Hatter and Furrier,* Apr. 1881, p. 11.

11. The legislature did not prohibit prison shoe making, which was actually being done at the time in Trenton State Prison. *Clothier and Hatter,* Feb. 1878, p. 21; Apr. 1878, p. 17; *Hat, Cap and Fur Trade Review,* Mar. 1878, p. 155; Feb. 1878, p. 133; also *Orange Journal,* cited in *Clothier and Hatter,* Apr. 1878, p. 25; HFNTA, *Semi-Annual Report,* May 1879.

12. *Hat, Cap and Fur Trade Review,* Apr. 1878, p. 183; *Clothier and Hatter,* May 1878, p. 13.

13. *Clothier and Hatter,* Apr. 1878, p. 25.

14. Ibid., p. 31.

15. Ibid., May 1878, p. 17.

16. *Hat, Cap and Fur Trade Review,* June 1878, p. 229; Convention of Hatters, "Proceedings of the First Convention, Sept. 1878," p. 6.

17. *Clothier and Hatter,* July 1878, p. 27; *Hat, Cap and Fur Trade Review,* May 1879, p. 183. In the end, 220 inmates of Concord State Prison worked at hatting.

18. Convention of Hatters, "Proceedings, Sept. 1878" p. 6.

19. HFNTA, *Semi-Annual Report,* May 1880; Connecticut Special Committee on Contract Convict Labor, *Report* (1880), p. 218.

20. The fullest exposition of the argument that the contract convict labor system was evil may be found in the *Clothier and Hatter,* April 1879, p. 29.

21. Connecticut Committee on Convict Labor, *Report* (1880), p. 266.

22. HFNTA, *Semi-Annual Report,* May 1879; Nov. 1880; Convention of Hatters, "Proceedings, Sept. 1878," pp. 6, 9; *Clothier and Hatter,* Apr. 1879, p. 38; *Hat, Cap and Fur Trade Review,* June 1878, p. 248. While the hatters' distortions are understandable, the hypocrisy of their professing concern for prison inmates while excluding ex-convicts from union hat shops is hardly becoming.

23. Convention of Hatters, "Proceedings, Sept. 1878," p. 6; Massachusetts Convict Labor Commission, *Report* (1880), p. 28.

24. Committee on Prison Labor of the State of New Jersey, *Report* (1879), p. 46.

25. Connecticut Committee on Convict Labor, *Report* (1880), p. 105.

26. *Hat, Cap and Fur Trade Review,* Feb. 1879, p. 26. In 1878 and 1879, fewer manufacturers joined the journeymen's campaign than they had expected.

27. The fact that the HFNTA did not take a direct role in directing the prison labor campaign is a reflection of that organization's limited authority and resources.

28. Convention of Hatters, "Proceedings, Sept. 1878," passim.

29. Convention of Workingmen of the United States of America, "Proceedings, Oct. 1879," p. 9.

30. *Clothier and Hatter,* Oct. 1878, p. 27; HFNTA, *Semi-Annual Report,* Nov. 1878.

31. *Clothier and Hatter,* Dec. 1878, p. 39; Feb. 1879, p. 34; HFNTA, *Semi-Annual Report,* Nov. 1878.

32. *Clothier and Hatter,* Dec. 1878, p. 39.

33. Ibid., Nov. 1878, p. 17.

34. *Hat, Cap and Fur Trade Review,* May 1879, p. 189.

35. HFNTA, *Semi-Annual Report,* May 1879.

36. Massachusetts Commission on Prison Labor, *Report* (1880), p. 13.

37. New Jersey Committee on Prison Labor, *Report* (1879), p. 36.

38. Massachusetts Bureau of Labor, *Annual Report* (1880), p. 56.

39. Massachusetts Commission on Prison Labor, *Report* (1880), p. 225.

40. Connecticut Committee on Convict Labor, *Report* (1880), p. 44; *Clothier and Hatter,* Apr. 1880, p. 5; Feb. 1880, p. 18.

41. Connecticut Committee on Convict Labor, *Report* (1880), p. 44; New Jersey Committee on Prison Labor, *Report* (1879), p. 5; Massachusetts Commission on Prison Labor, *Report* (1880), p. 6.

42. *Clothier and Hatter,* Apr. 1880, p. 5; *Hat, Cap and Fur Trade Review,* Apr. 1880, p. 180.

43. *Hatter and Furrier,* Dec. 1880, p. 7. This was the new name of the *Clothier and Hatter.*

44. *Hat, Cap and Fur Trade Review,* Oct. 1880, p. 55.

45. *Hatter and Furrier,* Dec. 1880, p. 7.

46. *Brooklyn Eagle,* 6 Nov. 1880.

47. Ibid., 3 Nov. 1880; 6 Nov. 1880; *Hatter and Furrier,* Nov. 1884, p. 4; HFNTA, *Semi-Annual Report,* Nov. 1880.

48. *Brooklyn Eagle,* 6 Nov. 1880. The *Eagle* also attributed Smith's victory to incumbent Chittenden's off-putting manner. He "acts like an oracle and alienates ordinary people," the *Eagle* noted.

49. *Hatter and Furrier,* Feb. 1881, p. 7.

50. Ibid., Mar. 1881, p. 4; Apr. 1881, pp. 3, 17; *Hat, Cap and Fur Trade Review,* Mar. 1881, p. 160.

51. *Hat, Cap and Fur Trade Review,* Mar. 1882, p. 167; *Hatter and Furrier,* Apr. 1882, p. 25.

52. *Hatter and Furrier,* May 1882, pp. 5, 13; June 1882, p. 40; *Hat, Cap and Fur Trade Review,* May 1882, p. 211. Even Superintendant of Prisons Baker's promise not to renew the hat contract did not console the hatters because they had little reason to trust him.

53. *Hatter and Furrier,* Jan. 1883, p. 6; Nov. 1882, p. 4.

54. Ibid., Jan. 1883, pp. 13–14; *Hat, Cap and Fur Trade Review,* Mar. 1883, p. 197.

55. John S. Perry, *An Analysis of the Vote on Prison Contract Labor Polled November 6, 1883* (New York: John S. Perry, 1883), passim. It was just as the finishers' struggle with prison labor ended that workingmen throughout the United States began to agitate heatedly on the issue. See E. T. Hiller, "Labor Unionism and Convict Labor," *Journal of the American Institute of Criminal Law and Criminology* 5 (1914–15): 851–79.

56. *Hatter and Furrier,* Nov. 1882, p. 4.

57. *Hat, Cap and Fur Trade Review,* July 1883, pp. 294, 297.

58. U.S. Bureau of Labor Statistics, *Annual Report* (1886), pp. 117–22.

59. *Hatter and Furrier,* Oct. 1880, p. 4. "The number of delegates at the Prison Labor Convention in Brooklyn last month wasn't so large as in New York last fall. Several Associations sent no delegates but said they would contribute." See also ibid., Nov. 1880, p. 17.

60. *Hatter and Furrier,* Aug. 1882, p. 17.

61. HFNTA, *Semi-Annual Report,* Nov. 1882.

62. *Hatter and Furrier,* Apr. 1881, p. 3; Aug. 1881, p. 8; Oct. 1881, p. 20; Mar. 1882, p. 11; *Hat, Cap and Fur Trade Review,* Mar. 1882, p. 167.

63. *Clothier and Hatter,* May 1878, p. 3; *Hat, Cap and Fur Trade Review,* Nov. 1878, p. 71.

64. *Clothier and Hatter,* Nov. 1878, p. 21. The Newark hatters honored George J. Ferry, ex-mayor of Orange and a leading manufacturer, for his role in lobbying by making him principal speaker at their grand demonstration against prison labor on 31 Oct. 1878. See ibid., Feb. 1879, p. 3; *Hatter and Furrier,* Feb., 1880, p. 18; Nov. 1881, p. 9; Mar. 1882, p. 11; *Hat, Cap and Fur Trade Review,* Mar. 1879, p. 135; Feb. 1883, p. 182.

65. *Hatter and Furrier,* Nov. 1880, p. 8; Nov. 1884, p. 8.

66. *Hat, Cap and Fur Trade Review,* Feb. 1883, p. 182.

67. Connecticut Committee on Convict Labor, *Report* (1880), pp. 108–11.

68. *Clothier and Hatter,* Nov. 1879, p. 28; *Hatter and Furrier,* Jan. 1880, p. 12.

69. HFNTA, *Semi-Annual Report,* May 1881; *Clothier and Hatter,* July 1879, p. 25; *Hatter and Furrier,* Nov. 1881, p. 9.

70. *Clothier and Hatter,* July 1879, p. 29; *Hatter and Furrier,* Jan. 1881, p. 3; Nov. 1881, p. 9.

71. *Hat, Cap and Fur Trade Review,* Dec. 1880, p. 94; Jan. 1882, p. 5; *Hatter and Furrier,* Dec. 1882, p. 13.

72. HFNTA, *Semi-Annual Report,* May 1880.

73. Ibid., Nov. 1880.

CHAPTER 7

Emergence of
A National Labor Policy,
1880–1885

T HE HATTERS' INTEREST in conciliation was not unique, nor was it pioneer-
ing. In Great Britain, trade unionists had created strong national organizations committed to a conciliatory labor relations policy in the years 1850–75.
While the Webbs' theory that the mid-nineteenth century saw the birth of
a "New Model" unionism is considered by contemporary scholars to over-
emphasize the discontinuity in British trade union development, even historians stressing continuity argue that during this period the unions' "central executives increased their power and tried to negotiate settlements."[1]

In coal, textiles, the manufactured iron trade, and the building trades,
large union organizations bargained with employers' associations. In order
to avoid strikes and preserve their contracts, the parties established boards
of arbitration and conciliation. Arbitration boards consisted of equal numbers of representatives of the parties to the agreement, who could name an
impartial arbitrator if they were unable to agree on a settlement themselves.
Conciliation, which was more commonly effected, was an informal process
by which selected employers and unionists not party to a dispute would
discuss the conflict with the antagonists and try to arrange an agreement.[2]

By 1880, arbitration and conciliation carried on by employer and union
groups had become commonplace in British industry, while in the United
States, movement in this direction was slower but unmistakable. American
trade unionists had begun organizing national unions before the Civil War,
but it was in the late 1870s and early 1880s that printers, carpenters, iron
and steel workers, and cigar makers began creating effective national
unions. Their officers, like the hatters', believed it was vitally important for
the national union to be able to prevent locals from embarking on disas-

trous strikes, particularly strikes against wage cuts during the depression of 1873. To that end, they campaigned for constitutional changes that would give central union bodies the right to authorize strikes. In order to make that right effective, they sought to build up strike funds which the national union could dispense in support of approved job actions. The strike funds were fed by union dues; the officers pressed incessantly to raise the dues even higher. Benefit features such as unemployment relief, burial funds, and sick pay rounded out the union strategy known as "business unionism."[3]

Simultaneously with the development of business unionism, American labor began to explore conciliation and arbitration. Shoemakers in Massachusetts took the lead in 1868, when the Lynn Lodge of the Knights of St. Crispin began requiring that shops bring their disputes with employers to an "arbitration" committee composed of journeymen drawn from outside shops. In 1877, Joseph Carruthers, reporting on the Knights' efforts for the Massachusetts Bureau of Labor Statistics, referred to this as "American-style" arbitration, as opposed to the two-party process used in England.[4] For another decade, Lynn shoemakers tried to work out either "American" or "European" style arbitration systems, without permanent success.[5]

At the same time, Pennsylvania iron and steelworkers and coal miners tried to establish joint arbitration committees with their employers. Coal miners and operators in the Pennsylvania anthracite fields tried arbitration as early as 1871, and sliding scale agreements on wages and prices brought temporary peace to the Pittsburg iron trade in the mid-1870s. The first arbitration and conciliation board to survive a wage settlement began in the New York cigar industry in 1879.[6] Thus, before the hatters began exploring arbitration in the 1880s, craftsmen in four of the most important segments of the American labor movement, shoemaking, mining, iron and steelmaking, and cigar making, had already experimented with the process.

It is clear that the interest of American managers and trade unionists in industrial conciliation was stimulated by reports of its success in England. For example, Joseph Gowen of the Reading Railroad cited the success of arbitration in England when he urged Pennsylvania miners to set up a joint board in 1871.[7] Moreover, after Joseph Weeks visited England in 1878 to investigate procedures for securing labor peace, Pennsylvania miners who had heard his report suggested that arbitration be adopted in the Pittsburg area coal trade.[8]

These early attempts failed, but after 1880, arbitration became an important part of American labor relations. In 1880, the state of New Jersey passed a law authorizing the establishment of a tribunal for industrial arbitration, and was soon followed by Massachusetts, Pennsylvania, and Ohio.[9] By 1885, support for arbitration as a means of rationally settling disputes came from such diverse sources as the governors of Pennsylvania and Ohio, the liberal Reverend Washington Gladden, the business union theorist Adolph Strasser of the Cigar Makers International Union, the conservative railroad union leader P. M. Arthur, and the Knights of Labor Grand Master Terence Powderly.[10]

Clearly the hatters' turn toward national unionism and a conciliatory trade policy in the early 1880s was not unique. The hatters were doing what many contemporary unionists were doing. It would appear that the explanation for this common response is that trade unionists shared an important common experience. All were responding to the intense competition among their employers to reduce labor costs. For American workers, the problem had intensified during the depression of 1873, when demand collapsed, prices fell, and employers cut back wages and employment levels. After the depression lifted, workers tried to raise their wages back to predepression levels, but found that their employers were competing with each other more intensely than before to keep down prices and labor costs by holding down wages and hiring less-skilled employees. When workers struck, they might defeat one employer, but, like a dandelion, the problem would reappear, and another strike would soon be necessary.

An anonymous poet expressed the difficult choices facing hat finishers' locals in the last quarter of the nineteenth century in the following way:

The Hatters' Soliloquy

> To strike, or not to strike —
> That is the question.
> Whether it is better in the minds of hatters,
> to strike when trade is brisk
> And orders must be filled,
> Or work according to agreement,
> Until the rush is over,
> And at the end of the "trade"
> Demand higher wages for the coming season —
> To meet — to argue — to resolve,
> And by a well-timed strike
> Raise the prices all round in a jiffy —
> Is a consummation hatters devoutly wish.
> For who would bear the heated slugs
> Or breathe foul steam for five dollars a day

With the thermometer at an even 100 in the shade
When by striking while the iron's hot
A raise of 25 cents might be gained on every dozen?
Who would? but that now and then
The dread of what may follow —
The lockout from independent factories,
To which no union hatter would return —
Doth give us pause,
Inclining us to hold on to what we have
Rather than go to districts we know not of
To be left out in the cold when trade is slack.[11]

Among the hatters, it was in the Danbury district that this pattern was most pronounced. After the finishers' successful consolidation and strike of 1872, the local had tried to control work and wages strictly; the town's manufacturers countered by importing and training as many foul men as possible. Danbury curler Granville O. Holmes described the struggle well:

As a rule . . . men in foul shops were compelled to work for much lower wages than men in fair shops . . . thus giving the employers of foul men a great advantage. . . . When the employer of fair men would reduce the price of his hats in the market to meet the competition of foul shops, it at once reacted on the workmen. The prices paid in fair shops would be lowered to that paid in foul shops when immediately, the wages of the foul men would go still lower. Thus matters went on from bad to worse, until the fair men refused to submit to any further reduction. . . . All shops were then declared foul (with one or two exceptions) in the Danbury hatting district.[12]

By the spring of 1881, only four of the town's nine largest hat shops were fair; in the next six months, three more firms went foul, leaving only 126 of Danbury's 1000 finishers fair, and few though they were, not all could be employed in the two remaining union shops.[13]

National unionism and industrial conciliation were two strategies trade unionists evolved to meet such situations. Organizing national unions meant that when it was important to resist an employer who sought to depress labor standards, the craftsmen would stand together to concentrate their forces in combat. Arbitration and conciliation in the interest of trade agreements meant employers and employees would be able to contain competition and maintain prices and standards. Though the two approaches appear to be quite different, in one way they were united — both were collective attempts to cope with the "anarchy of the market" that threatened skilled workers in the Gilded Age.

Steps Toward Collective Action

Richard Dowdall, newly elected president of the Hat Finishers National
Trade Association, kicked off the union's move toward a national trade policy of conciliation in the spring of 1880. Spurred on by anger at his home
local, Newark, for driving a major employer foul by insisting on a raise in
piece rates, Dowdall organized a campaign to elect delegates. First, the
Dowdall forces headed off a proposed "national consolidation," to take in all
nonunion hat finishers, by a vote of 23–10. Then, challenging the heart of
local power, the control of strikes, delegates approved two innovative national rules to make future consolidations unnecessary. Eliminating one of
the employers' major grievances, delegates voted to outlaw the journeymen's practice of striking for wages whenever trade became brisk. Instead,
shops were to negotiate bills of prices every six months and abide by them
regardless of the vicissitudes of trade.

Even more important, delegates approved an "American style" arbitration plan to make strikes unnecessary. In the future, when journeymen had
a grievance, rather than call a shop meeting to approve an immediate
strike, they were to take their complaint to the union local, which would appoint an arbitration committee composed of men drawn from shops not
party to the dispute to propose a settlement. Only if the employer rejected
the committee's decision could the journeymen strike.[14]

Although this arbitration plan resembled the method long used by finishers
to settle disputes among themselves, compulsory arbitration of grievances
against employers represented a radical break with craft tradition because it
stifled the journeyman's freedom to strike whenever he felt aggrieved, a
freedom central to the finishers' culture of work. Even toothless as it was,
lacking provisions for punishing offenders, the new national law represented
an unprecedented intrusion of the national association into the journeymen's
control of work.

President Dowdall elaborated the implications of the convention's actions
for the first time in his presidential report of November 1880. In order to
keep their employers fair, members were to refrain from demanding unrea-
sonably high wages and from enforcing overly strict work rules. If journeymen would not moderate their behavior voluntarily, the national association should have the power to force them to do so. Dowdall's words reflected
his confidence in his role as leader of the conciliation drive. "You have often
been compelled to a course of petty tyranny which reflects no credit on the
author and is productive of no good either to the employer or the employed.

We should be firm therefore, in resisting oppression and injustice, but we should always be sure it was such before committing ourselves to any action on it. No imaginary or sentimental grievances should be allowed to jeopardize the best interests of the Association or in any way to imperil the standing of our shops."[15]

Despite the steps taken by the convention delegates, many finishers and their locals were not anxious to give up the freedom they had previously enjoyed. In the fall of 1880, Newark hatters took the lead in upholding the old ways when they tried to undo their recent defeat by whitewashing 360 more foul men, including some former local members, and some who had always been foul. When the association proved unable to punish this defiance, the Orange, South Norwalk, and Newark locals consolidated once again, furthering the progress of skill dilution.[16]

Even worse, in 1882, the Danbury local tried to overcome its weakness once and for all by whitewashing more than 800 independent men but found that even at that heavy price, it could not bring all the town's shops fair. Three weeks after the hatters struck against three large foul employers, the local offered two measures of conciliation: first, if any journeyman had a grievance against his employer, he would have to present it to his shop committee to hear and settle, rather than present it to his shop crew during work hours, as had been the hatters' custom; second, "in case of dispute as to prices, work [was] to continue until the [union's] committee of arbitration [had] consulted with the bosses and made the result."[17] The foul factories spurned the hatters' olive branch, and the hatters had to admit defeat.[18]

Measures of Conciliation

Hat finishers' President Richard Dowdall decided to take advantage of the Danbury local's failure to win "the most determined struggle that has ever taken place in the history of the trade." He called a special convention of the national association to bring the union's constitution in line with the policy of union centralization and conciliation.[19] Delegates to the special convention, convened in Danbury on 24 April 1882, heeded President Dowdall's counsel. Proceeding in the direction first staked out at their previous convention, they passed "wholesale changes in [their] rules and laws, changes to benefit and unite more closely employers and employed," and thereby "prevent the new proliferation of foul shops."[20] These were the same "concessions" made by the Danbury strikers two months earlier.

Like the rule adopted at the convention of 1880, which required arbitration of all disputes, the resolutions of 1882 marked a significant step away from traditional craft policies, in the sense that they diminished the shop crews' and locals' customary ability to regulate their own affairs. In their effort to effect a new policy for the whole trade — conciliation — the finishers were opening the way for a new kind of trade unionism, one in which the power both to shape trade rules and enforce them resided in the national office.

After considerable debate, delegates amended the constitution to reflect the new direction in trade policy. By a close vote, they amended Article 3 Section 2, to enlarge the power of the national conventions; in the future it would take a two-thirds vote, rather than a majority, for the locals to repeal laws passed by the conventions. In addition, over the strong protests of the Brooklyn and South Norwalk delegations, delegates voted to alter Article 8 Section 6, to enlarge the board of directors' discretion in dealing with employers who had run foul shops and wanted to become fair journeymen.[21] Most important, at the suggestion of President Dowdall, a constitutional amendment empowered the board of directors "to make such laws or amendments to existing laws at any time the welfare of the trade may demand."[22]

Nevertheless, the finishers' attachment to traditional ways remained strong. Delegates limited the board's power to enact emergency legislation by subjecting all board action to "ratification by ⅔ of the local associations." Moreover, when the Danbury and Bethel delegations appealed for the one change which, they believed, would mollify employers in their district — a reduction in the apprenticeship term from four years to three — the convention turned a deaf ear. The traditional term was too sacred to give up; not a single delegate from outside northern Connecticut voted to reduce it.[23]

By 1883, the finishers were on their way to union centralization in the interest of a conciliatory trade policy. The prison labor fight had suggested the feasibility of such a course, and the Danbury struggle had revealed its necessity. Two successive conventions had limited the journeymen's, and their locals', prerogatives to hold shop meetings, set prices, and strike as they wished. Power to enforce such limitations was passing, slowly, to the national officers and the board of directors. Each concession was made reluctantly, with reservations, and the authority ceded to the association was far from total. Shops and locals remained the loci of power. It would take more shocks, of even greater magnitude than the Danbury struggle, to overcome the journeymen's adherence to tradition.

The South Norwalk Strike

Origins

The South Norwalk lockout and strike of 1884, "the greatest struggle between capital and labor" the hatters had ever fought, provided the impetus for the journeymen to make the break. Its origin lay in the depression in the hatting trade, which began in mid-1883, a full year before the general economic slump,[24] and continued without respite in 1884, a year that was so bad that the *Hat, Cap and Fur Trade Review* was moved to observe: "No such year has been known to any manufacturer now in business. Commencing in January 1884, a series of failures have occurred, covering over $1,000,000 of liabilities, from which no dividend, with a single exception, have been realized. This, added to a general and large decrease in values, a trade reduced fully one-third in volume and a financial disturbance of no small dimension, has made the year of 1884 memorable, and we have no doubt all are glad to take leave of it."[25]

For most manufacturers, the slump exacerbated an already chronic situation. Even in brisk periods, competition among hatting firms was so intense that it was standard practice in the hatting trade for factory owners to date their bills to jobbers months ahead and to discount them considerably.[26] Before the 1884 depression, a number of industrialists, led by George Ferry of Orange, New Jersey, had established an association to halt such practices, but their effort failed as individualistic entrepreneurs refused to live up to the common agreements. When the downturn did occur, it is not surprising that manufacturers did not react by trying to band together on a nationwide scale to solve their fundamental problem, excess competition; instead, they organized locally and reduced their costs by cutting wages.[27]

South Norwalk was an unlikely site for a testing ground.[28] An offshoot of the Danbury hatting trade, the town had grown to be an industrial center; as late as 1876 there had been but six hat shops.[29] Moreover, to produce the fine derbies that were their specialty, South Norwalk's twelve factories hired skilled journeymen, who were hard to replace.[30] Perhaps for that reason, the town lacked the tradition of labor strife that Danbury, Newark, and Orange knew so well.[31]

Nevertheless, in November 1884, four of South Norwalk's leading firms, which accounted for four-fifths of the district's hat production, joined together in a trade association to discuss means of making their businesses profitable. They decided that their miserable earnings were not wholly attributable to the depression; rather, they blamed the local unions for exacting noncompetitively high piece rates. Consequently, the associated firms resolved to impose a reduction in wages for the coming spring trade.

On 10 November, owners of the four hat factories posted a price list which provided for a 10 percent wage cut. They later claimed the bill had been put together after they had "visited other places, obtained the lists of prices paid in other trade shops, [and] examined the quality of work done in them."[32] Along with the new bill, the manufacturers demanded three changes in local union rules: (1) that the unions accept in principle uniform piece rates "for the same work in all their factories"; (2) that these rates should be "as low . . . as are paid in other places in 'trade' shops for the same work"; and (3) "that prices accepted by workmen at the start of the season be maintained during the season."[33]

At first, the shop crews' response was subdued. "In the factory of Mssrs. Adams Brothers, the workmen accepted the bill in every department of the factory except one, and in one department, that of sizing, actually went to work." Similarly, the men at Coffin, Hurlbutt and Co. "stated their willingness to work under the new bill for the season, actually went to work under it, saying they would call a meeting of the trade [the local] to work under the time condition of the bill."[34]

The response of the local was far different, however. Although the manufacturers' proposal was aimed only at the coming spring trade, the local ordered its shop crews to make sure that "no hats be taken out until the bill presented is taken down and abolished."[35] The local overrode its shop crews' inclinations to accept the wage cut because it saw the primary issue as something other than wages. "In the present depression of trade, everywhere, a modest reduction would have been accepted . . . if it had been offered in the proper manner. . . . But the bill was put up in the factories with scarcely a word of explanation except that some of the manufacturers stated that 'they had not made anything in three years and that they were going to make money now.' "[36] Such arbitrary behavior, coupled with employer demands for significant changes in work rules, was seen by the local as an unprecedented challenge to its accustomed power. It refused to surrender. On 19 November, twelve hundred men and women marched out of the four associated shops, and, to prepare for the battle, the trimmers organized a local, which they allied with the finishers' and the makers' locals. The contest was on.[37]

The employers were incensed by the journeymen's abrupt walkout.

"Among all the outrageous actions of the hatters' union of this city, this one . . . must be ranked foremost," they fulminated. Finding themselves ". . . confronted by the entire body of [their] work people . . . organized into one compact and hostile organization, each pledging itself to sustain the other in any demand their unscrupulous leaders might incite them to make upon" themselves, the manufacturers declared their shops "for the future independent of all 'trade rules.' "[38]

A dispute over wages had swiftly become a matter of principle. The manufacturers swore never again to honor the hatters' union rules; the journeymen swore to defend their union. Such at least was the official version of the strike. Although the manufacturers consistently claimed that they desired only to cut wages, they could hardly have expected the journeymen to accept unilateral reductions in their piece rates or succumb meekly to nonnegotiable demands for changes in union rules. Did they not expect their men to strike; did they not look forward to an all-out struggle? They certainly picked a good time for a battle; trade was slow, and could be expected to remain so for at least two months longer, so a short strike would cost the shop owners very little.[39]

On the other hand, in support of the employers' version of events, it is easy to imagine the factory owners' chagrin at seeing their shop crews accept the new price bill, only to be overruled by the local. Such a turnabout might possibly have led the industrialists to conclude that the union was a bad influence on men who otherwise were pliable. Throughout the strike, the owners were indeed to charge the local with playing such a role. Without conclusive evidence, suspicion about the strike's origin lingers.

The National Association Intervenes

As the South Norwalk journeymen squared off against their bosses, HFNTA President Dennis J. Hagerty intervened with a message of conciliation. Afraid that the local's militancy was plunging the union into a battle it could not win, because of the depression in trade, Hagerty urged the manufacturers to recognize the association and settle for a compromise.

Hagerty's semi-annual report, signed 1 December 1884, was a model of moderation. Acknowledging that intense competition was hurting the manufacturers, it suggested that alternatives to strife could restore profitability to the trade. Specifically, Hagerty suggested that the manufacturers organize a national trade association as a means of reducing competition. Recalling how cooperation between journeymen and employers had halted prison hat manufacturing, he proposed joint action on the tariff to raise both prices and wages. Cooperation was in the long-term interest of both manufacturers and craftsmen, he argued, because contented workers performed better than oppressed ones, who would strike whenever trade picked up. Besides, employers did not really benefit from wage cuts, since jobbers and retailers always seized on them as an excuse to reduce prices.[40]

Although the manufacturers did not respond to Hagerty's appeal, he was not easily discouraged. In the third week of December, Hagerty led a contingent of association officials to South Norwalk, where they proposed to mediate the dispute and arrange a compromise settlement.[41] Once again, the manufacturers refused to recognize the association's existence; Hagerty had to return to Brooklyn empty-handed.

Defensive Maneuvers

To win their strike and preserve their unions, the journeymen faced two tasks. They had to keep their members from being starved back to work, and they had to prevent the manufacturers from hiring adequate replacements. The first task was made all the more difficult by the hatters' customary improvidence. At the strike's beginning, the sympathetic *Norwalk Hour* noted that "hatters as a class spend money freely when they have it, and at the end of a trade, few have funds sufficient to last them until business resumes. If the strike continues much longer, many, unless they receive assistance, will want for the necessities of life."[42]

To raise funds for strike relief from sympathetic townsmen, the trimmers' Ladies' Social Union held a benefit "fair and supper" on Wednesday, 18 January. Volunteers contributed turkeys, cakes, and oysters; Heine's band provided music; and the women raffled off their fancy work. The evening was more a social success than a financial one; although it was repeated the following night, the net proceeds amounted to only $350.[43] The South Norwalk locals also hired a wandering minstrel show, H. B. Wood's Specialty Company, to tour the surrounding region to raise funds for the strikers. Show stops included Danbury, Bridgeport, and New York City.[44]

Despite such efforts, the striking hatters were strongly dependent on their craftmates for strike relief. Dennis J. Hagerty, HFNTA president, came to the scene of conflict on 4 December, to promise such support would be forthcoming. He brought "substantial funds from the hatters of Brooklyn," and intimated "there [would] be no lack of funds with which to continue the strike."[45]

In all, Brooklyn finishers sent more than $5000 to South Norwalk; after emptying their local treasury, they organized a theater benefit and a ball to raise additional money for the cause. Other locals contributed smaller but substantial amounts; the Orange journeymen, for instance, assessed themselves 2 percent of their earnings for the duration of the strike, despite being themselves victims of dull trade.[46] By April, the finishers' locals had sent $24,000 in strike support, and other unions, including the formerly hostile silk hatters, sent an additional $2000.[47] President Hagerty attributed such generosity to the fact that "the progress of the strike was viewed with great anxiety by the hatters all over the country. If the South Norwalk manufacturers were successful, and the men were forced to accept the reduction, manufacturers all over the country would soon follow their example."[48]

Yet even successful fund raising was inadequate to support 1200 strikers and their families for five months, and the unions did not even attempt to do so. As soon as the strike broke out, the locals tried to lighten their relief burden by finding alternate employment for their members. Their task was made easier by the fact that, in contrast to the journeymen of the hatting trade, who gave solid support to the strikers, American hat manufacturers remained aloof from the South Norwalk controversy. When jobbers and retailers began transferring their orders from the embattled factories, which were having trouble getting work out, the recipients of the new orders were perfectly willing to hire strikers to beef up their shop crews. In particular, more than two hundred journeymen found work in the fine hat shops of Brooklyn and in the remaining seven factories in South Norwalk.[49]

To reduce still further the number of strikers dependent on union funds, the journeymen turned to a tactic popular thirty years before. Three weeks after the strike began, several hatters formerly employed in the embattled factories organized a cooperative hat company and mapped plans to put out a sample line of high-quality goods. To raise the needed capital, they sold shares at $100 to prospective worker-owners, limiting each partner to five shares. Profits were to be divided pro rata, and only union men would be hired.[50]

The company put out samples "for any grade of hats" immediately, in premises leased from a fair employer, Raymond and Comstock.[51] At the same time, it set about building a three-story wood factory, which it hoped would eventually employ three to four hundred hands.[52] As in any orthodox business, the stockholders elected a president and board of directors to manage business.[53] By early February, the enterprise appeared to be a success. The original cooperative was employing fifty men and twenty-five women in its own freshly built factory, and a second cooperative association, organized on similar lines, was operating in leased premises.[54] Even a suspicious fire, which burned out both companies, causing $1500 damage, could not halt the cooperatives' progress.[55] They quickly rented space in new quarters and renewed operations; indeed, in April, they added a new wrinkle, opening their own retail outlet at 352 Broadway in New York City.[56]

John Swinton, labor's indefatigable reform champion, made the hatters' "remarkable experiment" a *cause célèbre* of the growing labor movement. In his modestly styled *John Swinton's Paper,* he praised the strikers extravagantly, hoping to rekindle his readers' interest in cooperation. "Shrewd Yankees as they are, whose fingers ache when they are idle, and who have been accustomed to do several things for themselves, they got the notion that they could even make and market hats, to the music of 'life, liberty, and the pursuit of happiness.' It is the most striking thing of the kind ever seen in our country."[57] With the help of Swinton's free publicity, the co-ops found markets throughout the United States, and survived after the strike had ended.[58] Unfortunately, like many of Swinton's enthusiasms, the cooperatives rapidly ceased to be a matter of public concern.[59]

Offensive Measures

Of course, to win their strike, the journeymen had to prevent their employers from hiring strikebreakers. Since few South Norwalk hatters were willing to defy their own unions, the issue turned on whether or not the manufacturers could import labor from out of town.[60] Considerable action took place at the railroad station itself.

When the first trainload of scabs from New Jersey arrived at South Norwalk's depot, "their coming was known to the trade and they were met by a large number of men who followed them to the [Mahackemo] hotel and tried to persuade (*sic*) them to return. There was considerable excitement for some time, and the lobby of the hotel was crowded, and all but three of the Jerseymen were induced to return the next day."[61] Soon the hatters were systematically guarding the train station, and "all newcomers, whenever possible, [were] brought to the hatters' headquarters," where union leaders "tried to get them to go home."[62]

Although the hatters adhered to a noncoercive policy, tension mounted over their efforts to turn back prospective scabs. Even the sympathetic *Norwalk Hour* came to believe that "the crowd of strikers on the depot platform, the rush for the 'fouls,' and the energy of the reasoning process grew with time until they became a nuisance. . . ."[63] The antagonistic *South Norwalk Sentinel* bluntly charged the union with attempting intimidation.[64]

Desperate for labor, the employers contested control of the train station. "In some cases, the manufacturers [met] strangers at the depot, and in one instance, they were escorted to a shop by the Mayor and a squad of policemen."[65] Soon the union men were complaining that such interference deprived them of an opportunity to present their case to the newcomers.[66]

The "battles of the depot" had their lighter sides as well. One is touched by an account of how a committee of strikers greeting newcomers were struck "bashful" by a group of "four young women" who arrived in town on the train. "Not feeling well enough dressed," the hatters could not bring themselves to speak to them, and inquire whether they were in town to break the strike.[67] The *Bridgeport Standard* of 9 December told an even better, if possibly apocryphal story.

> Many ridiculous scenes have transpired in the vicinity of the depot since the strike began, or rather since it assumed its present phase, i.e., the watching of trains for foul hatters, who are occasionally coming to work for the manufacturers. The one which came off yesterday . . . is to the point. The strikers, who in large numbers as usual, surrounded the train (except that they did not head off the locomotive) waited and watched for any stray hatters who had come to take their vacant places. Suddenly someone exclaimed, "There goes one," and a rush was made for rather a stoutish individual, with a larger satchel than is usually carried by a transient, who was heading for that portion of Main Street open on the depot grounds near the City Hotel. The unlucky stranger was immediately surrounded by three or four score of excited men, who blocked his way, and one of the leaders of the obstructing gang asked the new-comer if he were a hatter? to which the man with the large satchel answered: "Yes, something in that line." Then the crowd began to threaten, advise, and finally beg of him not to go to shop No. 2, saying he would be taking the bread out of their own and families' mouths. After listening to their talk, the stranger said, "Hold on a minute and I will tell you all about it." The crowd allowed him to mount a convenient box when he delivered his oration, which in substance was, that he was a veritable razor strop man, and he told his audience that he was glad to meet them, as his double patent nickle-plated strop, was the best in the world, and that it was only necessary to put one in a drawer with a razor to have that razor always keen edged and ready to shave face or hats, and he told them that as soon as he had eaten his dinner at the City Hotel, he should be glad to see them and sell them one of his patent strops.[68]

Offensive Weapons: Boycotting

Despite the strikers' determined and persistant efforts to deter out-of-town workers from taking jobs in South Norwalk, the manufacturers were able to recruit small numbers of strikebreakers.[69] The union men would not let matters rest, for in mid-December, they unveiled a new tactic — the boycott — which heightened the intensity of the already bitter struggle.

The boycott was a relatively new thing in 1884, and it is unclear how it came to South Norwalk. The most recent study of the phenomenon indicates that the practice originated in Ireland in 1880, as part of the Irish Land League's campaign for land reform in Ireland. It got its name from the ostracism practiced by Irish peasants against land agent Captain Charles Boycott.[70] Charles Stewart Parnell, the League's leader, described the system at a mass meeting in Ennis in the following terms: "When a man takes a farm from which another has been evicted, you must shun him on the roadside when you meet him. You must shun him in the shop; you must shun him in the fair green and in the market-place; and even in the place of worship. By leaving him severely alone, by putting him into a moral convent . . . you must show him your detestation of the crime he has committed. If you do this . . . there will be no man so full of avarice, so lost to shame as to dare the public opinion of right-thinking men in the country and transgress your unwritten code of laws."[71]

Word of the practice came to the American labor movement via Irish immigrant supporters of the Irish Land League. Yet in America, the boycott came to stand for a variety of activities and was not confined to Irish-American workers. Thus, in April 1881, Brooklyn unionists boycotted baker John H. Schultz for firing employees who joined a union; to bring Schultz to terms, the journeymen tried to cut off his sales by inducing grocers to refuse to sell his bread and by entreating customers not to buy it.[72] This is a consumer boycott, as we are familiar with the term today, and rather different from the activities of Parnell's Land League.

In the following year, Jersey City freight-handlers used a boycott to win their strike against the New York Central and Hudson River Railroad. They printed up a list of eighty-three strikebreakers and urged supporters to "shun them like a leper."[73] This form of ostracism seems more nearly like the Irish type and was clearly led by men with backgrounds in the Irish nationalist movement.

South Norwalk's boycott partly resembled the Irish kind, in that scabs who were townsmen were systematically either ostracized or insulted.[74] Since there were few such men[75] — all observers agreed that the women strikers were even more steadfast than the men[76] — the primary boycotting activity concerned workers from out of town and hardly resembled the tactics of the Irish Land League.

Within weeks of the beginning of the South Norwalk strike, an unofficial committee of striking hatters began to visit local merchants, demanding that they cease doing business with the owners of the foul factories, and their employees, if they wanted to retain the journeymen's patronage. Friend and foe alike agreed that the boycott was strikingly effective. One of the members of the associated firms, Coffin, Hurlbutt and Company, described the campaign's operations in vivid detail:

> Our situation is becoming intolerable and the whole community is influenced against us. We tried to board our men that we brought here, and not a boarding house would receive them. Even the restaurant keeper at the depot refused to supply them with food. He dared not do it, such is the state of the terrorism. We brought them down to this factory, and Mrs. Goodwin, the wife of our watchman, consented to supply them with food. . . . Today, she was waited on by a committee and told that if she continued to supply them with food, she should not purchase anything more in South Norwalk. They have the storekeepers under their control to such an extent that there is no doubt of their ability to carry out this threat. . . . We [the associated manufacturers] can't any of us pass from our houses to the factories without insult. Wherever we go we are followed by spies. . . .[77]

The merchants' acquiescence in the strike may have been forced in some cases by physical coercion, as the manufacturers charged,[78] but usually they went along with the boycott, as the *Norwalk Hour* noted with disgust: "We never dreamed intelligent men could be so cowed by threat, and our respect for the hatters increases when we consider how much they have accomplished with so little strain, as we compare their confidence with the timidity of the tradesmen."[79] The only case in which a striker was tried for intimidating and assaulting a boarding-house keeper resulted in a verdict of not guilty.[80] As a result of the effective boycott, the manufacturers had to "house [their] new men in [their] factories and feed them in the houses of the few of [their] old employees who remained faithful to [them]."[81] This was not good for the scabs' morale. "At Crofut and Knapp's shop #2, five or six men were at work on Thursday, the firm providing cots for them. . . . On Tuesday, the men, tired of working under such circumstances, climbed out of one of the shop windows and escaped."[82] Another foul hatter was so disenchanted with his experience living in a hat factory that he went back to

his home in Boston and blasted his former bosses in an interview with the
Boston *Globe*.[83]

Finding it hard to secure workers willing to live under such conditions,
the factory owners had to hire "toughs and prison birds." When New Jersey
prison officers came to South Norwalk "to arrest two men who were wanted
for highway robbery," and found them working in the foul hat shops, "the
fair hatters [were] wild with joy," for they considered it a public relations
coup.[84]

Public Relations and Violence

From the very beginning, the hatters had shown great concern for public
opinion. When President Hagerty came to town in early December, he
brought the strikers advice to "see that nothing is done by any of your number that would tend to lower you in the estimation of the public";[85] he was
"gratified" to find his counsel was not needed, for, as the *Norwalk Hour* reported, "the men are certainly deserving of great credit for the manner with
which they are conducting themselves. There is little or no drunkenness, a
remarkable fact when so many are idle and although knots of men are sta-
tioned all over the city, there is no disorder."[86]

To make their case to the public, the hatters hired a friendly attorney,
John S. Seymour, who wrote three lengthy circulars for publication in the
local newspapers. In his presentations, Seymour took the obvious tack of fo-
cusing on the employers' attempts to destroy the union while he minimized
the journeymen's wage goals. Parts of Seymour's letters were unusual and
noteworthy. In his letter to the manufacturers, dated 3 January, Seymour
posed the issues involved in the South Norwalk strike in moral, rather than
the customary pragmatic terms. When he dealt with wages, Seymour asked:
"Do you allow the laborer to share in the product of his labor which by right
he ought to have? 'Supply and demand' do not answer this question. . . .
Whether labor shall have its fair share of the product is not a matter of mere
private concern." When he dealt with the question of union recognition,
once again the attorney wrote not in terms of law, but of morality.

> You plausibly claim that you propose to run your business as you
> please, that a trades' union interferes with your business, therefore you
> suppress it. . . . The question is, what is your business? . . . And if
> [the journeymen] please to combine against your combination . . . if
> you forbid it, you attempt to run your business and theirs too as you
> please. You reduce your intelligent workingmen to a new level, you do
> all in your power to make him a machine and a slave. The slave driver

used to say to the world, I don't choose to listen to your theories of human rights, that is my business. . . . Then as now, it was capital taking more than its share of the product. The right of labor to combine was denied. Yet it was somehow found after a while that negro slavery was not wholly the slave driver's business. The relation of labor and capital never were and never can be simply the employers' business. . . .[87]

The unions were also careful to cultivate a moderate public image. Even after the radical rhetoric in the beginning of his public letter of 3 January, John Seymour struck a conciliatory pose. "It is a question if, after all that has been said of the evils of unionism, it is not better to have organized labor, which is always somewhat conservative, than disorganized labor which is radical, and which, when it unites, becomes a mob with no past to conserve and no future for which to provide."[88] To make labor harmony possible, Seymour proposed "European-style" arbitration.

You choose five men of your own number and the men five from their own number. These ten men would form the board. Their first duty would be to agree upon what the contest was about. There would first be danger from suspicion, bad blood, anger, strong language, boasts and threats, but the board would by and by settle down to business and having found out just what the fight was about would be able to examine carefully if not calmly the facts bearing on the claim on either side. And discussion and reason would do the rest. There would possibly be no need of a third element in the board to act as umpire, but in case the vote stood five to five on one of the important matters, the third element could be agreed on in the usual way.[89]

To prove the plan was not "new" or "visionary," Seymour cited its successful operation in the north England iron trade, the Northumberland and Durham, England, coal trade, the Massachusetts shoe industry, and the Pennsylvania iron trade.[90]

South Norwalk manufacturers were slower to appreciate the importance of public relations, and, during the first months of the strike, were consistently on the defensive, as their own statements made clear. "The most extravagant and untruthful statements have been given to the public by the 'strikers' or their agents. So far the manufacturers have submitted to misrepresentations and abuse, and have contented themselves with answering the questions of newspaper reporters and friends."[91]

In their first circular to the public, dated 25 December, the employers were careful to charge the journeymen with harming not only their business, but the town itself. "The union has retarded greatly the growth and prosperity of the city by preventing manufacturers from locating here. It has seriously interfered with the growth of our own business by rendering it impossible to manufacture low-priced goods successfully here."[92]

The owners' complaints were similar to those of Danbury's manufacturers three years before; the finishers demanded non-competitively high wages, enforced obstructionist work rules, and did not allow enough apprentices. Even worse, the local ignored its own rules whenever it proved profitable to do so. Finally, some of those rules most fundamental to the finishers' traditional culture seemed oppressive to their bosses since "[our employees have] constantly demanded of us that we should give work to men who could not properly perform it on the ground that the work should be equally divided."[93]

Although publication of the employers' circular won them some sympathy, the townspeople supported the strikers during the first two months of the strike. *The Norwalk Hour* summarized well: "It must be confessed that the sympathies of the people here are almost wholly sympathetic to the strikers, but there are many who are not satisfied with the high-handed methods of the strikers in the past."[94]

Violence

In mid-January, the manufacturers were able to turn public opinion around with charges that the strikers were guilty of outrageous acts of violence. From the strike's very beginning, "there were rumors of violence" and "sensational stories in the newspapers."[95] There was little violence, however, just a few incidents of rock-throwing, until, on 19 December, two strikebreakers were assaulted on one of their infrequent departures from the shop (Crofut and Knapp's Factory #2) they were living in. "They were set upon, and kicked and bruised, amid cries of 'kill the d — d s — s of b — s.' "[96] Later, a Danbury man, Daniel Coates, who blocked hats in South Norwalk, was assaulted as he made his way home from the Beantown train depot. He identified his attackers as "hatters, friends of the strikers."[97]

Although the employers, and their mouthpiece the *South Norwalk Sentinel,* made much of such incidents,[98] at first most townspeople shared the *Norwalk Hour's* view that "a few unprincipled schemers, a few reckless agitators who covet the notoriety gained during the strike, these with those they influenced, have caused all there has been of violence — the insulting epithets, the rushes, the stoning of a house, and the brutal street assault on a few of the fouls, too much by far, for the good name of the Association, yet less than could reasonably be expected."[99]

Finally, however, public tolerance balked at the explosion which shook Crofut and Knapp's Factory #2 on Friday night, 22 January. The employers and their *Sentinel* were quick to blame the strikers for what was believed to be a dynamite blast, although they refrained from blaming the union itself.[100] The *Hatter and Furrier* was less restrained; it charged that the dynamiting was due to an "outrage gang," along the lines of the Molly Maguires.[101]

The unions disclaimed responsibility for the blast, of course, and even charged the bosses with blowing up their own shop in order to gain public sympathy. To dramatize their innocence, the finishers' local hired the Pinkerton agency to search for the culprits, and offered a reward for their capture.[102] Nevertheless, the bloom was off the union cause; even after a mid-February fire burned down the strikers' cooperative hat factory, causing $1500 damage, the hatters had lost their aura of innocence.

Offensive Weapon: Consumer Boycott

The strikers were able to compensate for their loss of total public support in South Norwalk by adding a new weapon to their arsenal, the consumer boycott. On 11 January, a South Norwalk journeyman appeared before the New York Central Labor Union to ask for help. The group responded by passing a resolution asking its members to boycott all hats made by the struck hatting companies.[103] At the same time, John G. Saville, a leader of New York District Assembly 49 of the Knights of Labor, wrote to the Knights' *Journal of United Labor,* calling on members throughout the country to ask their local dealers to refuse to carry hats made in the embattled South Norwalk shops.

This link-up with the national labor movement changed the atmosphere in South Norwalk. For the first time, that normally peaceful town on Long Island Sound saw socialist agitators roaming the streets, talking of class conflict on a broad scale. Joseph Tammany, president of the finishers' local, distributed copies of New York's radical paper, *The Boycotter,* which urged journeymen everywhere to support militant class struggle.[104] Such scenes left their imprint on local politics for years to come.[105]

The consumer boycott's impact on the strike cannot be precisely measured. *John Swinton's Paper,* a booster of the campaign, reported from New York that "an energetic boycott has lately been begun here and elsewhere. . . . The cry of 'boycott' the South Norwalk hats is heard in all the unions and the names and trade marks are so familiar it will not be easy for them to recover the business which they are losing."[106] New York's Central Labor Union reported that twelve hat retailers in New York had acceded to its boycott demands.[107] Even the antistrike *Hat, Cap and Fur Trade Review* had to acknowledge that hat dealers throughout the country were reporting threats by local Knights of Labor assemblies to boycott all dealers who carried the wrong hats. For example, a Minneapolis dealer informed Coffin, Hurlbutt and Company of receiving such a threat, pointing out glumly that the Knights' assembly there had five thousand members.[108]

The manufacturers tried to play down the boycott's effectiveness; indeed, they claimed that backlash sentiment would even boost their sales,[109] but their actions spoke otherwise. Crofut and Knapp, the largest of the embattled companies, stopped selling its goods through its own New York retail outlet, channeling them through the less infamous Henderson and Bird store on Prince Street.[110] The disillusioned Boston scab reported that the manufacturers feared the boycott so much that they cut their names from the size markers they put on their hats.[111]

Apparently, the American labor movement deemed the boycott a success. After the South Norwalk strike ended, consumer boycotts proved more popular than ever before; so much so, in fact, that John Swinton protested their promiscuous use.[112] By the end of 1885, there had been more than 200 boycotts, and they had proved "more successful than strikes."[113] Hat manufacturers and dealers had been subjected to twenty-two such campaigns, trailing only newspapers and cigarmakers.[114]

Settlement

With the unions able to find jobs for most of the strikers and provide relief for the rest, the manufacturers bore the brunt of the strike. Crofut and Knapp had to keep one of its shops closed for the first fourteen weeks of the strike;[115] by the end of February, when the firm was finally able to secure enough workers to staff its second shop, the associated manufacturers had lost approximately $200,000 in trade.[116] While Crofut and Knapp was large enough to absorb such a loss, the smaller firms were not; early in March, A. Solmans found itself "financially embarrassed," unable to meet its due notes; and Coffin, Hurlbutt and Company, "not caring any longer to hold unproductive property," sold its factory to a Danbury firm.[117]

Consequently, on 14 March, the employers relented in their determination not to recognize the journeymen's associations. They wrote President Hagerty in Brooklyn, asking him to come to South Norwalk to arrange a settlement. Once there, Hagerty secured the manufacturers' agreement to meet an "arbitration [mediation] committee, composed of makers and finishers from outside districts"; he also induced the executive committee of the South Norwalk locals to agree to such mediation.

The president of the makers' and finishers' national associations then appointed a committee composed of union leaders from Newark, Philadelphia, Danbury, and Brooklyn. After two days of hearings, at which the manufacturers agreed in principle to recognize the unions, and the journeymen and women showed a willingness to make concessions, the committee adjourned and left South Norwalk, reserving its decision.

What happend next is unclear. According to President Hagerty, "the appointment of the Arbitration Committee broke the ice between the manufacturers and the trade associations." Before the committee prepared its terms of settlement, Coffin, Hurlbutt and Company, now under new ownership, "sent for a committee from the Local Trade and made their shop fair." A. Solmans entered into negotiations with the locals as well. The manufacturers' combination was broken.[119] The *Norwalk Hour* told a different story. It claimed that the national arbitration committee did propose terms for a settlement; all shops were to be open to the fair men; all the old price bills were to be restored; and the unions were to "get control" of the forming and sizing mills that had been foul before the strike.[120]

Whichever version of the negotiations is correct, the outcome is clear. Coffin, Hurlbutt and Company resumed operations as a fair shop, and, after negotiations with A. Solmans broke down, the three other firms remained foul as the strike continued.[121] At this point, the South Norwalk locals took the initiative which finally brought the strike to an end. On 3 April, they appointed an arbitration committee with full power to settle differences with the manufacturers. A week later, Crofut and Knapp and A. Solmans both reached agreement with the local committee, and on 13 April, the journeymen finally ratified the terms of settlement. Only Adams Brothers remained foul.[122]

Under the compromise settlement, the journeymen made substantial concessions; that is to say, they conciliated their employers. They accepted a bill of prices which entailed moderate reductions from prestrike levels and agreed to honor price bills for six months. Moreover, they agreed to hold but one shop call every three months, and that only to elect a shop committee. Perhaps more galling, the unions had to agree to take into membership twenty-five persons, selected by Crofut and Knapp, who had scabbed during the strike; fines imposed on such people could not exceed $200.

In return for these concessions, the locals gained recognition and the union shop; indeed, the trimmers' organization, which had not existed prior to the strike, gained full recognition. Future disputes over wages were to be settled by arbitration, conducted by committees of three employers and three journeymen. The unions agreed not to strike until arbitration had run its course. The settlement was no victory for the finishers' union.

Conclusion

The South Norwalk strike marked a point of no return for American hat finishers. For a dozen years they had reluctantly and slowly moved to establish a national union that could coordinate the workers' efforts to struggle against or to cooperate with their employers. The fruit of their hesitation had been a five-month struggle that had won the finishers no new power and cost them significant concessions. After the strike ended, there was no real question whether hatters would collectivize their efforts; local autonomy was dead, although the shape of the future was unclear.

Although the hatters' path to national unionism and measures of conciliation was different from that of other trade unionists, leading as it did from the prison labor fight to the great South Norwalk confrontation, the finishers' journey was in the mainstream of American labor development. The finishers reached their point of no return in the spring of 1885, when workers were flocking to the largest labor organization in America up to that time, the Holy Order of the Knights of Labor, which backed arbitration as a means to industrial harmony; this was the same time that local unions of skilled workers in many crafts were combining to establish national unions affiliated with the American Federation of Labor. For hatters, as for other skilled workers, collective action would prove an effective strategy for preserving valued traditions, but in so doing, it would change the hatters' culture as well.

NOTES

1. A. E. Musson, *British Trade Unions, 1800–1875* (London: Macmillian, 1972), p. 52.

2. I. G. Sharp, *Industrial Conciliation and Arbitration in Great Britain* (London: George Allen and Unwin Ltd., 1950). See also Keith Burgess, *The Origins of British Industrial Relations* (London: Croom Helms, 1975), passim; Sidney and Beatrice Webb, *The History of Trade Unionism,* (New York: Longmans, Green, 1902), pp. 322–23; Langson L. Price, *Industrial Peace* (London: Macmillian, 1887), pp. 37, 117.

3. Lloyd Ulman, *The Rise of the National Union* (Cambridge, Mass.: Harvard University Press, 1955); Bernard Mandel, "Gompers and Business Unionism, 1873–90," *Business History Review,* 28 (Sept. 1954): 264–73.

4. Carroll D. Wright, *Industrial Conciliation and Arbitration* (Boston: Rand Avery & Co., 1881), pp. 81–2; Massachusetts Bureau of Labor Statistics, *Annual Report* (1877), pp. 19–49.

5. Wright, *Industrial Conciliation,* pp. 84–97.

6. Ibid., pp. 19, 41, 46, 83.

7. Ibid., p. 81.

8. Ibid.

9. Edward Cummings, "Industrial Arbitration in the United States," *Quarterly Journal of Economics,* 9 (July 1895): 353–71.

10. Daniel J. Ryan, *Arbitration Between Capital and Labor* (Columbus, Ohio: A. H. Smythe, 1885); see also Washington Gladden, "Arbitration of Labor Disputes," *Journal of Social Science* 21 (1886): 156.

11. *Hatter and Furrier,* Aug. 1882, p. 15.

12. *Danbury News,* 15 Feb. 1882.

13. Ibid., 11 Jan. 1882; *Hat, Cap and Fur Trade Review,* Jan. 1882, p. 106.

14. HFNTA, "Proceedings of the Regular Convention, June 1880," pp. 367, 378, 381.

15. HFNTA, *Semi-Annual Report,* Nov. 1881.

16. Ibid.

17. *Danbury News,* 22 Feb. 1882.

18. The story of the Danbury strike is told in the *Danbury News,* 8 Feb.–15 Mar. 1882, the *Hatter and Furrier,* Mar. 1882, p. 7, and the *Hat, Cap and Fur Trade Review,* Mar. 1882, p. 154.

19. HFNTA, *Semi-Annual Report,* May 1882; *Hatter and Furrier,* Mar. 1882, p. 20; May 1882, p. 14.

20. HFNTA, *Semi-Annual Report,* May 1882.

21. HFNTA, "Proceedings of the Special Convention, May 1882," p. 407. The convention of 1880 had imposed restrictions on the board.

22. Ibid., p. 440.

23. Ibid., pp. 414, 422.

24. *Hatter and Furrier,* Nov. 1884, p. 7.

25. *Hat, Cap and Fur Trade Review,* Jan. 1885, p. 372.

26. See *Hatter and Furrier,* 1882–83, passim; *Hat, Cap and Fur Trade Review,* 1882–83, passim.

27. *Hatter and Furrier,* July 1885, p. 9; HFNTA, *Semi-Annual Report,* May 1884.

28. Orange manufacturers were first to organize rates, in November 1884, but they failed. *Hatter and Furrier,* Dec. 1884, p. 30.

29. *John Swinton's Paper,* 18 Jan. 1885.

30. *Hatter and Furrier,* Dec. 1884, p. 11.

31. *John Swinton's Paper,* 15 Mar. 1885.

32. *South Norwalk Sentinel,* 25 Dec. 1884.

33. Ibid.

34. Ibid. The journeymen's association presented a different version of events. It claimed that the hatters immediately perceived the new bill as an act of aggression and reacted accordingly. The owners' statement is here accepted, because it is less self-serving, and because it is consistent with the employers' stunned reaction to the walkout.

35. Ibid.

36. "Journeymen's Statement," printed in ibid.; *Norwalk Hour,* 3 Jan. 1885.

37. *Norwalk Hour,* 24 Nov. 1884; *South Norwalk Sentinel,* 21 Nov. 1884.

38. "Employers' Statement," printed in *South Norwalk Sentinel,* 25 Dec. 1884.

39. John S. Seymour argued as much in his letter to the *Norwalk Hour* on 13 Dec. 1884, and *South Norwalk Sentinel* on 1 Jan. 1885. Seymour was a lawyer for the unions.

40. HFNTA, *Semi-Annual Report,* May 1884.

41. *Hatter and Furrier,* Jan. 1885, p. 11; *South Norwalk Sentinel,* 25 Dec. 1884; HFNTA, *Semi-Annual Report, Supplement,* May 1884.

42. *Norwalk Hour,* 29 Nov. 1884.

43. Ibid., 10 Jan. 1885; *South Norwalk Sentinel,* 8 Jan. 1885.

44. *Norwalk Hour,* 20 Dec. 1884.

45. Ibid., 6 Jan. 1884; *South Norwalk Sentinel,* 11 Dec. 1884. The HFNTA could not itself give strike relief because it had no strike fund.

46. *Hatter and Furrier,* Dec. 1884, pp. 29, 35, 36; Jan. 1885, pp. 22, 25; Mar. 1885, p. 11; July 1885, p. 13; *John Swinton's Paper,* 15 Feb. 1885.

47. *John Swinton's Paper,* 1 Mar. 1885; *Hatter and Furrier,* Jan. 1885, p. 22.

48. *Norwalk Hour,* 6 Dec. 1884; *South Norwalk Sentinel,* 21 Dec. 1884.

49. *Norwalk Hour,* 13 Dec. 1884; *Hatter and Furrier,* Jan. 1885, p. 11; Apr. 1885, p. 11; Mar. 1885, p. 11; May 1885, p. 7. The *Sentinel* charged that one hundred more strikers took jobs in Danbury's foul shops. *South Norwalk Sentinel,* 8 Jan. 1885.

50. *South Norwalk Sentinel,* 11 Dec. 1884; *John Swinton's Paper,* 15 Mar. 1885.

51. *Norwalk Hour,* 13 Dec. 1884; 10 Jan. 1885; *South Norwalk Sentinel,* 11 Dec. 1885.

52. *John Swinton's Paper,* 22 Feb. 1885.

53. Ibid., 15 Mar. 1885.

54. Ibid., 8 Feb. 1885.

55. Ibid., 22 Feb. 1885; *South Norwalk Sentinel,* 19 Feb. 1885.

56. *John Swinton's Paper,* 5 Apr. 1885.

57. Ibid., 15 Mar. 1885. This was, of course, an exaggeration.

58. Ibid., 22 Nov. 1885; 12 Apr. 1886; 19 Apr. 1886.

59. Establishing cooperatives served a function beyond giving strikers temporary employment during a strike; it also threatened employers with new competition. Indeed, the *South Norwalk Sentinel* accused the cooperative owners of prolonging the strike in order to give their firms time to get established. *South Norwalk Sentinel,* 19 Feb. 1885.

60. *Norwalk Hour,* 6 Dec. 1884; 13 Dec. 1884.

61. *South Norwalk Sentinel,* 4 Dec. 1884.

62. *Norwalk Hour,* 13 Dec. 1884.

63. Ibid., 27 Dec. 1884; 24 Jan. 1885.

64. *South Norwalk Sentinel*, 8 Jan. 1885.

65. *Norwalk Hour*, 13 Dec. 1884; *South Norwalk Sentinel*, 1 Jan. 1885.

66. *South Norwalk Sentinel*, 1 Jan. 1885.

67. *Hatter and Furrier*, Dec. 1884, p. 11.

68. *Bridgeport Standard*, 9 Dec. 1884; reprinted in *South Norwalk Sentinel*, 11 Dec. 1884.

69. In the first week of December, Crofut and Knapp had "five or six" men working. The following week it had "ten or twelve." *Norwalk Hour*, 6 Dec. 1884; 13 Dec. 1884.

70. Michael Gordon, "The Labor Boycott in New York City," *Labor History* 16 (Spring 1975): 192–93.

71. *The Times* (London), 30 Sept. 1880, reprinted in Gordon, "The Labor Boycott," p. 192.

72. Gordon, "The Labor Boycott," p. 211.

73. Ibid., pp. 210–11.

74. *Norwalk Hour*, 27 Dec. 1884; *South Norwalk Sentinel*, 8 Jan. 1885.

75. *Norwalk Hour*, 10 Jan. 1885; *John Swinton's Paper*, 8 Feb. 1885.

76. *John Swinton's Paper*, 18 Jan. 1885; 8 Feb. 1885.

77. Manufacturer's statement to *New York World*, reprinted in *John Swinton's Paper*, 21 Dec. 1884. The boycott's effectiveness is confirmed by *South Norwalk Sentinel*, 25 Dec. 1884; 22 Jan. 1885; *Norwalk Hour*, 6 Dec. 1884; 27 Dec. 1884; 24 Jan. 1885.

78. "Employers' Statement," *South Norwalk Sentinel*, 25 Dec. 1884.

79. *Norwalk Hour*, 27 Dec. 1884.

80. *South Norwalk Sentinel*, 25 Dec. 1884.

81. Ibid.

82. *Norwalk Hour*, 6 Dec. 1884.

83. Ibid., 24 Jan. 1885. In the hatter's interview, he charged that the manufacturers kept their men in the factories primarily to keep them away from the cajoling strikers.

84. Ibid., 14 Mar. 1885.

85. HFNTA, *Semi-Annual Report*, May 1884.

86. *Norwalk Hour*, 6 Dec. 1884.

87. Ibid., 3 Jan. 1885.

88. Ibid.

89. Ibid.

90. Ibid.

91. "Employers' Statement," *South Norwalk Sentinel*, 25 Dec. 1884.

92. Ibid.

93. *South Norwalk Sentinel*, 25 Dec. 1884.

94. *Norwalk Hour*, 17 Jan. 1885.

95. Ibid., 13 Dec. 1884; *John Swinton's Paper*, 14 Dec. 1884.

96. *South Norwalk Sentinel*, 4 Dec. 1884; 11 Dec. 1884; 25 Dec. 1884; *Norwalk Hour*, 13 Dec. 1884, 27 Dec. 1884.

97. *South Norwalk Sentinel*, 15 Jan. 1885; *Norwalk Hour*, 17 Jan. 1885.

98. *South Norwalk Sentinel*, 25 Dec. 1884; 8 Jan. 1885.

99. *Norwalk Hour,* 27 Dec. 1884.

100. *South Norwalk Sentinel,* 22 Jan. 1885. It turned out that the explosion was caused by gunpowder and did little damage.

101. *Hatter and Furrier,* Jan. 1885, p. 11.

102. *South Norwalk Sentinel,* 22 Jan. 1885; 12 Feb. 1885. *John Swinton's Paper* repeated the unions' charge, 25 Jan. 1885.

103. *John Swinton's Paper,* 18 Jan. 1885.

104. *South Norwalk Sentinel,* 29 Jan. 1885; 5 Feb. 1885; 19 Feb. 1885.

105. The local workingmen organized a labor party in 1885 and 1886 and started up their own newspaper, the *Mechanics' Journal,* of which no copies survive.

106. *John Swinton's Paper,* 25 Jan. 1885.

107. Ibid., 1 Feb. 1885.

108. *Hat, Cap and Fur Trade Review,* Mar. 1885, p. 481. See also *John Swinton's Paper,* 5 Apr. 1885.

109. *South Norwalk Sentinel,* 29 Jan. 1885.

110. *John Swinton's Paper,* 5 Apr. 1885.

111. *Norwalk Hour,* 24 Jan. 1885.

112. *John Swinton's Paper,* 17 May 1885.

113. Ibid., 8 Nov. 1885.

114. *Bradstreet's Review,* 19 Dec. 1885, cited in *John Swinton's Paper,* 27 Dec. 1885.

115. *South Norwalk Sentinel,* 26 Feb. 1885.

116. Ibid., 16 Apr. 1885.

117. *Norwalk Hour,* 14 Mar. 1885; *John Swinton's Paper,* 15 Mar. 1885.

118. HFNTA, *Semi-Annual Report, Supplement,* May 1884, p. 8.

119. Ibid.

120. *Norwalk Hour,* 21 Mar. 1885.

121. *John Swinton's Paper,* 12 Apr. 1885.

122. *Hatter and Furrier,* Apr. 1885, p. 11; *Hat, Cap and Fur Trade Review,* May 1885, pp. 593–94; *South Norwalk Sentinel,* 16 Apr. 1885.

Advertisement for the hatters' union label
(from United Hatters of North America,
Annual Report, 1898).

Stripping Body from the Cone After Forming.

The Blower, by Which the Fur is Prepared and Cleaned for the Forming Machine.

Second Sizing.   Using a Rolling-Pin to Shrink the Body Further.

Stretching the Crown and Brim—One of the Shaping Processes.

Crown-Finishing.   Polishing the Hat After It is Pounced with Fine Sandpaper.

Curling the Brim to Give It the Proper Shape.

Finishing the Crown in the Hydraulic Press Which Gives It the Final Shape.

The process of hat manufacture was a complicated one. The three lower photographs illustrate hat finishing operations: the hatter uses the hydraulic presser to give the hat crown its final shape; the hatter polishes the hat with fine sandpaper; working with a mold, the hatter curls the hat brim (from *Scientific American*, Sept. 30, 1905).

Advertisement of new hat styles for the new season. Included are top hats made of silk, bowlers made of stiff fur felt, and tourist hats made of soft fur felt. (from *Hatter and Furrier,* May, 1983).

YLES 1883-4

MILLER & EVANS
MANUFACTURERS OF
SILK CASSIMERE, OPERA & LADIES RIDING HATS
67 PRINCE ST. N.Y.

STYLES OF
K HATTERS

IAN & CO.
LT HATS
HILADELPHIA

DICKERSON & BROWN
STIFF & SOFT HATS.
96 SPRING ST. N.Y.

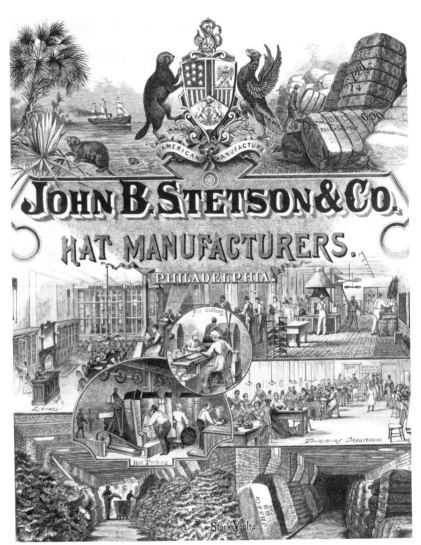

Advertisement for the John B. Stetson Hat Company, the nation's largest nonunion firm, showing interior scenes of the factory in Philadelphia. (from *Hatter and Furrier,* Jan. 1884).

ALL GOODS OF OUR MANUFACTURE

JOHN B. STETSON & CO.
PHILADELPHIA.

ARE

Identified by Quality Dies Expressed Hereon.

Exterior view of the John B. Stetson Hat Company factory with trademarks
of the company. (from *Hatter and Furrier,* Jan. 1884).

Advertisements for the principal protagonists in the 1885 Orange boycott, Frederick Berg and Lawrence T. Fell. Three years before the boycott, both men had been hat manufacturers (from *Hatter and Furrier,* Mar. 1882).

CHAPTER 8

The Orange Boycott

D URING THE WINTER of 1885, while the South Norwalk strike was raging, Orange hatters organized a community-wide boycott against a hat manufacturer who they believed was trying to prevent the women hat trimmers from organizing their own union. The boycott marshaled remarkable support for the trimmers' cause; nevertheless, it failed. The failure of the Berg hat boycott reinforced the lesson of South Norwalk: local action, no matter how effective, was not a viable strategy for a craft caught in the explosive expansion of a competitive industry.

The trouble began in the winter of 1885 when the Orange trimmers began to organize a trade union and called on the finishers, makers, and pouncers for aid. The women gained recognition in some Orange hat shops, but F. Berg and Company resisted organization. When the firm discharged Mary Deveraux, in March 1885, the trimmers' campaign unleashed tremendous social antagonisms. That Fredrick Berg became the center of a stormy conflict is paradoxical, for Berg's life in Orange embodied much of what gave the town its distinctive character.

Berg was one of Orange's hatters who made good; indeed, by 1880, his factory was one of the four largest. Berg's origins, though, could not have been more humble. He was born in Uberau, in Hesse-Darmstadt, the son of a poor farmer; his father was so dissatisfied with agricultural conditions at home that he uprooted the family and moved to Poland in search of better yields. When Poland proved no improvement, he returned to Uberau. Young Fredrick attended district schools and helped his father out on the farm until he was sixteen, when he followed his brothers' footsteps to Vienna, capital of the great Austro-Hungarian Empire. In Vienna, Berg apprenticed himself to the hatting trade. When he completed his term, in 1854, he began traveling throughout Europe, taking his place at the bench in numerous cities on the Continent. After two years, he ended up in the port of Danzig, where he received notice to report home to Uberau to face military service. Obediently, the young journeyman returned to Hesse-Darmstadt, where he drew a high number in the draft lottery and escaped conscription. At this point, free of social obligations, Berg emigrated to the United States.

Through a friend he met aboard ship, Berg learned of the opportunities for European hatters offered by Orange's hatting industry and came there straight from his disembarkment in New York. In Orange, which was growing rapidly because of the new soft hat craze, young Fredrick secured a position as journeyman in the small hat shop run by Christopher Nickel, a Bavarian immigrant. Following a classic path to success, Berg married his boss's daughter, Anna, and after the bridegroom served in the New Jersey infantry for nine months in 1862, the ambitious couple began saving up money to go into the business of hat manufacturing. Berg commenced operations in 1864, with $2000–3000 of his savings, and built his firm up slowly on a commission basis; by 1880, he was the first Orange manufacturer to sell his own hats directly to retailers, and his large brick factory provided work for 200 hands. He owned a large house in the pleasant upland western section of Orange on Hillside Avenue; he lived there with his wife, his six surviving children, one cousin, one boarder, and two caretakers.

In 1889, when Berg's sons were old enough to take over the firm's management, he went into the coal business; by then his personal worth approached $500,000. His interests extended to the Second National Bank of Orange, the Republican party and the Lutheran church; he discharged his civic responsibilities by serving on the board of assessments.[1] Fredrick Berg's wealth and status did not ensure him the obedience of his employees, however. When he fired Mary Devereux in 1885, most Orange hatters believed he was trying to stifle the trimmers' organizing campaign. In order to force the company to reverse its action, and to recognize the trimmers' union, the fair hatters struck Berg.

At first glance, it seems puzzling that the finishers would have risked so much to help workers outside their craft. After all, times had been hard in the hatting trade for two years, and to keep employers "fair" in the competitive hat industry was no easy matter. One explanation is that these trimmers were the sisters or daughters of many union men, or else were the sole source of support for their widowed Irish mothers. Another explanation is broader and more speculative; the mid-1880s were a time when women were organizing unions throughout the United States, particularly through the Knights of Labor, which had come to Orange in 1885 in conjunction with the South Norwalk strike. It may be that Orange hatters were imbibing a new brew of sexual solidarity, imported from other working-class communities.[2]

Whatever the explanation, hatters reinforced their strike by calling on their neighbors and friends to ostracize all those who went to work for Berg after he fired Mary Deveraux. Furthermore, they asked supporters not to shop at stores that continued to do business with Berg and its nonunion employees.[3] This meant that if a dairy sold milk to a strikebreaker, strike supporters were to cease buying milk there.

To effectuate the boycott, the hatters' union organized the shop crew discharged by F. Berg and Company. Members were assigned subdistricts of Orange, starting in the valley near the Berg factory. In their district, the men were to ask merchants to pledge their support.[4] After completing their rounds, the boycotters were to distribute circulars to neighborhood residents, informing them which merchants had joined the campaign and which had refused.

Although newspaper accounts were fragmentary, and biased against the hatters, it appears that most local residents supported the boycott.[5] On 28 March, the Orange Journal reported: "Nearly all storekeepers in the Valley have been requested not to sell anything to any employees of Berg's, and many complied with the request. Milkmen, peddlars, and saloon keepers were not exempt. The South Orange Skating Rink agreed to refuse to let any of Berg's employees have skates. . . . A mason's laborer named Heslin, whose wife was trimming hats for Berg and Company, was turned out against by his fellow laborers."[6]

When Captain A. M. Matthews, a coal seller, announced publicly that he would "rather have deserted to the rebels during the war" than to bow to the boycotters' demand that he cease selling coal to F. Berg and Company, the employees of Connett and Company, one of Berg's competitors, induced their employer to cease buying from Matthews. Another hat manufacturing firm, Clorer and Company, discharged one Higginbotham because he refused to move out of the house he shared with his older brother, a foul hatter at Berg's.

The solidarity between hatters and their neighbors should not be romanticized or exaggerated. Workers' strength in the Gilded Age came in part from their ability to coerce others not to scab, cross picket lines, or patronize noncooperative merchants. Thus it should not be surprising that Orange hatters resorted to physical force to bring some small proprietors into line. On the evening of 11 April, "a committee of hatters patrolled in

front of the various stores that [had] been placed on the hatters' black list.
. . . A committee which had been placed in front of [some] stores, and
some members of which were intoxicated, carried on their work in a most
high-handed manner, going so far as to enter the stores of both Walter
Vandell and Thomas Jones, and dragging customers out by main force.
. . . Several women, wives of some of Berg's hands, complained that they
had been followed around by men who had prevented them from trading in
stores by pointing them out to the proprietors."[7] At three stores in the valley, the proprietors refused to accede to the journeymen's demands. When
they called on the police for help, town marshal McChesney took command
and "accompanied [the women] to several stores and they obtained all they
wanted."[8]

Leading Orange businessmen launched a counteroffensive. "The prominent businessmen of Orange" posted circulars throughout Orange, asking
"Is America A Free Country," to announce a public meeting to fight boycotting and "preserve the rights of which as American citizens we are justly
proud." On the evening of 2 April, a crowd gathered at Liberty Hall to hear
speeches proclaiming boycotting to be a form of "czarist" tyranny, an insult
to American independence and freedom. At the end of his address, Captain
Matthews, carried away by the injustice perpetrated against him for defy-
ing the unions, pleaded with the audience to "see to it that boycotting is not
naturalized in this country."[9]

Orange's hatters were touchy about their reputations; they didn't want
Captain Matthews to have the last word. On 8 April, they called a public
meeting to present their side to the story. Richard Dowdall of Newark, ad-
dressing a throng of 1000 supporters, presented a statement by the hatters'
executive committees denouncing "the outrage" committed by a sympathiz-
er of the strikers, whose offense consisted of defacing the wall of a dwelling
house Berg was erecting. Julius Ellendorf then spoke, bringing a message of
solidarity from the journeymen of South Norwalk. Ellendorf countered the
patriotic rhetoric of Captain Matthews with his own version of American-
ism: "Mr. Ellendorf said he understood there was a man in this city who
denied to American citizens the right to organize for their own protection.
. . . Mr. Ellendorf characterized the action of the manufacturer as an attempt at enslavement and said, 'It is not the thing to do, for a man who has
turned his back upon tyranny and oppression in his own country to produce the same here. Let him remember that he was a poor man once and
that he may again be poor. Men are millionaires today and beggars tomor-

row. Wealth is no more secure. What a reflection it would be if he were again obliged to taken a maker's apron and work at the kettle.' "[10]

In the end, Orange hatters discovered the same lesson Julius Ellendorf and the Norwalk journeymen had learned: even an effective local boycott could not force a determined employer to give in to union demands. Even though the hatters were able to pressure scores of local merchants to cease doing business with the Berg hat company and its nonunion employees, Berg was able to secure food and house a crew of strikebreakers, and thereby continue producing and selling hats.

Even if the hatters' boycott tactic proved insufficient, it was not ineffective. When one looks at Orange's population, the explanation is not hard to find. More than one-fourth of the city's adult males were journeymen belonging to the striking unions. If one adds in the striking trimmers, and all the brothers, sisters, children, and parents of the strikers, at least 40 percent of Orange's population had a stake in the boycott.

It is not really hard to understand why local merchants such as saloon keepers and grocers acquiesced in the boycott — if they refused to, they stood to lose the patronage of a large number of their regular customers, whereas compliance would cost little. In short, the boycott was a tactic enabling a determined minority to exert pressure on a weak opponent — small, vulnerable proprietors.

There are indications that the strength of the hatters' boycott was based on more than their numerical weight in the community. For instance, in the battle of public opinion carried out in the local newspapers, the hatters' spokesman was Lawrence T. Fell, one of Orange's most popular and respected figures. Fell was a former journeyman who had opened his own hat factory and branched out into real estate. He was chairman of the local branch of the Irish Parliamentary Land League, and he was a state official, the New Jersey child labor inspector.

In a letter to the *Orange Chronicle* of 9 May, Fell commended the journeymen hatters for proposing to submit their dispute with F. Berg and Company to arbitration and criticized the firm for refusing to do so. Fell went so far as to imply that Berg's recalcitrance was hypocritical in view of the fact that Orange manufacturers had agreed not long before that arbitration was preferable to strikes as a way to resolve disputes. By making Berg's unwillingness to arbitrate the central issue, Fell exerted considerable moral pressure on local manufacturers to support the journeymens' position.[11] Furthermore, the hatters' desire to arbitrate had deeper implications: it indicated the union members' confidence that disinterested parties would support the hatters' right to organize F. Berg and Company despite the latter's claim that the capitalist's right to control his own property made arbitration wrong in principle. The hatters' proposal to settle the dispute called for both parties to name one satisfactory person each to hear the case; if the two people could not agree, they would name a third party to aid them in reaching a settlement. That the hatters were willing to submit to such a process indicates that they believed they had public opinion on their side.

The Berg Boycott and Gilded Age Politics in Orange

All in all, the Berg boycott is a puzzling phenomenon. It was a strikingly effective display of community solidarity, but it failed. It pitted workers against the local business elite, yet the leading public spokesman for the hatters was a businessman. Many workers supported the hatters' struggle despite the fact that the finishers' craft culture emphasized their difference from other workers, and their mobility from town to town.

In order to make sense of these seeming paradoxes, we must look beyond the particular event — the boycott — to the larger terrain of political life and social relations in Gilded Age Orange. Three themes emerge: first, the relationship between the hatters and the upper strata of Orange was complex. There were links of mutual interest and common values; there were structures of inequality and divergent economic interests. Second, hatters were deeply enmeshed in the social life of Orange's workers' neighborhoods. Third, hatters had multiple orientations toward social life based on their craft culture, class interests, ethnic identifications, and religious affiliations. Their ties were an intricate web, binding hatters to some of their neighbors in solidarity, and separating them from others.

Hatters and the Elite

At first glance, the Oranges — a term including the city of Orange and its suburbs — appear to have been a highly stratified community, with vast gaps between the affluent suburbanites and the toiling masses. Yet a closer look reveals a more complex picture.

Orange's suburbs were idyllic; their topography and climate attracted "an increasing immigration of the families doing business in the metropolis."[12] One mile west of downtown Orange stood two high ridges known as First and Second Mountains. Near the boundary between Orange and West Orange, they "rose abruptly to a height of 420 feet above the level of the city," running with intervals northeast and southwest. On the eastern slope of the mountains lived most of the Oranges' elite, including merchants and industrialists, as well as such national figures as General George B. McClellan, Thomas A. Edison, and George Huntington Hartford, director of the Atlantic and Pacific Tea Company. Other professional and commercial men preferred to live on the open plateau to Orange's east and south. Commuting to the great port cities was easy. The Morris and Essex branch of the Delaware, Lackawanna and Western Railroad systems sent trains from Orange to New York City twenty-eight times daily, and street cars ran between Orange and Newark every ten minutes.[13]

On all points of the compass, the white, Anglo-Saxon, and Protestant suburban residents enjoyed a favorable climate, because the mountains shielded them from both the "severe west winds of winter" and from the "sudden thundergusts of the southwest storms of summer." The Oranges became a health resort in the summer for wealthy persons "suffering with chronic lung diseases," or merely seeking a retreat from the hot, moist New York summer.[14]

For Orange's workers, who lived five hundred feet below the mountain ridges, it was a different world. No cool winds blew, and summers were discouragingly hot. Moreover, since the city was devoid of any sewage system, most of the region's waste flowed to the low land. Parrow Brook, which dribbled through the valley, was a "nuisance. Black dye stuffs, house drainage and general refuse found a handy depository in its murky depths."[15]

Workers lived near the city center, near the factory clusters, and along the railroad tracks. There were four clusters of hat factories, each bordered by railroad tracks, coal yards, innumerable saloons, and workers' homes. The cheap wooden one- and two-family houses were within easy walking distance of the factories, but what workers gained in convenience they paid for in noise, dirt, and disease.

Inequality in the Oranges was not a simple matter of city and suburbs, however, for not all of the Oranges' upper strata lived in the suburbs. Professionals and large proprietors made up nearly 10 percent of the city's population. Of these, according to a sample of twenty small residential areas, half lived in fashionable neighborhoods, on high ground: among them was Fredrick Berg, who lived up on Hillside Avenue. This section of north central Orange included thirty households headed by upper- and middle-class adult men, including four hat manufacturers, two stockbrokers, two lawyers, a dentist, five clerks, and three bookkeepers. Sixteen households employed and housed thirty-four servants. In the same area, there were only seventeen households headed by skilled male workers. None contained servants. There were six hatters, including three finishers, six building tradesmen, four other skilled workers, and two express drivers.

Berg's residence on Hillside Avenue, far removed from the haze and smoke, did not link him to the journeymen hatters, but fully half of the city's affluent lived scattered through the city's workers' districts.[16] For example, William McGall lived near his factory in the middle of industrial Orange Valley.

The spatial relationship between the Oranges' affluent strata and the working masses corresponds with the pattern of local politics. During the Berg boycott, some Orange businessmen rallied around their colleagues. In local elections, the suburban districts supported prominent Republicans, but this does not mean that they viewed workers as enemies or aliens. This becomes clear when we look at how the Oranges responded to an external threat to the region's major industry—hat manufacturing. During the winter of 1878, before America had fully recovered from a terrible depression, Orange manufacturers and journeymen learned that the administration of the Trenton State Prison was negotiating with a prospective contractor to put inmates to work finishing and trimming soft hats.[17] Orange and Newark journeymen hatters quickly sprang into action, organizing a committee to lobby Trenton lawmakers. George Ferry, Orange's mayor, testified before the legislature on the evils of contract labor. Captain Pierson, the Oranges' assemblyman, led the legislative effort, arguing that the hatting industry was important to the state. On 7 March, the Pierson bill gained approval, and prison hatting was dead.[18]

The demise of the proposal to produce cheap hats at Trenton State Prison did not mark the disappearance of the prison labor issue, for the hatters were determined to end all contract convict labor, particularly large-scale shoe manufacturing. In pursuit of this goal, which reflected their sense of connection to other workers, the hat finishers demanded that the local political parties recognize the legitimacy of the hatters' values, not simply their economic interests. That the Oranges' political organizations responded positively indicates that the hatters' social and physical segregation was not complete.

In the fall of 1878, the hatters began campaigning to halt contract shoemaking at Trenton State Prison, which was cutting into the sales of Essex County shoe shops. By mobilizing this effort, the hatters were fulfilling a promise they had made to the shoemakers' union the previous winter. The hatters kicked off their campaign with a monster rally of "mechanics and manufacturers" in Newark, in October 1878. Orange Mayor George Ferry, a hat manufacturer, was the principal speaker, and his speech expressed the sympathy Essex County's upper class felt for the working population in the wake of the harsh depression of 1873. "Wages are none too remunerative at the best, but when our legislators . . . so employ the convicts in the prisons as to produce a revenue, and wages are cut down, it is time that the mechanics of the state demanded that this thing should cease. . . ."[19]

In order to further the anti-prison labor cause, Orange hatters considered running one of the leaders for the assembly on an anti-prison labor platform, but the local political parties made this unnecessary. All Essex County's Democratic and Republican candidates for the state legislature made opposition to prison labor a prominent feature of their campaigns.[20] On election day, John Gill, a Republican hat manufacturer, as the victorious candidate for the state assembly from the Oranges, pledged to carry on the fight against prison labor.[21]

It was not until 1881 that the New Jersey state legislature passed a bill putting an end to large-scale shoe contracting at Trenton State Prison. Between 1878 and 1881, Orange hatters continued to play an active role in electoral politics, and local politicians continued to respond to their concerns. John Gill won reelection in November 1879 as a "friend of the workingman," for his efforts on behalf of the anti-prison labor cause;[22] in 1880, when the New Jersey state Democratic party pledged abolition of contract labor and the Republican party demurred, hatters' votes for gubernatorial candidate Edward Ludlow made New Jersey "the only Democratic state in the union."[23] Governor Ludlow repaid his debt to the hatters by pushing a bill greatly restricting prison contracting through the state legislature in 1881.[24]

The fact that all sections of the Oranges supported the hatters' efforts on behalf of other workers in the prison labor campaign, like the fact that Lawrence T. Fell played an active role in defense of the workers' rights in the Berg boycott, and the fact that the hatters offered to submit their dispute with Berg to arbitration, all indicate that support for the hatters' moral claims extended beyond the world of Orange's workers, into the world of businessmen and professionals. If one assumes that Orange's upper class were all firm believers in "free enterprise" capitalism, one is faced with a contradiction, but this was not the case. Many of the Oranges' civic leaders — men like Fredrick Berg and Lawrence T. Fell — were hat manufacturers who had begun their careers as journeymen. At least seventeen of thirty-seven Orange manufacturers in 1889 had worked at the bench a decade before—and they had absorbed many of the craft's values and traditions.[25]

As Lawrence T. Fell stated in his letter supporting the hatters' boycott of F. Berg, "Hat manufacturers of Orange have all been journeymen and knowing the rights of journeymen should be willing to concede the same."[26] Fell himself did more than "concede the hatters' rights." An Irish immigrant who had learned the hatting trade in Orange workshops, Fell abandoned his life as a journeyman to set himself up as a commission manufacturer in 1880. Three years later, when years of agitation by the state's labor unions finally induced the legislature to pass a Child Labor Act, the hatters' friend, Governor Ludlow, appointed Fell to serve as inspector of child labor. He used his post as a forum for lecturing parents and employers on the evils of putting children to work before the age of fourteen (boys) and twelve (girls); campaigned for compulsory education laws; and later, as factory inspector, helped secure passage of legislation to improve health and safety conditions in the factories.

When Fell was appointed to the new post in 1883, it did not appear as if he would play any significant role, for the legislation creating his post denied him effective enforcement power, nor did it provide him with any deputies to help him inspect the state's more than 9000 factories and other goods-producing workplaces. Moreover, Fell owed his appointment to his status as a businessman; the senate had previously rejected Governor Ludlow's first nominee, Richard Dowdall, a Newark hat finishers' union leader, for being a "demogogue."[27]

Despite these unpromising beginnings, Fell's career developed in unexpected ways. After inspecting numerous workshops and factories in his first year as child labor inspector, Fell was convinced that not only was child labor a serious problem, but that the law of 1883 was inadequate to cope with it.[28] He asked the state legislature to appoint two deputies to help him inspect the state's factories and workshops to enforce the law, but that was not all. Fell's year of service convinced him of the need for a compulsory education law, because "the ignorance of children is a threat to democracy," and also for "more thorough factory legislation."[29]

Leon Abbott, New Jersey's new governor, the son of a Philadelphia journeyman hatter, and a friend of Paterson labor reformer J. P. McDonnell, supported Fell's efforts. In 1884, he changed Fell's title to state factory inspector and authorized him to appoint two deputies to help him enforce the state's child labor and factory laws.

Fell showed his commitment to the labor movement by nominating J. P.

McDonnell, the Paterson labor reformer, and John Craigie of the Newark hat finishers as his deputies, and he continued in that direction. In 1885, Fell, Abbott, and McDonnell secured legislative approval of both a compulsory education act, and a factory health and safety law. The latter required proper ventilation in work places, prohibited overcrowding, provided for dressing rooms and water closets, required employers to give employees due notice, and required that industrial accidents be reported.[30] When, in 1886, with Governor Abbott's help, Fell gained three deputies to aid him in enforcing the law and three more inspectors in 1889, he was finally able to improve significantly the working conditions in New Jersey factories.[31]

Fell's leadership in using state power on behalf of working men, women, and children made him leader of Orange's hatters. They rewarded him by electing him mayor of Orange in 1892, but Fell's efforts also created enemies. New Jersey businessmen attacked Fell throughout his career, and although they failed to unseat him in 1886, they took the opportunity provided by the depression of 1893 to drive him out of office.[32]

Hatters and the Oranges' Working People

When all is said and done, the support of men like Lawrence T. Fell counted less for the hatters in their struggle against Berg than did the support of Orange's fellow workers. Despite the fact that the hat finishers preserved a unique tradition, spoke a special language, and cultivated their distinctiveness, they had sunk deep roots into their community and developed strong neighborhood ties.

This becomes immediately apparent as soon as one reads accounts of electoral politics in Gilded Age Orange. During the first half of the 1880s, hatters participated fully in civic life, not as members of a special interest group but as citizens with a variety of social roles and orientations. In their roles as concerned parents, finishers often ran for and won election to the school board, for example, where they participated in decisions about which teachers should be hired, where and when schools should be built, and how much teachers should be paid. As taxpayers, they frequently won election to the board of assessors, where they decided how much their fellow unionists, their neighbors, their local merchants, and their employers should pay in taxes. As concerned citizens, they gained seats on the town council, where they participated in decisions about whether or not to build a water works, where to improve streets and street lights, and what rights to grant local railroads and street car lines.[33]

The fact that finishers held all these offices was not simply a consequence of their numerical weight in the community — 500 journeymen could have been politically impotent. Instead, they won prominence in local politics by participating actively in the party system. Whether it was the Democrats or the Republicans who won local and national elections, there were always hatters reaping the benefits. For example, the journeymen received appointments to the Orange police force; there they enforced laws against vagrancy and drunkenness, kept order on picket lines, and intervened in marital disputes. Other finishers gained patronage jobs in the post office, where they maintained the town's communication system, carrying good news, bad news, and gossip to friends and neighbors. Of course, the fact that hatters received patronage jobs and won election to civic posts does not mean that they had gained political equality. As one might expect, the major posts, such as mayor, assemblyman, and senator, went to prominent businessmen and professionals, not to skilled workers, however numerous or cohesive they might be.

Orange was usually a Democratic town, and most hatters were Democrats, but journeymen played active roles in both parties and ran for office on both tickets. Trade loyalties influenced political behavior to some extent; hatters were more likely to vote for candidates from their industry, be they journeymen or manufacturers, than for outsiders, but the ethnic-religious dimension was probably more important. Orange's Irish Catholic community was Democratic, whereas the white Anglo-Saxon Protestants voted Republican.

It was to break up this alignment and unify hat finishers under one banner that three Democratic party leaders bolted from their party to organize a workingmen's slate in Orange's charter elections in the spring of 1886. All three were prominent in the hatting industry: Christopher McCullough as a foreman and former manufacturer, and John Seymour and John Denney in the finishers' union. Furthermore, McCullough and Seymour were activists in the Irish National Parliamentary League, where they assisted the leader, Lawrence T. Fell.

Irish Americans associated with the finishing craft were able to play a leading role in Orange politics because finishers were the best organized group within the city's largest industry, the Irish were a large, cohesive group within the finishers' union, and the finishers were the most successful of Orange's Irish workers. Their opportunity came as a result of the expansion of the hatting industry. After the soft hat boom began in 1854, Orange attracted large numbers of immigrants, particularly from Ireland and Germany, as well as large numbers of New Jerseyans. Then in the 1870s, hat manufacturers met their continuing need for skilled labor by hiring and training large numbers of apprentices, in particular American-born sons of Irish immigrants and of native parents. (In this context, "native" refers to children born in America to parents also born in America, as opposed to the American-born offspring of immigrants.) The consequence of this hiring pattern was that Irish immigrants and their sons made up more than a third of the Orange finishers' population in 1880, the native Americans another third, and German immigrants and their children a seventh, statistics that are staggering when one considers that the hatters were preserving and passing on a traditional culture with roots in the Middle Ages.

The expanding city developed a social structure in which inequality was expressed along ethnic lines. White, native Americans were able to take advantage of the opportunities created by urban growth to develop profitable businesses and enter the professions. Analysis of a random sample of the 1880 federal census indicates that native Americans held forty-three of the sixty-two nonmanual jobs.[34] (See Table 2.) English, German, and other northern European immigrants occupied the next rung in the Orange hierarchy. Nearly one-third of the adult males drawn from this population held nonmanual jobs. For the Irish, on the other hand, that figure was only one in ten; no blacks held nonmanual jobs.

Ethnic inequality extended into the workers' population. In every ethnic group, a majority of the adult males held manual jobs, but this generalization masks important differences. Few German immigrants (8 percent) or native Americans were unskilled workers (6 percent), but nearly half the Irish immigrants (41 percent) and all the blacks were.

There were also important differences in the kinds of skilled jobs held by workers of the several populations. The Irish immigrants and their children clustered in the hatting industry, whereas the German and native American skilled workers were more likely to be employed in the building trades and other crafts. Thus, it appears that Orange's large Irish population was able to rise out of the ranks of the unskilled primarily through the hatting industry, where yearly earnings were lower than in other crafts. The Irish hat finishers, whose craft was at the top of the hatting industry, were among the few sons of Erin to grasp a secure hold in the Orange economy.

Data on the occupations of young men and women in Orange's labor force reinforce the picture drawn from the adult males. Fifty-two percent of the native American males aged fifteen to twenty were either working as clerks or were in school; for young Irishmen, that figure was only 18 percent, and for the children of Irishmen only 11 percent. The only exception

Table 2. Occupations of Orange Adult Males According to Ethnic Background, 1880

Fathers' and Sons' Birthplaces

Fathers Born	Ireland				Germany				England		Other Europe				U.S.		Total	%
Sons Born	Ireland		U.S.		Germany		U.S.		England		Other Eur.		U.S.		U.S.			
	N = 66		N = 32		N = 35		N = 6		N = 6		N = 16		N = 14		N = 88			
Occupation	N	%	N	%	N	%	N	%	N	%	N	%	N	%	N	%	263	100
Hatter (inc. all crafts)	23	34	17	53	12	34	1	17	3	50	2	13	2	15	11	13	71	27
Other Skilled Worker	11	16	5	16	10	28	4	67	1	17	4	25	5	36	22	25	62	23
Unskilled	25	39	5	16	1	3	0	0	0	0	5	31	2	15	7	8	45	17
Clerk	0	0	0	0	2	6	0	0	0	0	0	0	0	0	11	13	13	5
Small Proprietor or White Collar	4	6	1	3	4	11	1	17	1	17	5	31	4	28	19	21	39	14
Large Proprietor or Professional	3	5	3	9	5	14	0	0	0	0	0	0	1	7	13	15	25	10
Other	0	0	1	3	1	3	0	0	1	17	0	0	0	0	5	6	8	3

Source: random sample drawn from U.S. Census, Orange, New Jersey, 1880

to this pattern of inequality was the fact that 72 percent of the children of German immigrants were either clerks or at school; this may indicate that the German population was achieving entree into the town's middle classes, although this point is not certain, for a youth's employment as a clerk may not have led to non-manual employment in later years.

Occupational data on Orange's unmarried women reveal a pattern quite similar to that characterizing Orange's adult men, except that the disparities between ethnic groups were somewhat greater as far as women were concerned. More than half the Irish women worked as servants in the homes of others, while only 7 percent lived at home without working for pay. By contrast, fully 60 percent of the daughters of native-born parents did not work for pay, and those who did work served in "genteel" jobs, as teachers, nurses, or salesgirls, or stayed home making dresses. Not a single native woman could be found in any of Orange's hat shops or ribbon factories, working alongside the daughters of Irish immigrants. More than any other fact, this symbolized the ethnic/class inequality of Orange's social structure. There is a striking parallel, for example, between the employment patterns of adult males and working women. Unmarried Irish and black women were at the bottom working as servants, just as Irish and black men were the unskilled laborers and servants. The daughters of Irish immigrants were in an intermediate status, working as hat trimmers and dressmakers, just as the adult sons of Irish immigrants tended to work as hatters. The native daughters were highest in status, staying at home or going to school, just as the native males held the town's best jobs. It would appear that inequality in the employment of women was more pronounced than in the employment of men.

If the Irish hat finishers had chosen to identify with the native and German skilled workers, Orange politics would have taken on a different cast, but the picture was more complex. An analysis of residence patterns of Orange neighborhoods does not indicate clear patterns of segregation between skilled and unskilled, nor among Irish, native, and German. To illustrate the mixed character of the neighborhoods where Orange workers lived, let us examine the one block on which more hat finishers lived than any other. It was on Madison Street, near the factories of Orange's Third Ward. In addition to eight hat finishers, there were two hat manufacturers, a florist, a policeman, a bartender, three building tradesmen, six laborers, a flagman on the railroad, two peddlers, and the employee of a junk shop. Of the young women, one worked as a cook, one was a servant, three worked as dressmakers, and three were hat trimmers.

Though the spire of St. John's Roman Catholic Church rose two blocks to the east, Madison Street was an "Irish" neighborhood only in part: thirteen of the twenty-seven households were Irish, while another eight were German. This pattern was typical of Orange; only seven of the eighteen workers' neighborhoods included in a residential sample contained an overwhelming Irish population of more than two-thirds. Even the native workers did not live predominantly in separate enclaves. In only one of the eighteen neighborhoods in the residential sample (William Street in central Orange) were more than two-thirds of the inhabitants the American-born children of American-born parents. In the ten other neighborhoods, no ethnic group predominated.

This analysis of Orange's residential patterns suggests that the hat finishers, who lived in the Irish communities, the mixed communities, and the native American bastions were in a position to play a key role bridging the workers of Orange. At the same time, it is clear that ethnic clustering in Orange was not so strong as to preclude substantial mixing of the city's workers. This could have produced class alliances across ethnic lines, or ethnic barriers to class alliances. In fact, there were both; the attempts of leading Orange Irish hat finishers to forge a majority that combined craft-, class-, and ethnic-consciousness met limited success and ultimate failure.

Multiple Orientations

The complexities of Orange politics are exemplified by the 1886 elections. The Workingmen's party nominated for mayor Christopher McCullough, an Irish Catholic foreman who had recently been an employer, despite the fact that the party had been organized in the hopes of luring Protestant skilled workers away from the Republican party! McCullough ran against George Hartford, the incumbent Democrat, who campaigned as a "civil service reformer." The Republican party faced a difficult decision; if it nominated its own candidate, it might ensure the victory of an Irish Catholic leader of organized workers. That wouldn't do. The party endorsed its rival, George Hartford, instead.

Democratic Party activists also faced difficult choices — to support the regular organization, or to follow the labor leaders. In the Second Ward, the Democratic party voted to endorse the Workingmen's candidates for councilmen, school board, freeholder, and assessor. In the other wards, the Democrats nominated separate slates.

The election results were mixed. The Workingmen's party gained the votes of more workers than the Democrats usually did, and the finishers voted for the labor slate almost unanimously, but Mayor Hartford narrowly won reelection by combining the preponderance of the normal Republican vote with a small Democratic vote.[35]

Hartford owed his election in part to Father Edward Fleming, pastor of Orange's largest Catholic church. On the Sunday before the election, Father Fleming urged his congregation to shun the Workingmen's slate, arguing that the Irish Catholics were well served by the two-party system.[36] His stance was in keeping with church strategy throughout the country; in New York's 1886 mayoral election, the church strongly backed Democratic nominee Abram Hewitt, an iron manufacturer, in his successful campaign against Henry George, champion of the city's Irish-dominated labor movement. Clearly, the church did not believe it could gain security in a political system based on class alignments.

In a letter he wrote to the *Orange Journal* after the election, Father Fleming, incensed that the finishers' union had voted to fine those members who voted wrongly, denounced the leaders of the Workingmen's party as opportunists, tools of the liquor interests, and hot-headed demogogues:

> I think . . . I have exposed only the worst class of the trade, the cads and the bullies who recognize no rights but those they assume to be theirs. They are an unmitigated nuisance. . . . The air of a hat shop is vitiated with their foul language and their blasphemies. . . . They are so loud in their demands of what they call their rights that when they break out periodically, and their actions are noised abroad, strangers are led to believe that Orange is something like a mining district of some Pennsylvania town. . . . It is time that the thinking, brainy men in the hatters' trade in this city should take their place as leaders.[37]

The *Journal* notes that such words would have been resented had they come from any other source, but coming from a priest who was a respected friend of the hatters, it was a different story.

Despite Father Fleming's opposition, the Workingmen's party did win numerous local offices, including council seats in the Second and Third wards, and positions among the assessors and on the school board. In the fall, John Denney, who had been elected a town assessor in the spring, ran as the Workingmen's candidate for the assembly in a district which included both Orange and East Orange. He surprised political observers by polling five hundred votes, only four less than the victorious Republican. Denney's strength reflected the recent movement of hatters into factory districts in East Orange contiguous to a working-class neighborhood in Orange, but the overwhelming Republican suburban vote of East Orange, combined with the Protestant Republican minority of Orange, denied Denney victory.[38]

Thereafter, Orange reverted to the two-party system. Nevertheless, the rise of the Workingmen's party had revealed the complexity of city politics. Industry, craft, ethnic, religious, and class identifications all influenced the political behavior of the finishers and their neighbors.

The relationship between class and ethnicity in Orange was complex. The Irish finishers' ties to other Irishmen formed the basis of their power in electoral politics as well as the basis for Lawrence Fell's career as an advocate of New Jersey's workers. Ethnic consciousness, however, was a hurdle to working-class solidarity as well as a basis for the Irish workers' power, for it separated native workers from the Irish in most election years. Even when the finishers' leaders tried to jump that hurdle by organizing a workingmen's party, ethnic solidarity stood in the way, in the form of Father Fleming's opposition to the new class alignment.

Conclusion

The analysis of Orange's occupational structure, residential patterns, and electoral contests helps us to understand why Orange hatters gained so much support in the Berg boycott as well as why that support was limited. A mixed picture has emerged; hatters had some support from Orange's shopkeepers and businessmen but were also opposed by the "leading businessmen" during their struggle with Berg for union recognition. They gained support from other workers for their boycotts and electoral forays, but ethnic divisions stood in the way of that support developing into a workers' alternative to the two-party system. And Irish solidarity buttressed the Berg boycott and undergirded the hatters' electoral organization, but these same ethnic ties impeded the development of the Workingmen's party.

That social relations in Orange were mixed, resembling class conflict in some respects and differing in others, should not be a surprise: social relations in Orange reflected to a great extent the relations between employers and journeymen in the hatting industry. During the Gilded Age, relations between hat manufacturers and finishers were changing slowly. Journeymen remained skilled craftsmen, largely in control of their work; employers remained small entrepreneurs, traditional in their business practices. Gradually, the manufacturers were changing in response to pressures from the commission houses, and as they became more rational in their approach to cutting costs, they increasingly challenged the hatters' autonomous status.

As they did so, journeymen had to turn to ever more collective measures of defense — formal local union rules, a stronger national union, cooperation with other hatters against prison labor. To the national leaders of the hatters' union, the message of the Berg boycott was clear: local action, no matter how strong, no longer sufficed. To halt the erosion of their skill standards, their traditions, and their control of the work process, hatters had to forge effective links with craftmates in other towns and workers in other industries. As the Berg boycott wound down, the Hat Finishers National Trade Association took bold initiatives to forge a new practice of solidarity.

NOTES

1. *Hatter and Furrier,* Nov. 1888, p. 25; David L. Pierson, *History of the Oranges to 1921* (New York: Lewis Historical Publishing Co., 1922), 4: 298–99.

2. Alice Kessler-Harris, *Out to Work: A History of Wage-Earning Women in the U.S.* (New York: Oxford University Press, 1982).

3. *Orange Chronicle,* 21 Mar. 1885. As we shall see in a later chapter, the boycott was a new weapon in the United States at this time. It was inspired by the Irish Land League's campaign against landlords.

4. *Orange Chronicle,* 21 Mar. 1885.

5. Ibid.

6. Ibid., 28 Mar. 1885.

7. *Orange Journal,* 18 Apr. 1885; *Orange Chronicle,* 18 Apr. 1885.

8. *Orange Journal,* 18 Apr. 1885.

9. *Orange Chronicle,* 28 Mar. 1885.

10. Ibid., 11 Apr. 1885.

11. Ibid., 9 May 1885.

12. U.S. Census Office, *Social Statistics of Cities, 1880,* p. 717; Pierson, *History of the Oranges,* p. 398; William H. Shaw, *History of Essex and Hudson Counties* (Philadelphia: Everts and Peck, 1884), p. 819.

13. Shaw, *History of Essex and Hudson,* p. 73; Pierson, *History of the Oranges,* p. 417.

14. U.S. Census Office, *Statistics of Cities, 1880,* p. 717; Shaw, p. 817.

15. Joseph Fulford Folsom, ed., *The Municipalities of Essex County, New Jersey* (New York: Lewis Historical Publishing Co., 1925), pp. 546–47.

16. To draw the neighborhood sample, twenty pages of the U.S. census manuscript schedule for Orange in 1880 were selected randomly. Each "neighborhood" included in the sample comprised the residents listed on three pages of the manuscript schedule, including one of those pages that were selected at random, and the pages immediately preceding and following it in the manuscript schedule. Therefore, each "neighborhood" included in the sample included 150 people, distributed in thirty households.

17. *Clothier and Hatter,* Feb. 1878, p. 17. The national context of the prison labor issue is discussed in the preceding chapter.

18. *Clothier and Hatter,* Apr. 1878, pp. 17, 25; see also *Hat, Cap and Fur Trade Review,* Feb. 1878, p. 133; Mar. 1878, p. 155.

19. *Clothier and Hatter,* Nov. 1878, p. 21.

20. Ibid., Oct. 1878, p. 29; Nov. 1878, p. 21.

21. *Hat, Cap and Fur Trade Review,* Nov. 1878, p. 71.

22. *Orange Journal* quoted in *Clothier and Hatter,* Nov. 1879, p. 28. The Democratic and Republican candidates for surrogate in the Orange elections of Nov. 1879, Captain Pierson and Colonel Zulick, both championed an end to prison labor.

23. *Hatter and Furrier,* Nov. 1880, p. 17.

24. Ibid., May 1881, p. 16.

25. David Bensman, "Business and Culture in the Gilded Age Hatting Industry," in S. Bruchey, ed., *Small Business in America* (New York: Columbia University Press, 1981), pp. 352–65.

26. *Orange Chronicle,* May 9, 1888; *Hatter and Furrier,* Nov. 1888, p. 25.

27. Herbert Gutman, *Work, Culture and Society in Industrializing America,* (New York: Alfred A. Knopf, 1976), p. 281.

28. In his report, he wrote, "I found that the child labor system had left indelible traces of mental and physical degradation. Old faces and dwarfed forms are the offspring of the child labor system. . . . We find childhood to be a period of killing drudgery for the children of the working people." New Jersey, Office of Inspector of Labor and Children, *First Annual Report, 1883,* pp. 5–7.

29. Ibid., pp. 8–9.

30. New Jersey Office of Factory Inspector, *Fifth Annual Report,* pp. 19–20.

31. Adelaide R. Hasse, *Index of Economic Material in Documents of the States of the United States: New Jersey, 1789–1904* (New York: Kraus Reprint Corp., 1965), p. 422.

32. Gutman, *Work, Culture and Society,* p. 280.

33. *Orange Chronicle* and *Orange Journal,* Mar. 1885–Apr. 1885, passim.

34. See Table 1. Thus, in 1881, out of the fifty-nine new members of the Orange finishers union whose background could be established, fifteen were the children of Irishmen, and twenty were of American background.

35. *Orange Chronicle,* 13 Mar. 1886; *East Orange Gazette,* 11 Mar. 1886.

36. *Orange Chronicle,* 6 Mar. 1886.

37. *Orange Journal,* 20 Mar. 1886.

38. *Orange Chronicle,* 23 Oct. 1886.

CHAPTER 9

The Search for
Labor-Management Cooperation,
1885–1889

ALTHOUGH THEY WERE determined to find a new way to defend their craft prerogatives, in the spring of 1885 the finishers were unsure which way to turn. As the South Norwalk strike came to an end, they adopted two different approaches to increase their power vis-à-vis their employers. The first was industrial conciliation. At the finishers' board meeting of 15 June, President Hagerty endorsed a plan for following up his previous proposal for mutually advantageous joint action with the manufacturers. Seconding a motion offered by Granville O. Holmes, a Danbury curler, Hagerty envisioned a national trade agreement between the unions and the manufacturers covering wages and work rules.[1]

Although such agreements were becoming common in unionized industries in the mid-1880s, it seemed "utopian" in the anarchic surroundings of the hatting industry.[2] Reacting with cautious approval, the finishers' board instructed the committee which it had appointed to confer with the makers and manufacturers to explore the agreement as well. The committee responded energetically to this instruction, sending letters to manufacturers throughout the hatting trade, urging them to organize a national trade association so that they could confer with the journeymen fruitfully.[3]

The finishers' second strategy was to enlist working-class support for union goals through boycotting nonunion manufacturers. By 1885, that tactic had become very popular throughout the American labor movement, in the Holy Order of the Knights of Labor, many national craft unions, and numerous central labor unions.[4] Moreover, the hatters had their own positive experience with boycotting during the South Norwalk strike when District Assembly 49 of the Knights of Labor campaigned hard on the finishers' behalf. Now the association began to make the weapon a permanent part of its arsenal.

To that end, in May 1885, Boston and Philadelphia journeymen joined the Holy Order as assemblies #3535 and #3589, following the lead of the South Norwalk local which had joined the order during the height of its long strike.[5] Reciprocating the hatters' good will, Knights of Labor assemblies throughout the country boycotted nonunion hat manufacturers in Orange and South Norwalk during the summer of 1885; F. Berg and Company and E. Brown and Company were singled out as targets to be shunned.[6] By the spring of 1886, the HFNTA and the hat makers' national association together organized District 128, a national assembly affiliated with the Knights of Labor, and ordered their locals to form their own assemblies.[7] Finishers' President Dennis J. Hagerty commented: "There is nothing about the Order that should prevent the entrance to it of any good member of our Association. I have been a member of it for five years, and I know there is nothing in it that interferes with a person's religion or politics. Our Association can join the Knights of Labor and still maintain our own self-government and integral laws. . . ."[8] The joint board agreed with Hagerty, approving affiliation by a vote of 17–1.

At the same time, the Order announced a national boycott campaign against John B. Stetson and Company of Philadelphia, the nation's largest nonunion hatting firm. Despite the fact that the farmers' alliance of Texas joined the drive against Stetson's, which sold mostly to the Western states, the big firm remained prosperous and foul.[9]

Affiliating with the Knights was only one part of the hatters' project to obtain working-class support. In the spring of 1885, within two months of the end of the South Norwalk strike, the HFNTA adopted a union label.[10] How the journeymen came to make that decision is unclear; certainly they had thought little of the idea previously. Only a year before, members of the Newark local had turned down with scorn the request of the cigarmakers' union to buy only cigars bearing the union label;[11] however, the idea of issuing a union label to make boycotts more visible, effective, and continuous proved infectious. On 3 June 1885, the national officers of the hat makers' and finishers' associations met to consider adopting a joint symbol. Under their plan, the unions would print, pay for, and advertise the label, distributing it only to those manufacturers who ran factories fair in both departments.[12]

Such a new idea did not, of course, meet with instant acclaim. The finishers' board of directors, troubled over whether or not employers should be eligible to use the label if one of their departments, but not both, was fair, delayed acceptance at first. Particularly concerned was the Brooklyn local, for within its jurisdiction were two factories that had union finishing shops and nonunion sizing shops. Nevertheless, within a month, the board decided to embark on the new, and possibly hazardous, course: its decision was that firms would be eligible to use the label only when both their departments were fair.[13]

Thus, in June 1885, the hatters' unions launched two campaigns, based on different assumptions and strategies, to improve their position. One, the label plan, rested on the assumption that the manufacturer-journeymen relationship would continue to be adversarial; the other, the trade agreement proposal, foresaw mutual cooperation instead. Despite the seeming contradiction between the two plans, the associations began implementing them simultaneously, to see whether one of them, or perhaps a combination of both, would bolster union efforts to preserve a traditional culture.

The journeymen faced two difficulties in implementing their new projects. The first was that both required considerable coordination between the two groups of craftsmen. Without it, the label scheme would fail, for if a factory's crew of makers went foul, its finishers would lose the protection of the label and vice versa. Similarly, if either group of journeymen took an action that caused a manufacturer to withdraw from the trade agreement, all his employees would be affected. Such coordination on a national scale was unprecedented, for the makers' association was only two years old.[14]

Making the problem of coordination more troublesome still was the fact that the structure of the two unions was so different. In particular, the decentralized character of the makers' association meant that the makers' officers could not force their locals to adhere to the policies agreed on by the two national bodies. Although the finishers' locals still had considerable power, they had come to have considerable respect for the national officers over three decades. Consequently, both the label plan and the trade agreement were vulnerable if the makers' locals continued to behave autonomously.

By the time the manufacturers responded to the unions' proposal for a trade agreement, in October 1885, the United Hatters, as the two associations began calling themselves when acting jointly, had already completed their preparations to issue a label.[15] When the joint boards began exploring the label in June, they did not foresee final approval until after the makers' October convention, perhaps because it was only at the national gathering, the associations' officers believed, that they could persuade the locals of the plan's efficacy. During the summer, the Philadelphia makers' local upset this timetable, however, by issuing its own label. Fearing that this premature action would jeopardize the whole scheme, which most locals had already approved, the joint committee responded quickly, deciding in late August to begin issuing the label "soon." Lest anyone doubt its resolution, the committee adopted a design for the label and authorized printing to begin within seven to ten days.[16]

On 6 and 7 November 1885, the joint boards made the important decision about how the plan would work. After considerable debate, they agreed that the national associations would sponsor the plan; that their national secretaries would have the labels printed and would distribute them to the locals; that the national treasuries, fed by levies on the locals, would pay all costs of the operation. Even the determination as to which manufacturers were eligible to receive the label would be based on criteria determined nationally.[17] Although the locals' representatives initially resisted giving their national officers so much responsibility and power, they became convinced that any local-based plan would cause excessive friction whenever one district applied unique standards of eligibility.

By deciding to join the Knights of Labor, issue a union label, and press for a trade agreement, the finishers inaugurated a new era in the history of their craft. Their locals thereby admitted that they could no longer control work in the shops within their jurisdiction, and that only a strong national association, which coordinated policy for all journeymen in the United States, could protect skill standards. To preserve their traditional craft culture, the hatters had to abandon one of its chief features, that of localism. Moreover, the contemplated joint action between finishers and makers necessitated by both plans spelled a diminution of the finishers' exclusivity. Affiliation with the Holy Order marked the passing of the hatters' longstanding isolation.

The joint union label plan was an initial success. Manufacturers in Danbury and Boston were eager to have labels put on their products immediately; by early 1886, Brooklyn and Yonkers factory owners began requesting them as well. By November 1886, eleven million labels had been distributed, far more than the associations had expected. The plan had become big business, and the locals readily paid its ever-mounting costs.[18]

They paid because the plan seemed to be achieving results; by April 1886, there were no foul shops left in Danbury, Boston, Brooklyn, and St. Louis. In South Norwalk and Orange, progress was slower, but even there, nonunion industrialists expressed interest in negotiating terms of an agreement to recognize the two associations in return for the right to use the union label.[19] Consequently, journeymen believed they had found a potent weapon; indeed, the Orange finishers toughened their bargaining stance vis-à-vis the foul manufacturers because of their faith in their new weapon.[20]

The early success of the union label cannot be attributed solely to the employers' fear of public boycotts. After all, the plan's effectiveness in dissuading the public from buying nonunion hats had hardly been tested; the unions had agreed to provide labels to retailers for all their stock on hand as of 1 February 1886, so there had been little time for a test.[21] Certainly Stetson and Company of Philadelphia seemed to be doing quite well despite a boycott campaign aimed directly against it.[22] Moreover, the United Hatters were not overly profligate in advertising the label; instead, they counted on the efforts of the Knights of Labor assemblies throughout the country to do the job for them.[23]

The explanation for the label's success lay elsewhere. One consideration that bore heavily on the manufacturers was the rapid growth of the Knights of Labor in 1885–86. With the associations inside the Order, employers assumed the label would be effective without testing it.[24]

More important, relations between journeymen and their employers were changing as negotiations over a national trade agreement got under way. With the prospect of cooperation in mind, fair manufacturers adopted the label, which they need not have done, as a sign of good faith. Foul employers turned fair, and used the label in order to join the negotiations. In Danbury, which had been the HFNTA's weakest link, the largest firms, including Tweedy Brothers, went fair in December 1885.[25]

Progress toward a general agreement was slow. Although the unions' joint label committee invited manufacturers to form a trade association to explore avenues to labor peace in June 1885, there was no official response until October. Then, Edmund Tweedy, one of Danbury's leading industrialists, decided that enough colleagues had expressed interest in the plan to make it viable. He called a meeting of factory owners for 28 October in New York City to discuss a joint agreement. Sixty-three manufacturers attended; together with another twenty-five who pledged to join but were not present, they represented 95 percent of the capital invested in the industry.[26]

Tweedy's opening address took up much of the first preliminary meeting. In it, he outlined his reasons for favoring conciliation with the journeymen. Explaining that he ran a foul shop because he considered some of the unions' rules unjust, not because he opposed unionism per se, Tweedy declared himself willing to recognize the unions if they became more reasonable. He found the fact that the journeymen had called on manufacturers to unite, when labor was "naturally distrustful of organized capital," to be strong evidence of their desire to change their ways.

Tweedy understood the associations' proposal to mean "the admission of all those at present employed in the trade into their associations, the bringing of all independent shops under reasonable association rules, the appointment of committees of conference, representing both parties, to consider matters of interest to the trade, and the adoption of joint measures which will give to the joint organizations the practical absolute control of the business." These were desirable goals, for they would mean an end to labor strife, would raise wages and profits, substitute arbitration for strikes, set regular times for bargaining on wages, eliminate excessive shop calls, and allow for the employment of reasonable numbers of apprentices.[27] Tweedy's primary goal was to use the unions to help the manufacturers organize their industry, to discourage prospective entrepreneurs from starting independent shops which used cheap labor. As he admitted, "If it were possible through the proposed organization and concert of action to prevent such injurious competition, surely the benefit to the trade would be immense."[28]

Tweedy's proposals met with warm interest. Before the meeting adjourned that night, its chairman appointed a committee to draft a constitution and bylaws for submission to the next session, called for 17 November.

Unfortunately, so rife was the hatting industry with competition and jealousy that it could not come together easily even in an attempt to freeze out newcomers and to raise prices. Most of the trouble stemmed from the fact that the New Jersey soft hat producers viewed the manufacturers association as an instrument of the Connecticut stiff hat manufacturers who, they feared, hoped to use it for their own advantage. But even though this perception was based on a misunderstanding — the New Jersey men did not know that the proposal for a trade agreement had originated with the journeymen — there were real differences among employers that inhibited the reaching of an agreement. Most important, those employers paying high piece rates, having more to gain than those paying lower rates, were more likely to favor making concessions to reach an agreement.[29]

As a result of the real and perceived problems, the Hat Manufacturers Association had a troubled birth. At its third meeting, on 1 December, with only thirteen of New Jersey's sixty manufacturers present, supporters of the proposed trade agreement adopted a constitution, deferring the issue of wages and all other trade rules until the journeymen could be consulted. The new organization began its life with but a limited consensus. Its constitution provided for the election of a conference committee to meet with union representatives but did not spell out the scope of that body's mandate. (If the association agreed with its committee's proposals, its decision would bind all members.) Recognizing the separate interests of the two branches of the industry, the constitution stipulated that there would be a soft and stiff hat department, and that members would vote only on matters affecting their own branch.[30] The movement was off to a shaky start.[31]

Bright Prospects for Peace

From November 1885 until June 1886, as the union label gained widespread acceptance, the Hat Manufacturers Association and the United Hatters progressed toward an agreement. The first fruits of conciliation ripened in Danbury, where the new local manufacturer's association signed a trade pact with the journeymen on 28 December, 1885. The agreement, which became a model for the industry, bound all employers, including many who had been foul, to run fair shops and to use the union label. In return, the locals agreed to:

1. Admit all of the men previously employed by the manufacturers. Those who had never belonged to the unions were to pay the regular initiation fee; those who had belonged and gone foul were to pay as much of the past year's dues as they had not paid.

2. Honor all price bills for six months. Each shop crew would negotiate wages with its boss.

3. Agree to the arbitration of all differences over prices by committees composed of equal numbers of employers and employees. All other difficulties were to be settled by employers and their shop crews.

4. Forego "disruptive" shop calls.[32]

Under the terms of the agreement, the Danbury finishers' local more than doubled its membership, admitting 336 journeymen who had never been fair, whitewashing 230 former members, and registering 74 apprentices. The initiation fees, totaling $3500, swelled the local treasury.[33] Moreover, the agreement's terms brought labor peace to Danbury for eight years, with only slight interruptions.

Although the Danbury agreements seemed to vindicate the policy of conciliation, the *Hatter and Furrier* deemed it premature. Would not a local settlement dull the Danbury businessmen's interest in national bargaining? Would it not confirm the suspicion of the New Jersey manufacturers? Such fears proved unfounded. In early February 1886, the conference committee of the manufacturers' association proposed terms of agreement to the unions' joint board of directors, albeit terms much stiffer than those demanded by the employers of Danbury. They asked the unions to:

1. Establish local and national arbitration committees comprised of equal numbers of journeymen and factory owners to settle all disputes.

2. Agree not to change their constitutions or bylaws without consulting the manufacturers.

3. Eschew disruptive shop calls.

4. Abolish restrictions on machine work.

5. Repeal the makers' law prohibiting makers from paying for damaged hats.

6. Issue union labels to manufacturers and jobbers for the stock on hand at the time the label plan went into effect.

Although the unions' joint board desired an agreement, it refused to approve the manufacturers' terms. The chief sticking point was machinery; at the makers' insistence, the joint board voted 8-7 that prices on machine work were to be fixed by locals "at a figure which would offer no inducement to use machinery."[34]

Although the makers' attempt to obstruct machinery might seem to have been an insurmountable barrier, both sides were determined to reach agreement. Consequently, when the joint board reported its conclusions to the manufacturers' committee, it laid aside the disputed issues for future consideration and ratified the rest.[35] So close did final agreement appear that the negotiators began considering a plan to replace the unions' unilateral label program with a jointly issued die and license to identify hats made under terms of the national agreement; in effect, this would have altered the label from an instrument used to protect labor standards to one aimed at reducing competition in the hatting trade.[36]

Progress continued in February and March as the hatters' local ratified the agreements of 6 February. Arbitration of disputes became standard in all the factories run by members of the manufacturers' association. Then, at the end of March, the unions stiffened their bargaining position. At a meeting on 29-30 March, the primary purpose of which was to affiliate the United Hatters with the Knights of Labor as District Assembly 128, the joint board decided that it would not sign a final agreement until all the members of the manufacturers' association turned fair.

President Hagerty presented this demand to the manufacturers' association on 7 April, promising the joint board's efforts to secure concessions by the locals if the HMA would exert its influence to turn all its members fair. The association agreed, and ratified the 6 February pact but requested that the makers' union change its laws on damaged hats and machinery, to facilitate efforts to persuade recalcitrant employers to recognize the unions.[37] Here we can see clearly how national bodies led their local affiliates in seeking national solutions to industrial strife.

On 1 June the joint board demonstrated its good faith by instructing all locals of the two unions to consolidate with the foul journeymen in their districts. The board threatened intervention by the national officers if the locals refused to comply. This threat was illegal, inasmuch as neither the board nor the officers had the power to so intervene in local affairs, but as the final signing of the agreement drew near, the leadership's confidence and prestige grew rapidly. The fruits of peace were proving sweet indeed,[38] for by this time, the goodwill engendered by the trade negotiations had enabled the label campaign to win unexpectedly quick success. Perhaps even more important, trade negotiations had helped the unions gain widespread recognition. By mid-summer, the finishers' locals acknowledged these achievements by giving their officers authority to effect consolidations.

Optimism about the prospects for industry-wide labor peace had reached unreal dimensions. How else explain the fact that when the United Hatters asked the Knights of Labor for help in boycotting the Stetson Company in Philadelphia, the *Hatter and Furrier* began boosting the Knights as agents of social tranquility? In 1886, a year when most American industrialists were preparing for a bitter class war, the *Hatter and Furrier* quoted Grand Master Terrence Powderly on the virtues of industrial harmony.[39] The bubble had to burst. Even though visions of labor peace might seem to be incompatible with nationwide boycott campaigns, the two phenomena were connected. Both reflected the fact that American business and American labor were becoming more collective. Businessmen were seeking ways to eliminate intense competition, and national unions were seeking to avoid protracted local strikes. National trade agreements and labor peace were possible outgrowths of this collectivization of economic and social life; highly organized class conflict, as symbolized by the eight-hour campaign of 1886 and the railroad strikes were others. Hatters, whose craft motto was "the interests of the journeymen and their employers is one and inseparable," pursued peace vigorously, but found it elusive.

The first major setback to the hopes of the hatters' and manufacturers' associations was the failure, in the winter and spring of 1885–86, of Orange journeymen and their employers to reach an agreement on the use of the union label. The problem arose from the fact that although all of Orange's finishing shops were fair, many firms sent sizing work out during the busy season to small "buckeye shops," which employed low-skilled foul men to do work as cheaply as possible. Situated right on the premises of the larger factories, the "buckeyes" were makeshift, temporary affairs, run on the tiniest of margins by entrepreneurs hoping to gain profit enough to start full-fledged shops of their own.[40] When the Orange finishers and makers, acting on the advice of their national officers, ruled that any firm weighing out work to a buckeye shop would be ineligible to receive union labels, the employers balked, for they valued the flexibility and low prices such shops afforded them.[41] A related problem was that the Orange unions ruled that only manufacturers who employed union men and women exclusively could put labels on their products. Since many firms had nonunion trimmers and pouncers, they too were disqualified.[42]

Such difficulties might have been resolved had the journeymen and employers been working together to reach a local trade agreement, as was the case in Danbury and Brooklyn, but the Orange finishers were so wrapped up in the label experiment that they did not press their employers for a trade pact.[43] Consequently, their employers treated the label question as a matter of "dollars and cents" rather than as a means to labor stability.[44]

At first, it seemed that the journeymen's intransigent posture might prove successful. By 16 January 1886, three of Orange's five largest shops had conceded on the issue of buckeyes.[45] Their desire to obtain the union label had superseded other considerations.[46] In the spring of 1886, however, the journeymen's hopes of gaining complete control of the Orange district met severe disappointment. At the same time that eight small firms began negotiating with the Orange unions over terms of a whitewash of their foul men, McGall and Allen and Company, the town's largest concern, decided to move on its own.[47] The firm discharged 200 of its nonunion employees, asking the locals to replace them with fair men. When fifteen of the firm's former employees, those who had once belonged to the HFNTA, asked to be whitewashed, the finishers' local refused, levying fines of $75 to $300 on the men instead because they had "scabbed" on previous strikes. The journeymen's vindictiveness infuriated William McGall, who had built a tiny commission shop into Orange's largest factory; he decided to resume operations as a nonunion firm rather than accept what seemed to him flagrantly unfair behavior.[48] Fredrick Berg, another large employer, followed McGall's lead, though he, too, had originally planned to turn fair.[49]

Expecting the union label to force McGall and Berg to back down, the Orange unionists held firm, but their confidence proved unfounded. Both companies remained foul until 1889; their prosperity undermined the union label. Moreover, the journeymen's intransigence embittered members of the Hat Manufacturers' Association, who believed McGall and Berg had been singled out for unfair treatment.[50]

More important was the hat sizers' refusal to surrender local autonomy. For almost two years, representatives of the hat makers' locals sat down to negotiate a national trade agreement with representatives of the finishers and employers, but to no avail. No matter how hard they tried, the sizers' leaders could not induce them to surrender local control of piece rates, to accept sizing machines, or to grant to the national officers the sole right to call strikes. The reason for the militancy of the makers' locals was not hard to find; employers had succeeded in developing machines that eliminated the need for some of the journeymen's skill, and thereby were able to challenge the makers' traditional control of work practices. Accepting union centralization meant acquiescing in concessions that undermined the craft, and this the sizers could not do.

Despite the makers' intransigence, leaders of the three parties continued to try to reach an agreement. The manufacturers' association began formulating national laws in April, presenting their proposals to a tripartite executive board meeting on 24 May. Quickly, the unions' joint board gave its approval, subject to ratification by two-thirds of the locals of each union. The rules were far more extensive than had ever before been considered. They provided that:

1. All disputes would be arbitrated without strikes.

2. Changes in piece rates or wages awarded by arbitration would be retroactive.

3. Each shop would set its own prices.

4. All wage bills would remain in effect for six months.

5. Journeymen would not restrict machine use.

6. Foremen, as employees of the manufacturers, would be subject to their discipline, and would be free to work at their trade.

7. The voucher system would be eliminated and manufacturers would refrain from giving work to nonunion shops.

8. Journeymen would work ten hours even if work started late in the day.

9. Privileges granted to one manufacturer would be granted to all, but all local rules would be subject to approval by the national unions.

10. The manufacturer agreed to accept all union rules not in conflict with the above nine resolutions.[51]

To strengthen the unions' alliance, and increase national control of the trade, the joint board added two proposals of its own to the manufacturers' resolutions:

1. Any local could not declare a shop foul until it received permission from the unions' joint board.

2. Local disputes between makers and finishers would be referred to an arbitration committee consisting of representatives of other locals.[52]

On 17 June, the manufacturers' association ratified the agreement, with slight reservations. The following month, the finishers' association followed suit, with three locals dissenting. At the same time, the Bethel, Bloomfield, and Millburn makers accepted the agreement; the *Hatter and Furrier* predicted ratification.[53]

This marked the farthest point the finishers were to go toward centralization in the interests of labor peace. Since the Norwalk strike had precipitated a change in policy, the finishers had taken long strides away from local autonomy. They had created a national label board, controlled by the national office. They had given the national officers power to effect consolidations and to declare shops foul. They had allowed manufacturers to co-determine work rules as a result of nationwide bargaining. They had even given up the right to strike.

Perhaps the greatest deviation from traditional principles was the finishers' decision to sacrifice labor solidarity in the interest of cooperation with their bosses. In May 1887, in response to a complaint by the Boston manufacturers that they could not get enough women, President Hagerty made an unusual trip to Boston to pay a visit to the trimmers' local. Hagerty asked the trimmers to relax their apprenticeship rules, fearing that the factory owners would abandon the trade agreement if the trimmers' unions could disrupt production on their own.[54]

Makers and finishers in Danbury went much further in their attempts to appease their bosses; in fact, they went so far as to acquiesce in the manufacturers' interference in the internal affairs of the trimmers' local. The trouble started when the Danbury factory owners proposed terms by which the local trimmers could join the Danbury trade agreement, to which the journeymen were already parties. The women declined, objecting to their employers' stipulations that shop-set prices would replace the customary minimum price rule. To the manufacturers' argument that their wage policy discriminated against shops producing cheap hats, the women answered that all hats took the same time to trim. When the 16 May deadline for capitulation passed, the employers locked out all except those who signed a document pledging to vote for surrender. Although this lockout violated both the trade agreement and the integrity of the trimmers' local, the journeymen sided with their bosses, successfully pressuring the trimmers to give in. Two months later, Bethel's hatters followed the same course when their employers locked out the trimmers there.[55]

Abandoning the Agreement

A dispute over the union label put an end to hopes for the trade agreement. Reasoning that since manufacturers in their districts were still operating foul sizing shops and therefore the union label was a failure, ten Brooklyn and Newark makers' locals had refused to make contributions to the joint label fund for several months. Finally, in August 1887, the national makers' association suspended both locals. At first, it appeared that this action might actually speed acceptance of the trade agreement, since the Brooklyn makers' opposition would no longer carry any weight. Indeed, the *Hatter and Furrier* continued to predict imminent ratification.[56] Moreover, on 6 September 1887, when the manufacturers acceded to the finishers' request to rescind their amendments to the June agreement, the pact finally went into effect. It covered only the finishers and manufacturers, however; the makers never did become parties to the agreement. In the long run, the label dispute signaled the movement's doom, for it rendered the makers' union so weak as to be ineffective.[57]

Despite the collapse of the makers' association, the finishers continued to pursue their conciliatory trade policy. At the June 1888 convention, for example, delegates voted to shorten apprenticeship terms from four years to three and to change strike and arbitration procedures so as to give union employers preferential treatment. Both changes were concessions to the employers, designed to keep alive the chances for a new trade agreement. Yet, while sweetening its carrot, the association did not lay aside its stick,

for the convention voted to maintain the label plan, and to renew its affiliation with the Knights of Labor, thereby alerting the manufacturers that the
journeymen had allies outside the industry.[58]

Then, in October 1888, when the finishers realized that the makers were
not strong enough to be reliable allies, they assumed the entire cost of the
union label and of the Knights' membership. National relations between
the two hatting unions came to an end, with distressing results. Immediately after the split, Brooklyn journeymen squared off in a bitter struggle when
the finishers refused to back a makers' strike for the right to reopen negotiations over piece rates when manufacturers changed their fur mixtures in a
way that made them harder to size. Violence ensued as the makers tried to
prevent their shopmates from crossing the picket lines.[59] Bitterness remained in the Brooklyn district for years afterward. According to the finishers' traditional principles, their own conduct was reprehensible, but,
once more, their desire to preserve good relations with the manufacturers
was paramount.

In this otherwise dismal picture, there was one ray of hope — the Orange
finishers' successful whitewash campaign in November 1889. Carefully preparing its effort months in advance, by convincing foul journeymen in
McGall and Allen's and F. Berg's nonunion shops to pledge to cease work
when called upon, the Orange local announced a strike at both factories on
19 November. After issuing ninety checks to McGall and Allen's men and
thirty more to Berg's, for $1 apiece, and after the Newark finishers' local an-
nounced it would whitewash all the independent men in shops over which it
had jurisdiction so that they would not break the strike in Orange, the
unionists gained a victory. Swallowing his vow to retire rather than run a
fair shop, William McGall accepted defeat "gracefully" on 23 November
and his colleague Berg followed suit three days later.[60]

Conclusion

At the end of 1889, the finishers' situation was mixed. Local trade agreements in Brooklyn, Danbury, Bethel, and South Norwalk had produced
four years of peace, uninterrupted by significant strikes and unmarred by
the opening of foul shops. In Orange, there was no trade agreement but a
successful organizing drive had brought hundreds of foul men into the
union, for the moment at least. The label plan was well established, giving
fair employers a good reason not to go foul.

There were many problems as well. Since there was no national trade agreement, manufacturers and journeymen had been unable to prevent new factories from opening on a nonunion, cheap labor basis. In Newark and Yonkers particularly, foul shops flourished, dominating the cheap hat trade. Moreover, three large factories in Philadelphia, led by John B. Stetson and Company, were prospering without the union label, diminishing its credibility.

Finally, the failure of both the manufacturers and the unionists to bring an end to the cutthroat competition characterizing the hatting trade left the journeymen vulnerable to cost-cutting pressures. When finishers became as vulnerable to technological change as the makers had been, they too had to abandon the strategy of conciliation.

NOTES

1. President Hagerty's version of the agreement's origin was:

There was a young man, a member of our association, who wrote to the national secretary and myself from Danbury, and asked us if we would be willing to meet him some time, as he had an idea he thought would greatly benefit the trade. . . . We appointed a meeting in Brooklyn with the gentleman in question, Mr. Holmes, and he stated that he had been thinking of the matter of proposing an invitation for conference with the manufacturers for some time. I knew this man to be just the kind of man from whom such an idea would be likely to emanate. We listened to the plan as he explained it, and he asked us what we thought of it. Mr. Phillips, our secretary, considered that the idea was rather Utopian; that it would be almost impossible for lion and lamb to lie down together without one of the animals getting inside the other after awhile. But after consideration we decided that there would be a great deal of good gained by forming such an organization. I knew in the first place that if there was an organization of this kind formed it would tend to prevent the continual clashing of interests between manufacturers and journeymen. We had just passed through the great South Norwalk struggle, and during that time, I had had some bitter experience from the results of a strife between employers and employees. I was just in a frame of mind in which I would gladly welcome any idea which would promise to bring about harmony between manufacturer and journeyman. After considering the matter for some time, Mr. Phillips and myself concluded that it would be well to call a meeting of the two National associations and lay it before them [*Danbury News,* Dec. 28, 1885].

2. *Hatter and Furrier,* June 1885, p. 11.

3. HFNTA, "Proceedings of the Board of Directors, 15 June 1885."

4. Michael Gordon, "The Labor Boycott," *Labor History* 16 (Spring 1975): passim; Leo Wolman, *The Boycott in American Trade Unions,* Johns Hopkins University Studies in Historical and Political Science, series 34 (Baltimore: Johns Hopkins University Press, 1916): 24; John R. Commons, et al., *History of Labor in the United States* (New York: Macmillan, 1918–35), 2: 314.

5. *Hatter and Furrier,* July 1885, p. 13.

6. Ibid., July 1885, pp. 9, 13; Sept. 1885, p. 7; Oct. 1885, p. 23. The effectiveness of these boycotts cannot be determined because complicating events soon intervened.

7. HFNTA and HMNA, "Proceedings of the Board of Directors, 29–31 Mar. 1886."

8. Ibid.

9. *Hatter and Furrier,* Mar. 1886, p. 16.

10. HFNTA, "Proceedings of the Board of Directors, June 1885."

11. *Hatter and Furrier,* Sept. 1884, p. 24.

12. HFNTA and HMNA, "Proceedings of the Board of Directors, 3 June 1885."

13. *Hatter and Furrier,* June 1885, p. 12.

14. Local unions of makers and finishers had worked together for decades, however.

15. *Hatter and Furrier,* July 1885, p. 28. The manufacturers' favorable response was foreshadowed by this journal in July, when it gave employers credit for initiating the proposal.

16. Ibid., Aug. 1885, p. 13; Sept. 1885, p. 11; HFNTA, "Proceedings of the Joint Board, 6 Nov. 1885."

17. HFNTA, "Proceedings of the Joint Board, 6 Nov. 1885."

18. *Hatter and Furrier,* Mar. 1886, pp. 15, 45; June 1886, p. 23; May 1886, p. 11.

19. Ibid., Jan. 1886, p. 8; Mar. 1886, pp. 15, 45; Apr. 1886, pp. 11, 16.

20. Ibid., Feb. 1886, p. 23.

21. HFNTA, "Proceedings of the Joint Board, 2–4 Feb. 1886."

22. *Hatter and Furrier,* Apr. 1886, p. 7; Feb. 1886, p. 11.

23. HFNTA, *Semi-Annual Report,* Dec. 1886.

24. From July 1885 to July 1886, the Knights' membership grew from 100,000 to 700,000. Gerald Grob, *Workers and Utopia* (Chicago: Quadrangle Books, 1969), p. 65.

25. *Danbury News,* 29 Dec. 1885.

26. Connecticut Bureau of Labor, *Annual Report* (1890), p. 136.

27. Ibid.

28. Ibid., p. 137.

29. *Hatter and Furrier,* Nov. 1885, pp. 16a–c; *Orange Chronicle,* 5 Dec. 1885, 26 Dec. 1885.

30. *Orange Chronicle,* 5 Dec. 1885, p. 12.

31. *Hatter and Furrier,* Dec. 1885, p. 12. The *Orange Chronicle* editorially supported Connett's contention, reiterating that the New Jersey manufacturers had acted in good faith but in ignorance of the facts. *Orange Chronicle,* 5 Dec. 1885; 26 Dec. 1885.

32. Connecticut Bureau of Labor, *Annual Report* (1890), p. 136; *Danbury News,* 29 Dec. 1885; 31 Dec. 1885. The finishers' local ratified the pact nearly unanimously.

33. *Danbury News,* 21 Jan. 1886. The makers' local admitted 320 men, whitewashed 20, and registered 54 apprentices, gaining $2500 in initiation fees.

34. HFNTA, "Proceedings of the Joint Board, 2–4, 6 Feb. 1886."

35. Ibid.

36. *Hatter and Furrier,* Feb. 1885, p. 11.

37. Ibid., April 1886, p. 12.

38. Ibid., June 1886, p. 23.

39. Ibid., Apr. 1886, p. 7; Feb. 1886, p. 11.

40. *Newark Daily Advertiser,* 2 Dec. 1885; *Hatter and Furrier,* Jan. 1886, p. 7.

41. *Newark Daily Advertiser,* 11, 12 Dec. 1885; *Orange Journal,* 12 Dec. 1885; *Orange Chronicle,* 5, 12 Dec. 1885.

42. *Newark Daily Advertiser,* 9 Dec. 1885.

43. *Orange Chronicle,* 5 Dec. 1885.

44. Ibid., 24 Oct. 1885.

45. Ibid., 16, 23 Jan. 1886. In addition, the Orange trimmers were successfully organizing a Ladies' Mutual Assistance Association. *Newark Daily Advertiser,* 3 Dec. 1885.

46. When John R. Lang went fair on 28 March, the *Orange Chronicle* reported that the Union Label had "accomplished what all the efforts of the journeymen could not. For a long time, J. R. Lang has made hats for Ferry and Napier on commission. Ferry and Napier couldn't put the Union Label in its hats. Some weeks ago, Ferry and Napier salesmen went West and found it impossible in many cases to sell goods to jobbers because they did not bear the Union Label. So Ferry and Napier made its factory in Matteawan, N.Y. fair and stopped weighing out to foul shops. So John R. Lang had to go fair or lose the bulk of its work." *Orange Chronicle,* 3 Apr. 1886.

47. *Newark Daily Advertiser,* 16 Apr. 1886; 17 Apr. 1886; *Orange Chronicle,* 17 Apr. 1886; *Orange Journal,* 17 Apr. 1886.

48. *Hatter and Furrier,* Nov. 1888, p. 25. McGall started with a commission shop worth $1500 in 1869; it was worth $250,000 in 1888. McGall's colleague, Fredrick Berg, had similar success.

49. *Orange Journal,* 24 Apr. 1886; *Orange Chronicle,* 17, 24 Apr. 1886; *Newark Daily Advertiser,* 19 Apr. 1886; *Hatter and Furrier,* May 1886, p. 23.

50. *Hatter and Furrier,* May 1886, p. 12.

51. Ibid., Apr. 1887, p. 8. HFNTA, "Proceedings of the Joint Board, June 1887."

52. At the same meeting, the makers indicated a desire to withdraw from the Knights of Labor. Hat finishers' President Hagerty defended the affiliation with the Knights, arguing it helped the union label; the board agreed not to disaffiliate.

53. *Hatter and Furrier,* July 1887, pp. 12, 15, 19, 31.

54. Ibid., May 1887, p. 11.

55. Connecticut Bureau of Labor, *Annual Report* (1890), pp. 146–47; *Hatter and Furrier,* July 1887, pp. 11, 32.

56. *Hatter and Furrier,* Aug. 1887, p. 8.

57. Ibid., Sept. 1887, p. 12.

58. HFNTA, "Proceedings of the Regular Convention, June 1888," pp. 49, 51.

59. *Hatter and Furrier,* Oct. 1888, p. 34; Nov. 1888, p. 37; Dec. 1888, p. 21; Jan. 1889, p. 23; Feb. 1889, pp. 15, 23; *Brooklyn Citizen,* 21 Dec. 1888; *Brooklyn Eagle,* 16 Dec. 1888; 18 Dec. 1888.

60. There was one tense moment, on 25 Nov., when 500 union men, "more or less intoxicated," surrounded Berg's shop to call on the foul men to quit work. Police feared a riot but none developed. *Newark Daily Advertiser,* 25 Nov. 1889; 23 Nov. 1889; 22 Nov. 1889; 26 Nov. 1889; *Orange Journal,* 23 Nov. 1889; *Orange Chronicle,* 23 Nov. 1889; *Hatter and Furrier,* July 1889, p. 24; Aug. 1889, p. 18; Oct. 1889, p. 16; Dec. 1889, p. 17.

CHAPTER 10

Machinery, Depression, and Survival: 1890–1895 and Afterward

As hat manufacturers enlarged their factories in the years 1885–90, they introduced a variety of simple machines to reduce labor costs. Such apparatuses as ironing machines,[1] pouncing lathes,[2] and brim edgers, shapers, and curlers[3] all constituted minor advances. In 1890, factory owners began adopting another machine which was radical in its design and impact. It was an hydraulic hat press, which worked as follows:

> The hat [was] placed, crown downward in an iron mould of the exact shape that [was] to be given the finished crown. A flat iron ring [was] placed upon the brim of the hat. A rubber bag of best quality [was] then lowered into the crown, and the part of the machine to which this bag [was] attached [was] firmly clamped down. The operator [threw] open a valve and a current of water [entered] the bag, distending it and pressing it outward against the inside of the crown. After a few seconds, the water [was] released, the bag raised, and the crown of the hat [was] found to have taken the exact shape of the iron mould in which it [had] rested.[4]

The press also imparted such a smooth finish to the hat surface that no ironing and little pouncing was necessary.[5]

Considering how thoroughly the hydraulic press transformed stiff hat finishing, the slowness with which American manufacturers took advantage of the new technology is surprising. Though the machines were in general use in English factories in the 1880s,[6] American manufacturers did not adopt them until 1891. The reason for the delay was not ignorance — George Yule, a New Jersey hat manufacturer, had produced presses for sale to finishing shops by 1880[7] but factory owners spurned his machines, believing they did not produce goods fine enough to suit American tastes.

Then suddenly, in 1888, English derbies became "a craze" in Eastern haberdasheries, cutting into the sales of American hat manufacturers.[8] No longer could the United States trade dismiss the imported pressed hats as "queer figures" of little value.[9]

Hoping to take advantage of the change in taste, Albert Turner, an English manufacturer of hydraulic presses, came to America in November 1889 to solicit orders.[10] He met early success, for that same month, one of Brooklyn's leading hatting firms, Dickerson and Brown, decided to install a press in its factory, in order to gain a share of the booming new trade.[11]

Although the hydraulic presses reduced the need for skilled labor, American journeymen were not alarmed at first. Dickerson and Brown's shop crew did not "make trouble" about the firm's installation of one presser; indeed, the men were so confident that they could do better work with their own hands that they voted to allow their employer to hire a press operator who did not belong to their union.[12]

Unfortunately, the journeymen's confidence proved unfounded; ten months later, imports of English derbies were still increasing, and many American manufacturers were installing the Turner hat pressers.[13] One firm, Roelofs of Philadelphia, commenced operations in May 1890 as America's first company to produce exclusively hydraulically finished hats.[14] Fourteen months later, Roelofs reported that it had boosted production from an initial three dozen daily to fifty dozen, an output which made it one of the country's largest producers.

As if to symbolize American acceptance of pressed derbies, in October 1891, the Turner Machine Company opened a factory in Danbury to supply the American market for hydraulic presses. Little more than a year later the plant's sales had so expanded that it was necessary to build a four-story addition.[16] Meanwhile, George Yule hastened to get in on the action, turning out presses in his Newark machine shop by October 1892.[17]

Of course, hydraulic finishing did not displace hand labor altogether.[18] Many purchasers of high-grade hats continued to buy hand-finished derbies.[19] In 1891, the Volk Hat Company of South Norwalk began to take advantage of such sentiment by advertising its products as handmade and therefore superior. Their promotional effort was so successful the firm had to double its capacity in 1892.[20] As late as June 1893, the *Hatter and Furrier* reported that, contrary to expectations, pressed hats were only holding their own, not replacing hand-ironed hats, in Brooklyn factories.[21]

Exactly how many finishers were displaced by the hydraulic pressing machine in the years 1890–93 is not known. In May 1892, James Graham, president of the Hat Finishers' National Trade Association, estimated that between four and five hundred journeymen were out of work because of the presser, and he identified that fact as the trade's major problem.[22] It is not clear whether all the idle men were actually victims of technological displacement, for stiff hat finishers were losing jobs for another reason at this time.

Beginning in the fall of 1891, the hat buying habits of American men changed; many who had previously considered derbies the only proper headwear to wear to work switched to the less formal, soft "tourist" hats.[23] Consequently, production and employment in soft hat factories, primarily in Orange, Newark, and Philadelphia, increased, while factories producing stiff hats lost trade. Some of the stiff hatters idled by this change in fashion moved to the soft hat centers to find work in their expanding factories, but others, those who were unwilling to move, or unable to finish soft hats, remained unemployed. Danbury and Bethel journeymen were hardest hit.[24]

We can get some idea of the extent of labor displacement from data collected by the U.S. commissioner of labor, who in 1897 wrote a special report on production by hand and machine methods. According to the report, it took a man operating an hydraulic press only twelve minutes to press a dozen hats in 1896; after pressing, a finisher using a steam-powered lathe required an additional two hours and thirty minutes to fine pounce the same dozen. At the same time, finishing a dozen stiff hats by hand took one journeyman three hours and thirty-six minutes, nearly an hour longer than by machine. Hence, the use of the presser and lathe reduced the amount of labor time required for hat finishing (leaving out curling) by one-fourth. The reduction in the journeymen's wages was less drastic. Employers paid their pressers and finishers a total of eighty-nine cents for a dozen hats, as opposed to ninety-nine cents a dozen for derbies finished by hand; the saving was only 10 percent.[25]

Whether unemployment was caused by technological displacement or fashion changes, it was a critical problem for finishers in 1892 and 1893. To help idle journeymen regain seats at the bench, the IHFTA convention changed the union's national rules. They did not try to fight the new technology, for finishers had come to believe such a course was futile since manufacturers would go foul rather than give up the cost advantages offered by mechanical improvements. Instead, the convention delegates moved to slow the growth of the labor supply by barring immigrants from entering the trade.[26]

This was not an ideal solution, as association President James Graham recognized, for the convention's decision was likely to annoy union employers, although perhaps not as much as restrictions on the hydraulic press would have. Since the ban on immigrants would apply only to employers of union labor, it would boost their labor costs even higher in comparison to their nonunion competitors; possibly, this would drive some manufacturers foul.[27] The finishers' situation in 1892 was difficult; the depression that struck the following year made it worse.

The Depression of 1893 and the Danbury Lockout

Although the introduction of the hydraulic presser in the years 1888–92 had strengthened the fair hat manufacturers' bargaining position vis-à-vis the finishers by reducing the value of the journeymen's skills and by rendering some men jobless, the employers did not move immediately to alter the agreements they had with their men. Manufacturers of soft hats were enjoying boom times while those who produced derbies were biding their time, hoping for a change in fashion to boost their sales once again.

But then, in mid-1893, a great depression descended upon America. Beginning in May 1893, financial panic induced a contraction of economic activity throughout the United States. The hat industry was caught up in the slump. Not only did sales decline in response to a sudden sharp drop in consumer purchasing power, but, in addition, hat manufacturers felt so unsure about the future that they cut back output for fear that jobbers would be unable to pay for their goods.[28]

At first, Orange's manufacturers were hardest hit, for they had expanded their plants to meet soaring demand only months before. In four months, from June to October 1893, the Orange finishing shops discharged fully 650 finishers, more than half their work force.[29]

Many of the men discharged from Orange factories sought work in other hatting centers, but few found jobs, for factories everywhere were operating on reduced schedules. In Danbury, factories that were just beginning to recover from two disastrous years fell idle once again.[30]

The onset of depression spurred Danbury's hat factory owners to change their relationships with their employees. In July 1893, in the midst of the financial panic, the local manufacturers' association sent letters to all the unions party to the joint agreement of 1886, requesting them to send representatives to a conference on 31 July, to discuss ways that Danbury's hatting industry could be revived.[31]

At the conference, the manufacturers argued that numerous union rules

were making it much more expensive to finish hats in Danbury than elsewhere, where machinery and cheap nonunion labor predominated. In particular, management representatives blamed rigid union rules for having
deprived local factories of a share in the recent soft hatting boom.

> The soft hatting industry has nearly left us and stiff hatting is rapidly
> losing ground, while in former times soft hatting was the principal in-
> dustry of this place.
>   It is safe to estimate that two-thirds of the heads in this country are
> covered by soft hats, while this industry has almost become extinct
> here. Where are these hats made? Not in Danbury. It is because the
> wages paid are higher than paid elsewhere.
>   We have the factories and the men, but the conditions surrounding
> the employment of men, owing to the restrictions of trade unions here,
> are such that it is impossible to successfully compete here. . . .[32]

The manufacturers also contended that restrictive labor practices were limiting their production of derbies.

> Stiff hatting is drifting the same way: the increase of product in New
> Jersey and Mass. has become of the most alarming proportions. Those
> districts, by the use of the most improved machinery and the cheapest
> labor, are taking our trade from us. . . . This was before the period of
> financial disturbance and distrust, and must not be confounded with
> it. . . .
>   In the past, the production of low and medium grades have been the
> main output, and these hats made for the masses are the first to suffer
> from unfair competition.[33]

Although it is not difficult to imagine the chagrin felt by Danbury manufacturers at missing out on the soft hatting boom, it is difficult to take their
complaints seriously. After all, as the manufacturers themselves admitted,
Danbury's soft hatting industry had been "rapidly decreasing" for the last
twenty years. Moreover, because of that decline, most of the town's soft hat
finishers had switched to the derby trade; Danbury no longer had an adequate labor supply to produce soft hats.[34] Finally, why should local factories, which employed fully skilled craftsmen, have been able to compete
with firms in Newark or Fall River which hired "the cheapest labor?" Danbury derbies were simply better than those made in low-wage towns; how
could they be expected to compete in price?[35]

Despite the fact that the employers blamed the unions for their troubles,
they did not couch their demands in belligerent tones. Indeed, the manufacturers explicitly reaffirmed their desire for continued harmonious relations;

they made no threats, nor did they demand unilateral concessions from the unions. Instead, they requested that representatives from management and labor confer to "formulate and agree upon some plan to remove the present obstacles and preserve harmonious relations."[36] Affirming their belief in the compatibility of the interests of labor and capital, representatives of Danbury's hat makers', trimmers', and finishers' unions agreed at the conference to discuss ways of restoring Danbury's prosperity,[37] but the workers' willingness to compromise fell far short of the employers' goals, and good intentions soon gave way to ill will.

The manufacturers' representatives to the joint conference, which began in August, opened negotiations with five proposals for concessions from all the unions and for additional concessions from each union individually. Each local was to agree

1. To promptly furnish all the help required by every factory operated by the members of the manufacturers' association.

2. To provide more apprentices.

3. To give employers "entire freedom to hire members by the day without any restrictions."

4. To give employers "freedom to employ helpers."

5. To improve the "method as to arbitration."

In addition, the negotiators for management asked the finishers' local to grant employers "freedom on all work done prior to and including pressing. Freedom on ironing and rounding machines, squaring, lureing, and entire freedom in packing room including lureing after trimming. Right to hire tradesmen by the day on any automatic machine. Also on blocking, curling, and setting machines, and planing. Ten per cent of the men employed at finishing by the piece." Finally, the manufacturers' representatives demanded additional privileges for those few Danbury factories producing soft hats. Those privileges included "pouncing before finishing, pressing, ironing and rounding machines, brim and crown pouncing machines in finishing room. Entire freedom after trimming. Right to hire tradesmen by the day on crown pouncing machines, ten percent of all the finishers."[38]

The manufacturers' demands challenged some of the finishers' fundamental craft prerogatives. Most important, the demand that employers be allowed to hire by the day as many hatters as they wished conflicted with the finishers' commitment to the piece rate system. If all men were to work by the day, how would they be able to keep control over the pace of their work? How would they retain their freedom to take off when they wanted?

In short, the manufacturers' demands threatened the journeymen's control over their work.

Although the finishers' representatives to the joint conference were unprepared to surrender basic craft rights, they did offer concessions. On 11 October, they presented to their unions a proposal representing the maximum they believed the finishers should concede. Their report was quite responsive to the employers' needs. It proposed giving management greater freedom in hiring helpers; speeding up arbitration procedures; and allowing a "reasonable proportion" of tradesmen to work by the day in "departments paid mainly by the piece." Moreover, the finishers proposed that the manufacturers be given the freedom they wanted in the soft hat department, subject only to the qualification "as to the number in each shop" by the day.[39] Since the loss of the soft hat trade appeared to be the major worry of the factory owners, the finishers' committee report seems quite responsive. Of course, concessions about soft hatting were easy for the journeymen to make since few finishers were actually employed in that area and any increase in work there was purely speculative.

Although the manufacturers had proven willing to moderate their demands, they had not agreed with the finishers' committee report. While the journeymen's representatives offered to allow "a reasonable proportion of tradesmen" to "work by the day in departments mainly paid by the piece," the employers continued to insist on the right to hire tradesmen by the day, conceding only that "a reasonable proportion of men" be allowed to work at piece rates. This appears to have been a difference of degree that might have been settled by negotiation; indeed, the manufacturers were later to say that they found that the report of the finishers' committee provided grounds for optimism.[40]

Nevertheless, it was not a foregone conclusion that the finishers' local's membership would ratify their committee's recommendations. As we have seen earlier, the rank-and-file craftsmen were not always disposed to follow their leadership's moderate course. Although the negotiating committee, looking out for the long-term interests of the trade, might counsel conciliation, the majority of the members, who were more concerned with their current problems and with reaffirming their manly militancy as well, might very well prefer to fight to maintain their old rights. Indeed, in the month that followed, the Danbury finishers' local met three times to consider whether to make concessions to their employers. At the third meeting, on 26 October, votes for several concessions and against others indicated that the local was not willing to follow their moderate leaders.

The slow pace of the finishers', makers', and trimmers' deliberations frustrated the manufacturers and caused them to split among themselves over how to gain sufficient concessions. On 7 November, the management of nineteen firms agreed to put maximum pressure on their employees by announcing that as of 27 November, the companies would sever all previous agreements they had with the various locals. Ten additional firms did not sign.[42]

At first, the finishers did not agree among themselves about what the nineteen manufacturers' announcement meant. Some journeymen saw it as the prelude to a lockout; others believed it was simply a bargaining ploy.[43] But two weeks later, however, the manufacturers' made their purpose clear; they would discharge all their employees on 25 November. After that, when the conditions of trade warranted it, they would begin hiring men on an independent basis. Tired of their employees' delays, the manufacturers decided to go foul whether or not the unions agreed to offer further concessions.[44] Just before the severance was to take effect, the finishers and makers met with the manufacturers' representatives one last time.[45] What proposals the union presented is not clear; in any case, the employers spurned them. The lockout had begun.

On 25 November, twenty factories belonging to members of the Danbury hat manufacturers' association shut down.[46] They discharged 3,859 men and women. Allied local industries producing hat boxes, wire, and machinery were also affected.[47] Danbury then experienced seven of the quietest weeks of its history. A reporter for the *New Haven Register* marveled at the town's tranquility: "For eight days there has been no police court, and Judge Walsh is beginning to feel his judicial throne rocking beneath him, for there have been in the streets of Danbury for the past four weeks upwards of 4000 unemployed men, and yet from that number there has been not a single arrest for drunkenness or disorderly conduct. Were Edward Bellamy to drop into town, he would certainly declare that in Danbury's quiet and well-nigh deserted streets he had found one of his model twentieth-century towns."[48]

We have seen that such orderliness had not always characterized hatters' strikes. During the previous Danbury strike, in 1882–83, and during the South Norwalk lockout, in 1884–85, angry journeymen had assaulted strikebreakers, threatened employers, and perhaps even resorted to arson and dynamite, but this time the locked-out men and women seemed less bitter, more resigned to hardship and more accepting of their fate. Moreover, the trade unions expended extraordinary effort to keep their members in line and to maintain morale. Each shop crew was instructed to act as if it were still "holding shop," still connected to its previous employer. The joint strike committee called regular shop meetings where journeymen discussed the latest developments; such gatherings kept the workers together and gave them something to do. When there was no news to discuss, the strikers were even treated to musical entertainments or subjected to temperance lectures. An eerie calm reigned.[49]

Things finally began to move on 10 January 1894, during the strike's seventh week, when the manufacturers announced they were preparing to resume operations on a foul basis. To dramatize their serious intentions, the manufacturers' association wrote Danbury Mayor Charles S. Andrews, asking him to protect their property and their employees when their shops reopened.[50] The unions responded mildly, offering to resume negotiations, but the manufacturers balked. They did not want a repetition of what had happened in the fall, when they had bargained with union committees for two months, only to see the locals reject their committees' recommendations. The employers' association insisted it would reopen contract discussions with union representatives only if the latter were fully empowered to effect an agreement.

This was no trivial demand. The hat finishers had rarely authorized officers or delegates to commit the members to trade terms. Agreements on prices and work rules were usually subject to membership ratification, but now the hatters complied. For years they had been giving over more power to their arbitration and vigilance committees, their local officers, and the association leadership; now they surrendered their control of the terms of the trade agreement. The finishers' desire for a settlement was strong indeed.

The employer and union representatives met for four days in "the best of harmony."[51] The journeymen were willing to make substantial concessions to keep the shops fair; indeed, they ultimately agreed to adopt the employers' original demands for revising the trade agreements — those proposed in August 1893 — as the basis for settlement.[52] In the finishers' case, this meant abandonment of the piece rate system for a large proportion of the work force. Never before, not even in the headiest days of the proposed national trade agreement, had the finishers been willing to compromise on an issue so basic to their craft tradition.

Even so, the factory owners were not satisfied. Some were determined to open their shops independent of the unions, regardless of the proposed concessions, and the trade association was bargaining for them as well as those willing to resume fair status. Consequently, after the hatters' representatives offered to accept the manufacturers' original terms, the factory owners added another demand, that the unions guarantee not to interfere, currently or in the future, with any foul shop run by an association member.

The journeymen would not accept the pledge of noninterference, arguing that agreement would be tantamount to saying "you can have this and that so as to run a fair shop, and if you don't like that you can run an independent shop and we guarantee not to interfere with you." It was better to let the factories go foul, with the possibility of organizing them later on,[53] and so the negotiations broke up without agreement. Despite the dashing of the unionists' hopes of retaining all the association shops, calm still prevailed in Danbury. Although the manufacturers began circulating the strikers, offering to hire anyone willing to work, they made no effort to bring workers in from out of town, for they remembered the upheaval that attended attempts to import labor during the strike of 1882–83. For their part, the unions prepared to picket all foul shops peacefully, without threats or violence.[54]

It was generally understood that some of the nineteen factories would open fair, however. On 21 January, six employers met the members of the unions' joint executive committee to discuss terms for opening their shops with full union recognition.[55] At first, the unions' position was that since only six firms were involved, the journeymen were not obliged to offer as many concessions on trade rules as they had allowed the full manufacturers' association. Faced with the prospect of losing all nineteen shops, however, the finishers and makers changed their minds on 22 January. Now it was up to the trimmers.[56]

The women had minds of their own. They did not want to give up control of work on the sewing machines and they were willing to fight for their rights. Had the finishers and makers not intervened, the trimmers would have stayed out on strike even if that meant losing control of every single shop.[57]

The men, however, were determined to salvage something from the long struggle. On 26 January, representatives of the makers and finishers informed the trimmers that if they did not settle, the two locals would sign agreements to open the six shops. As they had done in 1890, the male hatters showed they were willing to abandon the women's cause. Faced with this threat, the trimmers capitulated. Six factories would open fair.[58]

At this point on 26 January, the independent factories still lacked an adequate labor supply. Only one shop was running foul, while three shops were closed altogether. The struggle could have continued for weeks or even months, had the strikers patrolled the railroad stations, picketed the factories, boycotted and threatened strikebreakers, and called a national consumer boycott against hats produced in the foul factories. That is what they had done in South Norwalk during the depression years 1884–85, but the Danbury hatters believed further resistance was futile. Their employers were determined to go foul, and they had the depression, low-skilled immigrant journeymen, and laborsaving machinery all working to their advantage. The journeymen chose to surrender, hoping that if they avoided a bitter struggle they could recoup their losses later. On 31 January, the three trade unions gave their members permission to apply for work at the independent shops on whatever terms the employers offered.[59]

The Danbury lockout was a serious defeat for hat finishers throughout the United States. The shops that reopened foul in February had gained significant advantages over competitors operating fair.[60] Union men everywhere could expect their employers to press for similar concessions, especially because the strike's outcome proved the journeymen could be beaten.

The finishers did not merely wait for disaster to strike. If the strike weapon were feeble amidst general depression, then perhaps the union label would be more effective. At a time when the IHFTA could not afford to publish its semiannual report, it spent $3800 to promote the label.[61]

Were the funds well spent? Apparently many manufacturers thought so. Their advertisements for "union made" hats filled the pages of the *American Hatter* and the *American Hat Review*.[62]

The hatters' unions bought labor peace in more painful and expensive ways as well. If employers demanded reductions in piece rates, the hatters took them, if not always happily. For example, in April 1894, at Ellor Brothers' factory in Watsessing, New Jersey, the men struck against a proposed wage decrease but compromised after their employer demonstrated to them that his competitors were getting their finishing done for less.[63] If a shop crew was not willing to accept a wage cut, its local might step in to make sure the firm did not go foul; this happened in Orange, in June 1894, when the finishers' associations ordered the men at the No Name Manufacturing Company to halt their strike and return to work at lower wages.[64] In one case, officers of the IHFTA actually intervened in an apparently minor dispute in Orange. The employees of F. Berg and Company had struck over wages; when an arbitration committee sided with management, the men not only refused to go back but they persuaded the Orange local to back their refusal. Fearing that the loss of Berg's large shop would set a dangerous precedent, association President James Graham traveled to Orange to order the men to resume work regardless of the local's action.[65]

The finishers had to swallow things even less to their taste than wage cuts. A correspondent for *The American Hatter* reported that "things have been done by the Orange manufacturers in the past year which a few years ago would have almost caused a riot in the factory, but the men have accepted them with scarcely a protest, even among themselves." For example, "The owners of one of the largest factories in the (Orange) district some time ago had a lot of hats upon which they wanted extra good work done, and they told the men that they wanted them finished by men of their own selection, without reference to the order in which they were expected to get work. . . . [The finishers] realized the uselessness of making a fight and throwing themselves out of all work, and they accepted the situation."[66]

Such concessions bought the finishers labor peace, but the cost was too high. During the summer of 1895, the hatting trade recovered from depression. Factories which had been running part time for three years were now working overtime and making good profits, for the tariff of 1894 had cut the cost of imported fur.

The Orange hatters had never been happy about the wage cuts forced on them by President Graham in 1894. With trade booming, and profits pouring into their employers' coffers, there was no way they would accept the status quo.[67] At the Orange local's meeting of 13 August, delegates agreed it was impossible to make living wages under the existing bill of prices. They agreed to demand an across-the-board increase of twenty-five cents per dozen at all shops in the district. Within a week, almost 700 finishers were on strike.[68]

The local's action was unusual, for shops usually bargained separately with employers over wages. Moreover, F. Berg and Company had a signed wage bill in effect at the time the finishers demanded general advances. That fact put the local in the bad graces not only of F. Berg but also of the international association, which had long ruled that shops could not demand that their employers revise existing wage bills.

Indignant at its men's bad faith, Berg and Company demanded that the international order its shop back to work. As they had done so often, the journeymen declined to recognize the association's authority. The Orange local refused to meet with the IHFTA national board at its headquarters in

Brooklyn. The ball in its court, the board ordered Berg's men to work, under their current bill of prices. If they did not comply, the shop could be declared open to all journeymen.[69]

Orange finishers were not impressed. When board representative Michael McKiernan from Newark spoke to the meeting of the Orange local on 18 August, his request that the delegates comply with national policy was tabled unanimously. "A spirit of rebellion against the National Association was openly manifested. . . . It was charged the National Board didn't represent the men who elected them."[70]

Without their association's backing, the Orange finishers prosecuted their strike against local employers, but with little success. Only five small firms agreed to terms while Orange's three largest firms persevered; on 22 August, F. Berg and Company, Connett, Read and Company, and Cummings, Matthews and Company agreed to remain independent, under penalty of forfeiting a cash bond.

Within two weeks, Orange finishers concluded that their position was untenable; they could not battle intransigent employers, implacable union leaders, and hard times simultaneously. On 1 September, local unionists approached management at Berg's, offering to send union members back to work under the previous bill of prices. By doing so, the local restored itself to the international's good graces, but Berg's was uninterested. The firm had no immediate incentive to resume good relations with the association, for it had been able to hire a full crew of men on a nonunion basis. For the longer term, the management preferred to free itself of the unions' interference. Matters rested there until 18 October, when Orange finishers called off their strike. Four shops, employing 500 men, had been lost to the union. Few journeymen had won a wage increase. Morale in the Orange district, and throughout the international, was at low ebb.[71]

Conclusion

The years 1890 through 1895 brought defeat to the hat finishers' craft union strategy. Strike losses in Danbury, in 1893–94, and in Orange the following year, cost the association control of twenty-three shops and a thousand jobs. Moreover, the association had had to surrender significant craft prerogatives to forestall further losses. The strike defeats and membership losses threatened the international's very existence. For one thing, it was almost impossible to press the union label when so many large and well-known firms were operating without it. Furthermore, the union's treasury was so low that financing the label campaign precluded publishing official union proceedings.[72]

The finishers' defeat resulted from a number of causes. Improved machinery decreased demand for skilled labor. Compounding that problem was the depression of 1893, which enabled employers to find nonunion men to do much of their work; furthermore, during the prolonged slump, some desperate union men went foul as well. Finally, the union's defeat can be attributed to internal union problems. The Orange local's defiance of the national policy of conciliating employers also contributed to the collapse of craft unionism.

American hat finishers did rise up from defeat to impose their values on the workplace in the years following the depression of 1893, but to do so, they had to modify their perspective on craft and union. Under pressure, the hatters created a new and effective trade unionism, albeit one far removed from the craft-centered localism with which their story began.

NOTES

1. *Hatter and Furrier,* Feb. 1890, p. 34; Mar. 1892, p. 23; May 1892, p. 27a; June 1892, p. 27; Sept. 1892, p. 35.

2. Ibid., Dec. 1885, p. 24; May 1888, p. 17; May 1889, p. 27; Apr. 1889, p. 29; Oct. 1889, p. 39; Sept. 1892, p. 35; May 1891, p. 38; Sept. 1891, p. 39.

3. Ibid., Oct. 1884, p. 28; Nov. 1884, p. 28; Dec. 1884, p. 23; Sept. 1885, p. 11; Oct. 1885, p. 11; Mar. 1886, p. 24; Oct. 1886, p. 60; Mar. 1887, p. 39; Apr. 1887, p. 35; Oct. 1887, p. 39; Sept. 1888, p. 32; Feb. 1889, p. 34; June 1889, p. 47; Nov. 1889, p. 64; Feb. 1890, p. 23; Feb. 1892, p. 39; David Mills, *The Twentieth Century Hat Factory* (Danbury, Conn.: The Lee-McLachlan Co., 1910–11), p. 100.

4. Mills, *The Twentieth Century Hat Factory,* p. 102.

5. The hydraulic press was used only on stiff hats at this time, and only replaced the blocking, ironing, and some of the pouncing operations. It did not displace curling until the twentieth century. Ibid., pp. 102, 105.

6. Edward Knight, *Mechanical Dictionary* (Boston: Houghton, Osgood and Co., 1876), p. 1078; (1884), p. 446; Edward Spon, *Spon's Encyclopedia of the Industrial Arts, Manufactures, and Commercial Products* (London: E. & F. Spon, 1879–82), p. 1116.

7. *Hatter and Furrier,* Nov. 1889, p. 41; *Appleton's Cyclopedia of Applied Mechanics* (New York: D. Appleton, 1893), p. 40.

8. *Hatter and Furrier,* Apr. 1889, p. 11; Aug. 1889, p. 9; Aug. 1890, p. 15.

9. Ibid., Sept. 1887, p. 9.

10. Ibid., Nov. 1889, p. 64; *Hat Review,* Nov. 1889, p. 4.

11. *Hatter and Furrier,* Nov. 1889, p. 64.

12. Ibid.

13. Another response by American hat manufacturers, staunch Republicans as they were, was to push for increased tariffs on imported hats. They were successful in gaining congressional action but not in keeping out the hats.

14. *Hatter and Furrier,* Aug. 1890, p. 15.

15. Ibid., July 1891, p. 70; Feb. 1892, p. 30.

16. Ibid., Oct. 1891, p. 51; *Hat Review,* Aug. 1893, p. 62.

17. *Hatter and Furrier,* Apr. 1892, p. 38b; Apr. 1893, p. 33.

18. No soft hats were yet finished on hydraulic presses.

19. *Hatter and Furrier,* Sept. 1892, p. 35.

20. Ibid., June 1892, p. 56.

21. Ibid., Sept. 1892, p. 35. The reason for the delay in acceptance of pressed hats is probably that the hydraulic machinery had still not been perfected. In January 1894, the New York correspondent for the *Danbury News* reported that: "The recent improvements in the method of hydraulic pressure has again brought the process up to a higher standard and makes it a strong opponent of 'all hand-made work.' The disagreeable features in the American pressed hat a few years ago have been corrected as far as possible, and many of the retailers, who have steadily refused to use them after the first experiment, are again disposed to give them a trial. Whether the process under its present favorable conditions will now become a permanent fixture in hat making depends largely on the coming season." *Danbury News,* 27 Jan. 1894.

22. IHFTA, "Proceedings of the Regular Convention, 2–12 May 1892," p. 6.

23. *Hatter and Furrier,* Nov. 1892, pp. 19, 23, 31; Dec. 1892, p. 23; Feb. 1893, p. 27; Mar. 1893, p. 23; Apr. 1893, p. 25; May 1893, p. 27; *Hat Review,* May 1895, p. 49.

24. *Hat Review,* Dec. 1892, pp. 14, 23, 31; Feb. 1893, p. 27; Mar. 1893, p. 23; Apr. 1893, p. 22; May 1893, p. 24.

25. U.S. Commissioner of Labor, *Report on Production by Hand and Machine Methods* (1897), pp. 1190–91.

26. IHFTA, "Proceedings of the Regular Convention, May 1892."

27. IHFTA, *Semi-Annual Report,* May 1892.

28. *The American Hatter,* June 1893, pp. 18, 21; July 1893, p. 19.

29. Ibid., Oct. 1893, p. 21.

30. Ibid., Sept. 1893, p. 17; *Danbury News,* 27 Oct. 1893.

31. *Danbury News,* 21 Nov. 1893; *The American Hatter,* Nov. 1893, p. 44.

32. Circular from the manufacturers' association, dated 31 July 1893, reprinted in *Danbury News,* 21 Nov. 1893.

33. Ibid.

34. The admission comes from a circular issued by the manufacturers' association on 17 Nov. 1887. It was included in the circular they released on 20 Nov. 1893. *Danbury News,* 21 Nov. 1893.

35. E. H. Taylor made this point in his letter to the *Danbury News,* 23 Oct. 1893. In addition, the *Danbury News's* regular correspondent from the New York wholesale hat center agreed that it would "never be possible to reduce the cost of hats made by intelligent and experienced labor down to the figures which satisfy the ignorant, slovenly and unskilled mechanics of some districts and the machine-made goods of

other localities. But why should Danbury strive to cope with such localities as (Fall River and Newark)? The character of the hats produced is dissimilar in almost every respect." The *New Haven Register* made the same point in an article about the Danbury lockout reprinted in the *Danbury News,* 18 Nov. 1893.

36. Danbury hat manufacturers' association, circular dated 31 July 1893, reprinted in *Danbury News,* 21 Nov. 1893.

37. *The American Hatter,* Nov. 1893, p. 44; *Danbury News,* 20 Nov. 1893.

38. *Danbury News,* 12 Oct. 1893.

39. Ibid., 12 Oct. 1893.

40. Danbury hat manufacturers' association, circular, dated 31 July 1893, reprinted in *Danbury News,* 21 Nov. 1893.

41. *Danbury News,* 20 Oct. 1893.

42. Ibid., 9 Nov. 1893.

43. Ibid., 11 Nov. 1893.

44. Ibid., 20 Nov. 1893.

45. Ibid., 24 Nov. 1893; 25 Nov. 1893.

46. Ten other factories belonging to association members remained open, but had few orders.

47. *Danbury News,* 25 Nov. 1893.

48. *New Haven Register,* n.d., reprinted in *Danbury News,* 18 Dec. 1893.

49. *Danbury News,* 28 Nov. 1893; 29 Nov. 1893; 1 Dec. 1893; 7 Dec. 1893; 21 Dec. 1893; 28 Dec. 1893.

50. Ibid., 11 Jan. 1894.

51. Ibid., 16 Jan. 1894.

52. Ibid., 19 Jan. 1894.

53. Ibid.

54. Ibid., 22 Jan. 1894.

55. Ibid.

56. Ibid.

57. Ibid., 26 Jan. 1894.

58. Ibid., 27 Jan. 1894.

59. Ibid., 1 Feb. 1894. Because hat orders were still light, only one-fourth of the men applying for jobs at the foul shops were hired. Two thousand hatters remained out of work. Those with employment paid one-tenth of their wages into a fund for the jobless.

60. *The American Hatter,* Mar. 1894, p. 29.

61. Ibid.

62. See, for example, *Hat Review,* Jan. 1895, p. 80; Feb. 1895, p. 42; Mar. 1895, p. 32.

63. *The American Hatter,* Apr. 1894, p. 18. The next month, a Brooklyn hat manufacturer cut his finishers' piece rates; it was the first such reduction in Brooklyn in many years. Ibid., May 1894, p. 26.

64. Ibid., June 1894, p. 13.

65. Ibid., Oct. 1894, p. 23.

66. Ibid., Aug. 1894, p. 24. There were many similar instances. For example, in May 1894, the Orange finishers' association voted to allow F. Berg and Company to

hire a nonunion curler to work on a curling machine; at the same time, the local voted to permit C. B. Rutan to bend the rules on use of the ironing machines. Brooklyn manufacturers were able to get their small work crews to do more work than usual at lower than normal piece rates. *The American Hatter,* Feb. 1894, p. 26; *The Hat Review,* May 1894, p. 40. Reinforcing the Orange hat finishers' efforts to blunt their employers' demands for wage cuts and concessions was a strike by immigrant nonunion hatters in Newark in the fall of 1894. Led by Jewish socialists, the strike had the effect of boosting hat orders in Orange's fair factories. The story of the strike is told in *The American Hatter,* Sept. 1894, p. 25; Aug. 1894, p. 28; *The Hat Review,* Sept. 1894, p. 32; Oct. 1894, pp. 18, 26; Dec. 1894, p. 34.

67. *New York Times,* 3 Aug. 1895; *Orange Chronicle,* 17 Aug. 1895.

68. *American Hatter,* Aug. 1895, p. 47; *Newark Evening News,* 14 Aug. 1895.

69. *American Hatter,* Aug. 1895, pp. 47–48; *Newark Evening News,* 16 Aug. 1895, p. 1. IHFTA, "Proceedings of Board of Directors, 1895," pp. 95–6.

70. *American Hatter,* Aug. 1895, p. 47.

71. Ibid., Sept. 1895, p. 33; Oct. 1895, p. 39; *Orange Chronicle,* 7 Sept. 1895.

72. IFHTA, *Annual Report,* (1895).

CHAPTER 11

Hatters Unite
Behind the Union Label,
1896–1915

W‍RITING IN THE DEPTH of the depression, with the terrible defeat at Berg's on his mind, James Graham, president of the finisher's national association, told his followers that "only the union label saved the union from complete destruction."[1] As the depression lifted, hatters made their label the keystone of their efforts to defend craft status and tradition.

They knew this strategy was no panacea. They had promoted their label for ten years and had struck and boycotted on its behalf many times without winning security. By the winter of 1895–96, they knew that to make their weapon effective, they would have to accomplish a number of things. First of all, the IHFTA had to make sure that the label was credible to consumers. If manufacturers could argue convincingly that some hats which lacked the label were produced by highly skilled men under decent conditions, the association would have a hard time generating sales resistance against label-less hats.

Secondly, the union had to be able to argue to manufacturers, wholesalers, and retailers that such a large proportion of men's fur felt hats produced and sold in the United States bore a union label that the remaining hats could be, and were indeed, discriminated against by the buying public. A union firm like Dunlap's of Brooklyn might find it hard to justify meeting union work rules and wage standards if it saw the label-less hats of competitors selling briskly.

Thirdly, the union would have to be consistent in its rules. If conflict among locals or leadership cliques produced sudden shifts in label policy, the union would antagonize employers and confuse consumers. Moreover, the union would have to maintain a high degree of discipline and administrative efficiency to make sure that no union labels found their way to foul factories, and that no fair hats were sent to market without labels sewn in.

Finally, the association needed substantial financial resources to advertise the label throughout the United States. More union members and higher dues would create a stronger label.

The hatters realized that to strengthen the union label, they would have to enlarge and centralize their association, and they were in no mood for halfway measures. For forty years, ever since they had organized a national union in 1854, they had slowly and reluctantly been beefing up their association; this time was different. The depression of 1893 had brought the hatters to a crisis point, and they responded decisively.

On 13 July 1896, the International Trade Association of Hat Finishers of North America met in special convention in New York City to perfect their union. The first order of business was revolutionary — the merger of the hat finishers' association with that of the makers to create the United Hatters of North America. The new organization did not obliterate craft distinctions entirely. Its constitution permitted finishers and makers to continue electing their own shop committees and local officers, and even to legislate separately those work rules that applied only to one branch of the trade. Nevertheless, the United Hatters bound the craftsmen tightly together. Henceforward, decisions about administration and distribution of the union label, when to strike and when to settle, whether or not to whitewash foul men, and how to relate to other unions would all have to be decided jointly.[2]

Eleven years earlier, when the finishers and makers had begun working together to promote the union label, many finishers had objected to tying themselves to "outsiders" they considered less skilled, and untutored in craft principle. Over the course of a decade, however, it had become clear that the fate of the two groups was closely intertwined. The merger, and the special convention, proceeded without controversy.

The special convention of 1896 accomplished more than the amalgamation of two unions into one, for the United Hatters of North America was far more centralized than either its predecessors had been. The new constitution created a strong central authority, the general executive board, consisting of four national officers elected by convention delegates. The board's authority was broad, if ambiguous, but the bottom line was clear: only the GEB could authorize a strike.[3] Moreover, "in cases wherein local officers fail[ed] to perform the duties prescribed for them by the laws of th[e] association, they [were to] be removed from office by the President and Secretary of the Association."[4]

The constitution also provided for a board of directors to represent the locals. While inferior to the GEB, the board had substantial power; it alone could make a foul shop fair. If a local proposed generous terms to a manufacturer to induce him to turn fair, the board could veto those terms if it believed them detrimental to the union as a whole; perhaps more important, the board could declare a shop fair even when the local having jurisdiction was not satisfied with the terms of the whitewash.[5] Clearly, it was the locals who lost power under the new constitution.

The rationale for the transfer of power from the locals to the national boards is not hard to find — framers of the constitution wanted to make sure that shortsighted militants, concerned about pay increases, work rules, or elections to local union office, would not be able to impede the association's national strategy. Article 19 of the new constitution makes this very clear: any time a dispute arose between a shop crew and its employer, the controversy was to be heard by a body consisting of equal numbers of journeymen and manufacturers from outside the shop. If this panel could not resolve the problem, a "disinterested" party was to be brought in for binding arbitration.[6] Finally, convention delegates gave practical evidence of their desire that the national association take on added power and responsibility by levying dues amounting to 1 percent of a member's weekly earnings.

Thus, in the wake of their defeat in Orange, the hatters rearmed themselves. They merged to form the United Hatters of North America. The new organization's constitution gave four national officers power to execute national policy to make the union label a credible weapon against manufacturers.

The Union Label Campaign

The fortified association set about using the union label to bring foul shops under union control. The general executive board took the first step in September 1896, when it voted to affiliate the United Hatters with the American Federation of Labor. Soon thereafter, two representatives attended the federation's annual convention in Cincinnati.[7]

When the IHFTA had adopted a union label in the spring of 1885, it had affiliated with the Knights of Labor, rather than the AF of L, not for any ideological reason, but simply because the Knights were involved in several boycotts at that time and seemed better situated to promote the union label. Within a year or two, the hatters' District Assembly #128 of the Knights of

Labor was moribund; the finishers promoted their label without the aid of either national union body.

In 1896, when the United Hatters thought once again of affiliating with a national federation, the Knights of Labor was a mere shell of its former self; the AF of L now contained most of the organized workers of the United States. Moreover, the AF of L had become deeply involved in the labels and boycotts of its member unions.[8] Each issue of the *Federationist,* the AF of L's monthly journal, contained a "We Don't Patronize" column, and soon the names of foul hat manufacturers were listed there.[9]

To reinforce the *Federationist'*s message, John Phillips, the hatters' national secretary, sent letters to local trade unions and central labor bodies, telling them about the United Hatters' label. Within nine months of the merger, Phillips had written to six thousand labor bodies, requesting them not only to advise their members of the hatters' campaign but also to send delegations to retailers, asking them to sell only hats bearing labels.[10] Throughout the United States, the labor movement responded. For example, in 1898, promises to pressure retailers came in from such diverse groups as the Metal Polishers Union of Toledo, Ohio; the Musical Association of Topeka, Kansas; the International Association of Machinists in Detroit, Michigan; and the Brotherhood of Railroad Trainmen, in Hannibal, Missouri.[11]

The hatters' locals followed up the national letter campaign. Boston's hatters induced the Massachusetts Federation of Labor to request its affiliates to back the hatters' label.[12] Soon afterward, the Boston journeymen organized a "union label ball" to which they invited prominent leaders of trade unions and community organizations. Placards advertising the hatters' "label ball" were placed in store windows throughout the town, and a wagon bearing a large sign depicting the union label was pulled through the streets by a team of horses.[13]

How successful were the hatters in creating a demand for union labels? That is a question difficult to answer precisely. The none-too-sympathetic *American Hatter* conceded that "many hat manufacturers consider using the union label to be good business despite some unjust union rules."[14] Reinforcing this judgment is the fact that the United Hatters had considerable trouble with retailers and manufacturers who put bogus labels in their hats, apparently in the belief that this would improve their marketability.

Thus the merger of the finishers' and makers' associations had proved a moderate success by October 1899. By aggressively promoting the union label throughout the American labor movement, the stable and centralized United Hatters had been able to induce dozens of firms to go fair.

Economic Troubles and Union Legislation

Unfortunately, the economic conditions that had undermined the hat finishers' association continued to cause problems. Increased use of machinery, in both the making and finishing departments, had materially reduced the demand for skilled labor; the resultant influx of less-skilled men reinforced the union's weakness at the bargaining table. Hatters suffered more unemployment and underemployment than they had in the 1880s, and when they were working, their conditions were worse. Employers demanded that journeymen work longer hours, with greater regularity, and at a faster pace than they were accustomed to; foremen discriminated against "men with grey hairs" who could not keep up the pace and excluded less-skilled men when it suited them to do so.[15]

While the hatters' primary response to the deterioration of their status was to promote the union label, they adopted more direct means as well. The simplest way to oppose speedup was to agree not to produce more than a "reasonable" amount of work a day, no matter what the employer and his foremen might decree. Philadelphia makers were strictly enforcing a "stint" in September 1899, while finishers were "agitating" to do so.[16]

The stint was not the only means of limiting output. In December 1898, Boston finishers amended their local bylaws to prohibit men from working during the lunch break. The *Journal of the United Hatters* approved: "We believe this is a step in the right direction, as there are so many men unemployed that something must be done to shorten the hours of labor. This applies especially to a large shop where the men may do 2–3 hats apiece during the noon hour, and if they are not allowed to do it, it will make room for a few more of our men."[17] Hatters also tried to reduce unemployment by instituting a fifty-five hour week. The Orange local began enforcing such a limit in July 1899; the national association adopted the hours limitation at its convention of 1900.[18]

The United Hatters also tried to equalize wages at levels above those they had fallen to during the depression. In Danbury, the settlement of the disastrous strike of 1894 had set piece rates substantially below what journeymen customarily received. Four years later, Bethel journeymen complained that this price differential was causing their shops to lose work to

Danbury's.[19] With great heat and statistical wizardry, the Danbury hatters defended themselves. They claimed that their wages were not really substandard, it was only that they were producing cheap hats; furthermore, their employers would risk losing the union label rather than increase piece rates.[20] Danbury's large membership made its power within the association immense; although the general executive board approved a proposal to establish a minimum price for finishing and making, $1 and seventy-five cents per dozen, respectively, and approved another proposal to establish a uniform bill of prices for finishers, the Danbury locals prevailed to defeat both in the board of directors.[21]

Undaunted, Bethel proposed another strategy to improve the journeymen's status, and this one met with greater success. In 1899, the little local submitted to the general executive board new definitions of making and finishing, including all employees in both departments under union jurisdiction, whether they worked as machine tenders, in other semiskilled jobs, or as full-fledged craftsmen. Redefining the union's jurisdiction was necessary, the Bethel men explained, because concessions granted by the unionists to their employers during the depression had given many "snap" jobs to nonmembers and enabled foremen to fill hat shops with foul-hearted men while journeymen languished without jobs.[22]

On this issue, the United Hatters triumphed. Those employers who balked at hiring union men to fill the jobs newly designated as belonging to making or finishing, or who balked at requiring some of their employees to join the union, backed down when the association threatened to revoke their union label.[23]

Machine tenders were not the only outsiders admitted to the United Hatters in the late 1890s. Pouncers entered the Orange local in 1899; then, at the national convention of 1900, delegates voted to add coners, slippers, and hardeners to the United Hatters of North America's jurisdiction.[24] These men were less skilled than the makers and finishers, few had trade union experience, and none shared the hat finishers' craft culture. Nevertheless, the coners, slippers, hardeners, and pouncers probably had more in common with the United Hatters' membership than did another large group of workers admitted in 1899 — the Hebrew Hatters of Newark.

The story of the decision to incorporate eleven hundred Hebrew hatters will soon be told, but here it should be noted that they were considered to be inferior craftsmen, from an utterly alien cultural background, who produced cheap hats under conditions that would make union men shudder with disgust; nevertheless, the United Hatters of North America voted to grant them cards.[25]

Declension of An Artisan Culture

Perhaps the decision to whitewash the largest group of aliens the hatters had ever absorbed symbolizes as well as anything can the declension of the hatters' culture. Pursuing the union label policy had necessitated relinquishing many vital features of the hatters' culture of work.

Hat finishers had relied on apprenticeship as the vehicle to pass on high skill standards as well as the craft's traditions, but after 1896, the United Hatters had had to admit large groups of men who had never served apprenticeships, who had never developed high degrees of manual skill, and who knew little of artisan lore. Exclusivity had been sacrificed.

Moreover, even "old-time" hatters were slowly and subtly changing. Foremost among the hatters' values at work was the craftsman's freedom to decide when he would work and at what pace. When employers began taking advantage of high unemployment levels to pressure their men to work hard, fast, and long, the association had responded with countermeasures that protected hatters in a new way. However effective the stint and the fifty-five hour week may have been, they clearly represented a concession by the United Hatters that it was no longer possible for individual men to control their labor.

Hat finishers had cultivated manly independence, granting status and respect to journeymen for standing up to foremen, rather than conceding their rights, and shop crews often had struck to defend members who incurred the bosses' wrath. In the post-depression years, however, shop crews were not supposed to meet more than once a month, and all grievances other than those concerning piece rates were supposed to be resolved through arbitration; strikes over wages had to be approved by the national union. Under these conditions it is hardly surprising that journeymen would lose some of their independence. And so they did, Edward Moore complained, in a *Journal* editorial entitled "Indifference, Apathy and Cowardice," "Some men are afraid to discipline the manufacturers. In the struggle that is now going on . . . we cannot afford to be cowards."[26]

One of the principal means the hatters had used to prevent the development of cowardice had been the control of hiring and firing, but here, too, old ways were passing. The *American Hatter* noted in September 1899 that the manner in which makers and finishers are now employed by the foremen is one of the trade matters which have undergone a great change in the past few years. According to the rules of the journeymen's union, a member when desiring work in a factory must have a member already employed in the factory accompany him. . . . This plan is apparently followed at the current time, but few men are put to work who have not either privately asked for work or had some friend do it for him, the matter of going on turn being simply a matter of form. Formerly, the rules of the union imposed a penalty upon a member who asked for work in any other than the prescribed form, and the rule probably still exists, but such a thing as enforcing it is now unheard of.[27]

The decay of the custom of "going on turn" symbolized and made possible the hatters' loss of the power to assure their members equal access to employment. Foremen took on younger and more highly skilled men first; less-skilled and older men were first to be "bagged."[28]

Although few journeymen abandoned the principle of equality, equality was impossible to enforce in practice. Unemployment was a chronic problem, skill standards had been breached, the union membership was far more heterogeneous than it had ever been. The hatters had to admit that "machinery [was] ridding shops of old men who can't keep up with the work."[29] J. W. Sculley, a South Norwalk hat finisher, put the matter apocryphally, but well: "There seems to be no place in some of the shops for 'the average' or the aged one. Hatting has long since ceased to be a trade, and deserves to rank with the professions. Particularly this is true in the curling department, where the individuality of man plays so important a part, and where the impossible is so much sought for."[30] Rather than attempt to force employers to retain veteran journeymen, the hatters explored setting up a retirement home. Such was the price of survival.[31]

Edward Moore summarized what was happening to the hatters in a *Journal* editorial. "There don't seem to be that real fellowship among jours that existed some years ago. It is a common sight to see a stranger walk into a shop nowadays and look around without being greeted with a How-de-do from a man in the shop. I wonder if we will ever get back to the old days when jours were jours in the real sense of the word."[32]

Toward Class Consciousness

It would be one-sided to understand the transformation of the hatters' culture as simply a matter of decline. While the hatters' sacrificed exclusivity, while they lost some of their manly independence, while they gave up control of the pace and duration of their labor, while they relinquished their insistence on equality among craftsmen, they began to develop a new outlook, a new set of values and priorities. In short, they grew class conscious.

In the pages of the *Journal of the United Hatters,* over the years 1898 to 1903, union leaders drew for the membership a picture of American society in which hatters were part of a working class struggling against the mighty power of industrial capitalism. Thus, in September 1898, Edward Moore expressed his antagonism against the owners of capital in virulent terms: "Not long ago, a hero of peace, named James Morris, was martyred at Oskosh, Wisconsin, fighting not for false patriotism — that often is but a shield for selfish greed, and used to make opportunities for the rich to fleece the poor — but fighting in the sacred cause of labor. . . . For this he was foully murdered by a brute in the employ of the Paine Co."[33]

Usually, the *Journal's* tone was more restrained, less inclined to single out villains, but, repeatedly, the United Hatters' leadership continued to point to industrial capitalism as American workers' great enemy. In a thoughtful editorial, in September 1899, Moore warned his readers that "the freedom of the American workingman is seriously threatened. . . . Boasting of Old Glory will not free us from industrial slavery. . . . While the machine is displacing the workingman, the trusts and the great department stores are driving out 'the business man.' "[34] Neither Edward Moore nor the association claimed to have a solution to such thorny problems, but they were willing to look beyond the little world of the hatting trade for possible solutions.

> Attempts are being made . . . to restrict the trusts. They have proved as futile as the attempts the workingman made to prevent the introduction of machinery.
>   Would the problem be solved if we restricted factories to a certain size? Would it be advisable to secure the immense benefits that come from the cooperative efforts of the trusts for the whole people?[35]

The United Hatters' leadership was now willing to consider radical solutions. This was something new. During the years 1873–93, when America was the scene of intense social and industrial conflict, the hatters had ignored the radical prophets. The railroad strike of 1877 had filled American businessmen with a profound fear of communism — the armories which dot our central cities are testimony to that fear — and drove many active trade unionists into the Socialist Labor party. In the mid-eighties, massive strikes in many American cities impelled workers to question the increasing power of concentrated wealth and brought labor's champion Henry George and his single tax theory celebrity throughout the land. The hat finishers, though, wedded to their craft traditions, had remained oblivious to all these developments. They preferred to hope that, in the long run, "the interests of the journeymen and their employers are one and inseparable."

In 1900, however, as the hatters fought with all their resources against F. Berg and Co., the *Journal* indicated that its mind was open to the possibility that "the interests of journeymen and their employers" were separable and, indeed, in conflict. In May 1900, it printed, without editorial comment, the presidential campaign platform of a trade unionist who had abandoned the liberal capitalist faith — Eugene Victor Debs. Debs's platform as candidate of the Social Democratic party called for a shorter work week, public works, national insurance for industrial accidents and unemployment, and social equality.[36]

Another champion of American workers, Henry Demarest Lloyd, made his way into the Hatters' *Journal* during the same spring. Lloyd, author of *Wealth Against Commonwealth,* exposer of Standard Oil and other trusts, and ally of the Chicago labor movement, traveled in New Zealand in 1899 to study social legislation and labor conditions. His report on sanitary inspections of factories, half-day closings on Saturdays, compulsory arbitration, and the eight-hour day gave hatters food for thought.[37]

As the *Journal* reported and commented on economic and political developments of interest to labor, it showed itself to be similarly unafraid to challenge contemporary militarism, patriotism, and imperialist enthusiasm that swept American society in 1898 as it went to war against Spain. Though many hatters went to war, and received respect from their fellows when they returned, the *Journal* looked at the war from the perspective of the working class; it did not identify the hatters' interests or viewpoints with that of America as a whole. In Editor Moore's opinion, this was a "rich man's war."[38] Expanding American markets in the Caribbean might be good for businessmen, the *Journal* editorialized in April 1899, but "how will that benefit those who can not find employment? Boasting of Old Glory . . . will not free us from industrial slavery."[39] Specifically, the *Journal* cited the case of a U.S. Army general who was sent into Warren, Idaho, during a bitter mining strike, and, in Moore's words, "declared trade unions unlawful." "The result of the War [is] fast pushing workingmen into slavery," he concluded.[40]

In a moving commentary on the death of James Morris, a striker in Oskosh, Wisconsin, Moore poetically contrasted the fate of American workingmen struggling for their rights with that of our soldiers fighting to expand the business system's profitability.

The Heroes of Peace

They fight their battles in shop and mine,
They die at their post and make no sign,
And the living envy the fortunate dead,
As they fight for a pittance of butterless bread. . . .

Fame, where is your story and where is your song
For the martyrs of peace and the victims of wrong?[41]

Finally, as the war wound down, and the hatters prepared for their great showdown with Berg and Company, the *Journal's* pages began to bristle with quotations from famous American and English critics of capitalist injustice and inequality. In April 1899, the *Journal* reprinted a poem by George E. McNeill, the Knights of Labor's publicist and philosopher; his "Poor Man's Burden" was decidedly antiwar and antitrust. Next issue, the paper assembled a series of aphorisms by Henry Thoreau, Ralph Waldo Emerson, and William Morris on the dignity of labor. Moore's successor at the editorial desk, George Byron, continued this practice, edifying his readers with thoughts like:

"Beneath a ragged coat may be a noble soul."
"Non-resistance to oppression is nothing short of complicity."
"Capitalism makes criminals of men; I would make men of criminals."

It is not really surprising that the United Hatters' national officers should have come to identify the union's interests with that of organized labor and the working class in general. For them, the union label strategy could only work if the Hatters achieved recognition from other unionists as brothers and allies. Moreover, the United Hatters' officers came into repeated and frequent contact with other union leaders. For instance, in December 1896, just months after the merger creating the United Hatters of North America, two officers, Robert Barrett and John Phillips, attended the American Federation of Labor convention in Cincinnati. Such meetings always resemble hothouses, for delegates are shut in hotels together for days at a time, without much contact with the outside world. Since the hatters' delegates were there to garner sympathy and support for the union label, they must have spent long hours meeting as many unionists as possible, recounting the hatters' woes and listening to similar stories from their colleagues. One would expect Barrett and Phillips to return to the United Hatters' national offices filled with a new sense of identification with the labor movement and a determination to pass this sense on to the membership. Just after the convention's close, President Barrett's semiannual report read:

> Organized labor has given our label such valuable support that we cannot use language strong enough in which to convey our thanks. . . . The advantages gained during the last eight months by the label and by advertising it extensively are well known to your officers and to many of the rank and file. . . . [We] are anxious to increase demand for the label and we do not know any better way to do this than to advertise it to the fullest extent of our means, and to affiliate and keep in touch with the labor unions of the land.[42]

This is just what President Barrett and Secretary Phillips did. Their experience with the federation in Cincinnati was repeatedly reinforced as they sought to strengthen and cement the hatters' relationships with sister unions. Learning which union leaders were the key contacts in gaining support from national unions, central labor bodies, and significant local associations became part of the United Hatters' leadership's task.

Of course, the rank-and-file member of the United Hatters' did not share such experiences with his union leaders. More than half of them lived in communities where there were not many other trade unionists, and where, consequently, their contacts with the wider world of organized labor was quite limited. In towns like Orange, New Jersey, and Danbury, Connecticut, the AF of L had little existence outside of the United Hatters, and whatever labor community existed was heavily influenced by the hatters' unions and their traditions. Under these circumstances, it would be surprising indeed if rank-and-file hatters developed consciousness of their membership in a working class organized to combat industrial capitalism as quickly and as fully as their leaders did.

Unfortunately, the historical record does not allow us to gauge readily the ideological orientations of the mass of hatters. What information we have comes mostly from the national and local officers of the United Hatters and reflects their perspectives. That leadership did comment on the membership's outlook, however, and what Edward Moore tells us confirms our expectations. In his editorial "Indifference, Neglect and Cowardice," Moore complained that many finishers and makers were participating actively in fraternal organizations such as the Knights of Columbus or the Ancient Order of Hibernians but were not doing so in their own trade unions. Furthermore, Moore charged, many workers were ignoring their "duty" to other trade unionists. Indeed, he went on, they were "going foul" on cigarmakers, brewers, bakers, shoemakers, and tailors by buying goods without labels. Finally, "in the struggle that [was] going on between the privileges of the dollar and the rights of man," too many hatters were acting cowardly, giving in to their bosses, rather than joining with their brothers to stand up for justice.[43]

Complaints like Mr. Moore's are as old as trade unionism, and reflect the different institutional positions of the national leaders and the rank-and-file. We should not, though, conclude that the national leadership had developed a class consciousness thoroughly out of step with the membership's traditional craft orientation. The pages of the *Journal of the United Hatter* indicate that local activists and leaders had undergone significant changes as well.

For example, in 1899, the Bethel and Danbury locals became embroiled in a dispute over what Bethel hatters considered to be their neighbor's excessive concessions to their employers. In March of that year, the secretary of the Bethel union sent to the *Journal* a poem which put the controversy in the context of the entire struggle between capital and labor.

> Oh these indeed are fight times,
>   of every kind and sort
> When we're not fighting Spaniards,
>   we're after other sport,
> We have to drive the Marshalls out, and Thom,
>   lest they will ruin us.[44]
> Oh! Let us be united, then all our battles we shall win.
>
> We've got to knock Mark Hanna out,
> We've got to lick the trusts,
> We've got to pound monopolies,
>   until they up and bust;
> We must have equal privileges,
>   if we run our union right,
> Tell Danbury drop her bugaboo,
>   and help us in the fight.[45]

Dispatches from the tiny Chicago hatters union even more clearly demonstrate how thoroughly local activists might identify their cause with those of fellow unionists. Chicago's entire report in March 1899 concerned itself with the struggle between the Allied Printing Trades Council and the Chicago *Record* and the Chicago *Daily News*. All the city's unions were "paying a weekly assessment to carry on the war, and we all consider it of the greatest importance that we win. . . ."[46]

Chicago's hatters were not alone in support of the strikes of fellow trade unionists. During the winter and spring of 1898–99, the Boston local assessed its members 1 percent of their earnings to support the strike of Marlboro, Massachusetts, shoemakers; South Norwalk makers not only donated money to the Marlboro strikers but also contributed cash to striking cigarmakers in far-off Canton, Illinois.[47]

Local hatters' unions did more than vote to support strikes on a few occasions; they took working-class solidarity as an ideal to act on. Danbury finishers fined members patronizing nonunion barber shops fifty cents. The Philadelphia finishers' association established a committee to dissuade its members from buying nonunion bicycles, cigars, and shoes.[48]

It was the hatters of Orange and Newark who went furthest in promoting label-consciousness. In 1898–99, they organized a consumers' league to foster competition among shop crews over which could collect the most union labels. Results of the competition were printed in the *Journal of the United Hatter.*[49] A year later, Orange journeymen claimed credit for organizing local bakers for the first time, for driving "trust-made" tobacco out of town, for helping to establish a union shoe shop, and for introducing union-made soap to local stores.[50] Similarly, Danbury finishers campaigned to organize all the town's barber shops in 1898, but their efforts did not stop there, for the hatters wanted the "barbers' union to reciprocate. . . . Many barber shops sell scab cigars."[51]

Clearly, the hatters were not mere passengers on American labor's bandwagon. Along with Samuel Gompers and his cigar-makers, they were pioneers in the effort to make American workers label conscious and thus conscious of their interdependence. President Barrett expressed the matter clearly in his semiannual report of 1898: "[T]here is another feature of our business that must not be lost sight of, if we wish to keep our association where it belongs, in the front ranks of organized labor. Fraternalism is invoking rapid strides in all grades of society, and will yet prove to be the greatest friend of mankind in its struggle against the centralized power of aggregated wealth and its tendency toward imperialism."[52]

The Hatters' Label Challenges

Soon after he uttered these remarks, President Barrett's prophesy was severely tested. The United Hatters' attempts to alleviate unemployment by limiting the work week to fifty-five hours precipitated the most important boycott in the hatters' history.

Trouble started when the union firms in Orange refused to limit the work week to fifty-five hours as long as fair hatters working in nonunion shops such as F. Berg and Company and E. V. Connett and Company continued to labor unlimited hours. The Orange local faced a dilemma; it could withdraw fair journeymen from the foul shops, thereby increasing unemployment, or it could attempt to force the large and prosperous foul firms to go fair. The United Hatters chose the latter course; in October 1899 it withdrew 150 fair men from F. Berg and Company and called on workers throughout the United States to boycott Berg hats.[53]

Because it regarded this boycott as a test of the union label, the United Hatters went to extraordinary lengths to remove Berg's from the list of prosperous foul firms. Responding to a report that Berg was planning to staff the factory with "Hebrew hatters" from nearby Newark, the new president, John Moffitt, approached the representative of the Jewish journeymen, Joseph Barondess, about how to prevent large-scale scabbing.[54] The issue was a delicate one because, only eight months earlier, Edward Moore had denounced the Hebrews as hoodlums, while the Newark local had rejected merger proposals.[55] Nevertheless, Moffitt and Barondess agreed to let bygones be bygones. The United Hatters of North America's board of directors voted to grant union cards to more than 900 Jewish journeymen, effectively preventing their employment by Berg.[56]

Many hatters, led by Moore, who was apparently anti-Semitic, protested the invasion of less-skilled aliens; indeed, Moore led part of the Philadelphia local out of the United Hatters, so strongly did he resent the whitewashing. Most journeymen, though, considered winning the fight against Berg to be paramount. Moore was replaced as editor of the *Journal,* the Philadelphia local was reorganized, and several Newark factories producing cheap hats were made fair.[57]

Meanwhile, the United Hatters prosecuted its boycott against Berg with unprecedented vigor. Six agents were hired to organize support. They were assigned to represent the association in San Francisco, California; Louisville, Kentucky; New Orleans, Louisiana; Ohio and upper Pennsylvania; Missouri, Nebraska, and Colorado; and New England. Their message, as formulated by the Orange hatters' association in February, linked the campaign against Berg to broader social issues. "The United Hatters calls upon union workmen and friends of union labor everywhere to refuse to buy or sell hats bearing the name of Berg and Co. . . . The firm is backed by millions of capital, and it is only by showing them the strength of organized labor that they can be brought to respect . . . the union principles."[58]

Six agents promoting the boycott throughout the United States does not seem a formidable force, but President Moffitt's ingenuity allowed the organizers to concentrate their efforts. Apparently using an informant inside Berg's, Moffitt learned where the company was shipping its orders and directed his agents to build up local pressure against Berg outlets. The United Hatters' efforts even reached down to the little buckeye shops to which Berg sent out some of its work. Ferreting out the teamsters who transported hat bodies to and from the buckeyes, Moffitt bribed them not to make deliveries.[59]

While there is little direct evidence of the boycott's effect on sales, it is possible to infer that the impact was substantial. The *Journal* reported that retailers returned many shiploads of hats to Berg because they couldn't sell them without a label.[60] While one might be inclined to discount this claim, the actions to Berg and Company tend to reinforce it. If Berg could sell hats without labels, why did he send hats to Austin, Drew and Company for packing, so that fraudulent labels could be sewn in?[61] Most persuasive of course was Berg's decision to surrender to the union's pressure early in September 1900.[62] Under terms of the agreement, Berg agreed to hire only union men in the future, in all departments of his shop. Since the company thereby became subject to all the rules of the Orange local and the United Hatters, Berg had to agree to limit hours to fifty-five per week; finally, the firm increased piece rates by 27.5 percent.

The United Hatters did not have to make comparable concessions, for they had "won" this strike-boycott decisively. On one issue, the journeymen did have to tread carefully, however, and that was what to do with the men who had "scabbed" during the strike. Berg and Company was not in much of a position to insist on the United Hatters taking in the men; after eleven months of turmoil, management was more concerned about winning back its old customers. If the hatters refused to allow the scabs to join the union, however, those men would not disappear, no matter how much the unionist might desire that to happen. Rather, they would remain in the area, ready to take their places at the benches of any employer desiring to operate on a nonunion basis, and that was a possibility the United Hatters did not welcome, for it had plans to organize the entire district and to establish a beachhead among the cheap soft hat shops of nearby Newark. Consequently, the hatters did not exploit their opportunity to punish the men who had made it possible for Berg to weather the strike for so long. Instead, the union took in the strikebreakers, fining them no more than $250.[63]

So fortified, the United Hatters set about organizing E. V. Connett and

Company, Orange's remaining major foul hat firm. Eighty fair finishers left Connett to take their places at the newly opened benches at Berg; the company then was warned that it would be placed on the AF of L's "We Don't Patronize" list if it did not agree to recognize the United Hatters. Within two days, E. V. Connett and Company followed Berg's lead. Suddenly, all Orange valley's hat shops were fair.[64] The local unionists, firmly in the driver's seat, were now free to vent their wrath on the journeymen who had left their association during the strike of 1894–95 to remain at Connett, working foul for the past five years. Not only were the fines levied on the Connett crew higher than those levied on Berg's men, but a few of Connett's were denied union cards altogether.

Meanwhile, in Newark, the United Hatters accomplished their goal of organizing a major producer of cheap soft hats when Meyer Mercy, one of the country's largest and oldest foul hat companies, agreed to recognize the association in return for a whitewash of its crew. Perhaps it is not surprising that the triumph over Mercy was viewed by many hatters with mixed emotions; after all, Mercy's firm paid low wages to low-skilled men to produce cheap soft hats for sale in a murderously competitive market. Many journeymen in Newark and elsewhere wondered what membership in the United Hatters meant, if the "clod-hoppers" who made up Mercy's shop crew would be able to enter the association on a full and equal basis.[65] When Mercy reneged on his promise to raise wages promptly, the decision to whitewash the disreputable establishment made the United Hatters' leadership look bad indeed.[66] Yet, though President Moffitt conceded that the union's action at Mercy's was perhaps a bit hasty, the association did not revoke the firm's right to issue the label. Soon, that decision paid dividends.[67]

Progress and Its Price:
Loewe v. Lawlor

The hatters' successes organizing Berg and Mercy ushered in the best three years in their history. After Berg surrendered in 1900, the *American Hatter* conceded that "just at present, the United Hatters of North America seem to have convinced a large number of large manufacturers that the union label is a desirable and necessary addition to their hats."[68] Dozens of manufacturers recognized the union in the years 1900 to 1903, including major firms like Connett's of Orange and Mallory's of Danbury.[69] When Roelofs of Philadelphia succumbed to a nationwide boycott in 1902, only 12 of America's 190 hat manufacturers remained nonunion.

The hatters' success paralleled, and was connected to, the upsurge of the American labor movement. Membership in trade unions shot up from 447,000 in 1897 to 2 million in 1904.[70] The AF of L's new strategy, which combined "business unionism" with working class solidarity through union label boycotts and sympathy strikes, appeared invincible.

Labor's success rested on the fact that unionists were organized collectively while businessmen were not. When business began to collectivize, at the turn of the century, labor's progress ground to a halt. In steel, tobacco, sugar, and oil, competing firms joined together in trusts or holding companies. David Parry organized smaller businessmen into the National Association of Manufacturers and employers organized dozens of industrial associations, such as the National Erectors Association and the National Stove Founders Association. All three developments spelled trouble for organized labor. U.S. Steel, established in 1901, soon rendered impotent America's largest union, the Amalgamated Association of Iron and Steelworkers. The National Association of Manufacturers launched the open shop drive in 1904, and employers' associations launched campaigns to neutralize sympathy strikes and label boycotts.

Hatters were to be the most famous victims of the new business strategy. Their trauma began in 1902, hard on the heels of the union's exhilarating victory over Roelof's. Hoping to eliminate all foul shops, the United Hatters selected Dietrich E. Loewe's Danbury hat factory as its next target. During the summer of 1902, hatters' President John Moffit asked Loewe to recognize the union and put its label in all his hats. If Loewe refused, Moffit warned, the union would place his firm on the AF of L boycott list. The union had spent $23,000 boycotting Roelof's and was prepared to spend a like amount to turn Loewe's fair,[71] but Loewe was prepared to counter Moffit's threats. With his friend Charles H. Merritt, another Danbury nonunion hat manufacturer, and Merritt's son Walter Gordon, Loewe had organized the American Anti-Boycott Association and solicited pledges of support totaling $20,000.[72] So buttressed, Loewe told Moffit he would not budge. On 20 August 1902, the United Hatters called on Loewe's men to strike. All but ten turned out, fair and foul alike. The struggle was on.

After several months, Loewe assembled a shop crew and resumed producing hats. Now it was time for the boycott. To legitimate their campaign, the hatters put Loewe on the AF of L list of companies "We Don't Patronize." Then the union began to strike at Loewe's distribution network. After obtaining a list of Loewe's orders, the hatters systematically set out to dissuade retailers and wholesalers from carrying Loewe's hats. Wherever

Loewe's hats were sold, an agent of the United Hatters appeared. In Richmond, Virginia, for example, two hatters spent "several weeks" to get the local trade and labor council to put a retailer, T. D. Stokes and Company, on their unfair list.[73]

On the West coast, the San Francisco labor council passed a resolution on 3 July 1903, in response to an appeal by the hatters' union: "Union firms do not usually patronize retail shops who buy from unfair jobbing houses or manufacturers. Under these circumstances, all friends of organized labor, and those desiring the patronage of organized workers, will not buy goods from Triest and Co. . . ."[74]

The hatters' tactics hurt Loewe as they had Roelof; Loewe lost more than $33,000 in 1902 and 1903, but he would not surrender. Instead, he turned to Daniel Davenport, legal consultant to the American Anti-Boycott Association. Davenport developed a legal strategy based on the theory that the Sherman Anti-Trust Act (1890), which stated that "every contract, combination in the form of trust or otherwise, or conspiracy in restraint of trade or commerce among the several States, or with foreign nations, is hereby declared to be illegal," applied to the labor boycott. This was a novel idea, for everyone knew that the Sherman Act had been aimed at the robber barons, not at trade unions. Nevertheless, Davenport counted on the fact that the law did not state that it applied only to business practices. If the Sherman Act covered labor, then under its seventh section Loewe, as the person injured by an illegal restraint of trade, could sue for triple damages. But whom should Loewe sue? Davenport introduced another wrinkle: he argued that the individual members of the United Hatters should be held liable for damaging Loewe's business, whether or not they participated in any way in the strike, boycott, or even the decision to boycott.[75]

To carry out his plan, Davenport put young Walter Merritt to work combing the real estate and bank records of Danbury, Norwalk, and Bethel, compiling a list of all union members who owned property. Out of more than 2,000 Connecticut unionists, Merritt found 248 hatters who owned homes or had bank accounts.[76] Under a Connecticut statute, Loewe could attach without notice the real and personal property of the men he accused of injuring him.[77] On 12 September 1903, Merritt gave his list to Sheriff Peter Doolan of Fairfield County, who served papers on the town clerk of Danbury and on several banks.[78] At the same time, Loewe filed suit in the circuit court for the District of Connecticut asking for treble damages under the Sherman Act.

Dietrich Loewe — or was it Walter Gordon Merritt? — realized that the townspeople of Danbury might not appreciate this legal action. In a letter published by the *Danbury News* on the day Sheriff Doolan served the papers of attachment, Loewe defended himself in terms of values all Danburyites shared:

> Having for a long time worked as an employee like the men with whom we now differ, we have never lost sympathy, and aim to have a good understanding with them. Activated by a desire to deal honestly, fairly and generously with all who work in our shop, bearing in mind that they were free and independent American citizens, with a pride in their manhood deserving of respect. . . . This is a country of liberty, some are Protestants, some Catholics, some believe in unionism, and some do not, but whatever their creed or belief all must be treated with fairness and permitted to earn a livelihood. We are unwilling to black-list the citizens and youth who do not belong or cannot obtain entrance into the unions. We believe with our honored President, Theodore Roosevelt, that the principle of the open shop is the only true and correct basis for individual liberty.[79]

Fortunately for Loewe, his case was to be fought in the federal courts, not in the court of public opinion, where workers had repeatedly triumphed. It was to be a long struggle.

Because Loewe's suit struck at the AF of L's organizing strategy, the AF of L helped formulate the legal defense and recruit nationally prominent attorneys, including John W. Davis, the Wall Street lawyer who later ran for president on the Democratic ticket. Counsel for the defense filed a demurrer in circuit court, arguing that the boycott did not come within the scope of the Sherman Act, which was aimed at trusts, not combinations of laborers. Furthermore, their brief argued, "the character of the combination must be determined by its designs, means, and effect. The design is to unionize the plaintiff's factory."[80]

The district court did not render judgment on the hatters' defense for three years. In the meantime, hat manufacturers, emboldened by Loewe's example, began to defy the United Hatters and its union label. Knox of Brooklyn, one of the best-known names in high quality hats, went foul in 1903. Even worse, Roelof of Philadelphia resumed its nonunion status in 1904 and remained foul in the face of a nationwide boycott called by the AF of L. Soon the trickle was a flood: the number of union hat shops decreased from 178 in 1902 to 100 in 1907, and in the union shops, the workers' power diminished. Employer pressure forced the United Hatters to rescind its restrictions on machines and to relax its rules on the employment of unregistered boys in 1907.[81]

By that time, the legal drama had resumed. On 7 December 1906, District Court Judge James P. Platt rejected Daniel Davenport's novel arguments: "The Supreme Court has not yet broadened the interpretation of the Sherman Act. What it may do if the matter comes before it is, in my opinion, very uncertain."[82]

While the hatters celebrated, Davenport relentlessly pushed on. If the lower courts were unwilling to stake out new legal grounds, he would have to try the higher courts. The next step was an appeal, on a writ of error, to the circuit court of appeals.

The issue before the appeals court had been identified by Judge Platt: did the Sherman Act apply to labor boycotts or not? Let the Supreme Court decide, the appeals court ruled. So the hatters' fate, as well as the fate of the AF of L's boycott strategy, rested in the hands of the Supreme Court.

Chief Justice Melville W. Fuller read the Court's unanimous decision on 3 February 1908. What he said could not have been worse for organized labor: the Sherman Act did apply to combinations of workers, Fuller ruled. To buttress this conclusion, Fuller cited with approval the reasoning of a Louisiana district court, in the Amalgamated Council case, which held that Congress had taken up the antitrust issue in response to the evils of "massed capital," but during congressional deliberations had developed a broader conception of the problem. Consequently, Congress wrote the law in such a way as to prohibit "all combinations in restraint of commerce, without reference to the character of the persons who entered into them."[83]

Justice Fuller did not conduct his own investigation into the legislative history to reach this conclusion. Rather, he drew almost verbatim from Davenport's brief of counsel for Loewe. Fuller wrote, "The records of Congress show that several efforts were made to exempt, by legislation, organizations of farmers and laborers from the operation of the act, and that all these efforts failed, so that the act remained as we have it before us."[84]

This was not true. In fact, "the Congress which passed the Sherman Act, actually, not once but twice accepted such amendments without even a roll call." Those changes did not appear in the final bill because Senator Edwards dropped the amendments as superfluous when he redrafted the bill for the judiciary committee.[85] Justice Fuller's inaccurate historical conclusions are all the more curious because he was aware of a Massachusetts district court decision in the Patterson case, which held that "if the interpretation contended for by the prosecution were adopted, the inevitable result will be that the Federal courts will be compelled to apply this statute to all attempts to restrain commerce among the states, . . . by strikes or boycotts. . . . It is not to be presumed Congress intended thus to extend the jurisdiction of the courts of the United States without very clear language."[86]

Justice Fuller's historical reconstruction may have been weak, but his conclusion was firm: he reversed the district court decision and ordered a new trial. In doing so, Fuller established three principles: the Sherman Act applied to labor; urging consumers to boycott goods that crossed state lines was illegal; boycotting retailers of goods that have been shipped interstate was also illegal.

Loewe v. Lawlor was disastrous for organized labor, but worse was to come. On 4 October 1909, Loewe's suit against the Connecticut hatters resumed in district court. Walter Gordon Merritt, now a law school graduate, examined witnesses, and Judge Platt presided once again. Because the Supreme Court ruled that the Sherman Act applied to boycotts such as the one conducted by the United Hatters and the AF of L, the unionists could defend themselves only on narrow grounds. Their primary argument was that the individual defendants had not participated in the boycott and therefore were not liable for damages. Judge Platt was not impressed. His charge to the jury left little room for doubt as to the verdict: "I must impress upon you that it is your positive duty to accept it as the law of the case that the defendants are parties to a combination. . . . The only question, therefore, with which you can properly concern yourself is the matter of damages."[87] The jury did its duty, as interpreted by Judge Platt. The hatters were found guilty and assessed a sum three times the damages set at $74,000 plus $10,240.12 costs.

As if their legal defeat was not bad enough, the hatters lost "the most severe" strike in their history in 1909–10. The trouble began in 1909, when Walter G. Merritt convinced the hat manufacturers' association to order its members to cease using the union label and to require all members to post a $25,000 bond to make sure all held firm in their stance. The employers' unity made the unions' task impossible. The hatters struck for twelve months, longer than they had ever struck before; their union paid out nearly half a million dollars in strike benefits, an unprecedented sum; friendly unions chipped in $240,000 to support their struggle; nevertheless, when the United Hatters called off the strike, important firms, like Schoble and Company, of Philadelphia, and Crofut and Knapp of South Norwalk, remained foul.[88]

Though the hatters' prospects looked bleak, they pursued the legal avenues open to them. In 1910, their lawyers filed an appeal of the verdict of the district court on the grounds that Judge Platt had erred by instructing the jury how to decide the case. When the circuit court of appeals upheld their contention, on 10 April 1911, the hatters had to go back to court for a new trial, this time in the unfriendly court of District Judge James L. Martin of Vermont. When the jury interrupted its deliberations to ask Judge Martin whether it could award Loewe more than he had asked for, the outcome was certain; judgement against the unionists amounted to $252,130.[89]

The hatters' legal setbacks propelled them into politics. In 1910, United Hatters' treasurer James Maher won election to Congress where he worked to secure legislation exempting labor from antitrust prosecution. The Democratic victory of 1912, in which not only hatters but the entire AF of L participated, enabled Maher to gain his goal. On 15 October 1914, Congress enacted the Clayton amendment to the Sherman Act. While Samuel Gompers of the AF of L hailed the bill as labor's "Magna Carta," subsequent court rulings limited its impact drastically, and its passage did not save the hatters.

The final blow came on 5 January 1915, when the Supreme Court heard the hatters' appeal of the 1912 district court decision. Justice Oliver Wendell Holmes uttered the last words — the hatters had to pay.[90]

AF of L support was a small solace. The contributions collected on Hatters' Day helped Connecticut journeymen keep their homes, but the United Hatters of North America had declined steeply during the years of legal struggle. The hatters' practice of solidarity — which grew throughout the nineteenth century until it embraced the whole world of organized labor — had enabled trade unionists to defeat their divided employers. When capital organized, in employers' associations, giant corporations, and citizens' alliances, and when capital gained support from the federal courts, then the skilled workers' solidarity proved insufficient.

Labor only recovered when the Great Depression weakened the business system, and when labor regrouped, it did so on a different basis. When autoworkers sang "Solidarity Forever" at the sitdown strikes in Flint, Michigan, skilled and unskilled workers sang together. Their union immersed itself deeply in electoral politics. In short, labor's world in the thirties was a world of centralized authority and collective action which the hatters, in their first hundred years of struggle, could have barely imagined.

In retrospect, what appears most impressive about the hatters' story is how well they adapted to their changing environment. The centralization of hat manufacturing had threatened to undermine the journeymen's autonomy; new machines displaced the craftsmen's skill; heavy immigration produced widespread unemployment. Nevertheless, hatters adapted by expanding their practice of solidarity. Even though controlling their work locally, in the shop, was central to the finishers' culture of work, they created one of America's first national unions. When the national union found it could not stop the influx of low-skilled men into the trade, hatters pioneered in the negotiation of trade agreements with their employers. When employers abandoned the trade agreement, finishers merged with allied craftsmen to form an amalgamated union, the United Hatters of North America, which joined with its counterparts in the American Federation of Labor to promote workers' solidarity nationwide. The hatters had preserved their culture of work, not by clinging to archaic customs, but by creating new institutions and new forms of struggle.

NOTES

1. United Hatters of North America, *Semi-Annual Report* (1895).

2. International Association of Hat Finishers of America, "Proceedings of the special convention, 13-18 Jan. 1896."

3. *Constitution* of the United Hatters, Article 19.

4. Ibid., Article 9, Section 11.

5. Ibid., Article 10, Section 10.

6. Ibid., Article 19.

7. United Hatters of North America, *Semi-Annual Report* (Dec. 1896), p. 4.

8. Phillip Taft, *The A.F. of L. in the Times of Gompers* (New York: Harper, 1957), pp. 264-5.

9. American Federation of Labor, *American Federationist* (1897-99), passim.

10. United Hatters of North America, *Semi-Annual Report* (1897).

11. United Hatters of North America, *Journal* (Aug. 1898), p. 5.

12. Ibid., (Sept. 1898), p. 1.

13. Ibid., (Oct. 1898), p. 5.

14. *American Hatter,* Aug. 1899, p. 29.

15. United Hatters of North America, *Journal* (Sept. 1899), p. 2; (Sept. 1900), p. 3.

16. Ibid., (Sept. 1899), p. 2. Many skilled craftsmen enforced stints in the late nineteenth century, but hatters had considered them inimical to the craft tradition that individual workmen determined their pace and hours of labor. See David Montgomery, "Workers' Control of Machine Production," *Labor History* 17 (Fall, 1976), 485-509.

17. United Hatters of North America, *Journal* (Dec. 1898), p. 1.

18. Ibid., (Nov. 1899), p. 6.

19. Ibid., (June 1900), p. 7; (Feb. 1899). p. 1.

20. Ibid., (Mar. 1899), p. 3.

21. Ibid., (Nov. 1899), p. 6; (Dec. 1899), p. 4; (June 1900), p. 6.

22. Ibid., (Apr. 1899), p. 5.

23. Ibid., (Apr. 1899), p. 5; (Sept. 1899), p. 3. After the Bethel rules were adopted, forty finishers' and twenty-five makers' jobs came under union control. Also see ibid., (Aug. 1899), p. 1.

24. Ibid., (June 1900), p. 7; (July 1899), p. 1.

25. See p. 199.

26. United Hatters of North America, *Journal* (Apr. 1899), p. 4.

27. *American Hatter,* Sept. 1899, p. 41.

28. The *American Hatter* noted that in Orange, "all of the local men, including many who can not ordinarily get steady work are now working." *American Hatter,* Oct. 1898, p. 21.

29. United Hatters of North America, *Journal* (June 1900), p. 4; (Aug. 1900), p. 4.

30. Ibid., (Sept. 1898), p. 6.

31. Ibid., (Aug. 1900), p. 4.

32. Ibid., (Nov. 1898), p. 1.

33. Ibid., (Sept. 1898), p. 4.

34. Ibid., (Apr. 1899), p. 4.

35. Ibid.

36. Ibid., (May 1900), p. 3.

37. Ibid., (Mar. 1900), p. 5.

38. *American Hatter,* Oct. 1898, p. 25: "The demand for men has practically ceased. The soldier boys found their benches practically waiting for them. If a manufacturer had all the men he really wanted, he found room for the jour who went to war, and the journeymen who did not go were perfectly willing to divide with their soldier comrades, whether there was plenty of work or not."

39. United Hatters of North America, *Journal* (Apr. 1899), p. 4.

40. Ibid., (June 1899), p. 4.

41. Ibid., (Sept. 1898), p. 4.

42. United Hatters of North America, *Semi-Annual Report,* (Dec. 1896), p. 5.

43. United Hatters of North America, *Journal* (Apr. 1899), p. 4.

44. These were nonunion hat manufacturers.

45. United Hatters of North America, *Journal* (Mar. 1899), p. 7.

46. Ibid., (Mar. 1899), p. 1.

47. Ibid., (Dec. 1898), p. 2.

48. Ibid., (Sept. 1898), p. 3; see also (Aug. 1898), pp. 1, 3.

49. Ibid., (Sept. 1899), p. 4; (Oct. 1899), p. 5. In September 1898, the *Journal* began printing a list of goods members should boycott. In 1900, delegates to the national convention voted to bar any delegate to the next convention who did not wear union labels in his shoes, clothing, and, of course, hat.

50. Ibid., (Feb. 1900), p. 4. Danbury and Bethel hatters helped organize several trades and breweries in 1896–97, according to President Edward Barrett's semiannual report of June 1897, p. 3.

51. Ibid., (Sept. 1898), p. 3.

52. United Hatters of North America, *Semi-Annual Report* (June 1898), p. 5.

53. United Hatters of North America, *Journal* (Oct. 1899), p. 6. *American Hatter,* Oct. 1899, pp. 15, 24. Although only 150 of Berg's 474 employees were unionists, all but 31 struck.

54. United Hatters of North America, *Journal* (Nov. 1899), pp. 1–2.

55. Ibid., (Feb. 1899), pp. 2, 4.

56. Ibid., (Nov. 1899), pp. 1–2. In January, some additional foul men in Orange and Reading, Pa., were whitewashed.

57. Ibid., (Apr. 1900), p. 2; (June 1900), pp. 6, 8.

58. Ibid., (Feb. 1900), p. 1. See also United Hatters of North America, "Proceedings of the Convention of 1900," 7–18 May, pp. 80, 155, 207, and 274.

59. United Hatters of North America, "Proceedings of the Convention of 1900," 7–18 May, p. 268.

60. United Hatters of North America, *Journal* (Apr. 1900), p. 2. The Newark *Evening News* reported that Berg had lost $200,000 as a result of the strike. See 18 Sept. 1900; 1 Sept. 1900.

61. Ibid., (Apr. 1900), p. 2.

62. *American Hatter,* Sept. 1900, p. 48.

63. Ibid.

64. Ibid.

65. Ibid., Sept. 1900, p. 4.

66. United Hatters of North America, *Journal* (Oct. 1900), p. 3.

67. Ibid.

68. *American Hatter,* Sept. 1900, p. 4.

69. Donald Robinson, *Spotlight on a Union* (New York: Dial Press, 1948), p. 78.

70. Selig Perlman and Philip Taft in John R. Commons, et. al., *History of Labor in the United States* 4, (New York: Macmillan, 1918–35): 13.

71. Robinson, *Spotlight,* p. 85.

72. Walter Gordon Merritt, *History of the League for Industrial Rights* (New York: League for Industrial Rights, 1925), p. 4.

73. Walter Gordon Merritt, *Million Against One: A Conspiracy to Crush the Open Shop* (New York: American Anti-Boycott Assn., 1904), p. 11.

74. Robinson, *Spotlight,* p. 86.

75. *Loewe v. Lawlor,* U.S. District Court, District of Conn., 1906, 148 Fed. 924.

76. Robinson, *Spotlight,* pp. 87–88. The hatters' holdings totaled $130,000, for an average of less than $600 each, the equivalent of a year's income.

77. Albert Finkelstein, "The Story Behind the Danbury Hatters' Case," *Voice* of the Union of Cement, Lime, Gypsum and Allied Workers, July 1949.

78. Robinson, *Spotlight,* p. 88.

79. *Danbury News,* 12 Sept. 1903.

80. Robinson, *Spotlight,* p. 90.

81. Ibid., pp. 94–95.

82. *Loewe v. Lawlor,* U.S. District Court, District of Conn., 1906, 148 Fed. 924.

83. Irwin Lichtenstein, "Labor Unions and the Federal Anti-Trust Law," *Chicago Federation News,* 1 Nov. 1941, pp. 2, 3, 5, 8.

84. *Loewe v. Lawlor,* U.S. Supreme Court, 1908, 389.

85. Irwin Lichtenstein, "Labor Unions and the Federal Anti-Trust Law," *Chicago Federation News,* 1 Nov. 1941, pp. 2, 3, 5, 8.

86. *United States v. Patterson,* U.S. District Court, Massachusetts, 1893, 55 Fed. 605.

87. *Loewe v. Lawlor,* U.S. District Court, District of Conn., 1909, 142 Fed. 216.

88. Robinson, *Spotlight,* p. 94.

89. *Loewe v. Lawlor,* U.S. District Court, District of Conn., 1911, 130 Fed. 633.

90. *Loewe v. Lawlor,* U.S. Supreme Court, 1915, 235 U.S. 522, 35 S. Ct. 170, 59 L. Ed. 341.

Conclusion

In 1800, THE JOURNEYMEN hatters of Danbury organized a trade union. This was something new — the first time hatters had organized an association to represent themselves collectively in their dealings with the master craftsmen. It came about because the hatting industry had expanded. When the continental wars shut off the export of English hats to the United States, Danbury's master hatters had expanded production to fill the vacuum. In a rapid sequence of changes, masters increased their work force; their shops could no longer be contained within households; and journeymen began to see themselves as employees, with needs and interests distinct from those of their employers.

The first hatters' union in Danbury institutionalized the new relationship between employers and employees, but it came into being to preserve the hatters' ancient culture of work. The new union's regulations included apprenticeship rules that echoed the Elizabethan statutes of the sixteenth century; preserved work sharing customs practiced by French artisans in their compagnonages; and imposed controls on a traveling system remarkably similar to that practiced by English and French journeymen of the eighteenth century.

Here, then, is the history of American hatters' trade unionism in the nineteenth century: the craftsmen acted ever more collectively to preserve traditional ways of working and living. Throughout the nineteenth century, the hatters' adaptation to changes in their industry enabled them to preserve much of their tradition.

In the Gilded Age, when factories in seven northeastern cities produced hats for sale throughout the country, the members of the Hat Finishers National Trade Association were a diverse lot. In Orange, New Jersey, for example, one-third of the craftsmen were American-born children of American-born parents, another third were native-born children of immigrants, particularly from Ireland and Germany, and the remainder were themselves immigrants, generally men in their forties and fifties, who had come to America from Ireland and Germany about three decades earlier. Though diverse in background, hatters were socialized during their years of apprenticeship to share a common culture of work. At the heart of the finishers' culture was their insistence on remaining free from their employers' authority; a big-hearted, "manly" journeyman let no one tell him what to do or how to do it. He would rather walk off the job, and often did, than tolerate an affront to his dignity. Even among themselves, craftsmen were extremely sensitive to slights, strongly assertive of their own proud independence. But they were not individualistic. They were extremely conscious of their standing within their peer group; they competed vigorously for prestige within the craft, accepting their peers' judgements of success and failure. Verbal play, puns, and practical jokes were the common coin of their competition and served to lessen the pressures generated by intimate group life.

Hat finishing was skilled work, and the men took pride in their labor; each new trade season was the occasion for exuberant plunges into arduous activity. Hatters valued leisure as well, finding the seasonal unemployment endemic to their industry a boon as well as a burden. Moreover, finishers enjoyed variety; traveling from shop to shop and town to town was a hallowed tradition within their culture. Young men especially moved frequently from one hatting center to another; older men just as often changed employers. Hard drinking was another carry-over from their craft's preindustrial days, and if a hangover caused a man to lose work on Blue Monday, he could make up for lost time on Tuesday, Wednesday, and Thursday, working with a will among his like-minded shopmates.

Finally, hatters were a practical sort, little prone to philosophical speculation or social experimentation. Their gregariousness suited them well for electoral politics; many finishers ran for office or participated in the campaigns of others, but their efforts were usually confined to local Democratic and Republican parties. The journeymen were primarily craft-conscious; they usually shunned radical or class movements.

Gilded Age hat finishers preserved their independence from the bosses' authority, maintained their ability to enjoy leisure, and safeguarded their equality as journeymen by enforcing strict union rules about how work was to be done. At the heart of the finishers' policy was piece work; men were paid for as much work as they chose to do. As long as this rule remained in effect, journeymen could decide how fast they would work, and when they would rest, and they could ensure that each shopmate shared in whatever orders were on hand. Personnel policy was also important. Foremen had to hire hatters in turn, without discrimination, and did not fire their hands in slack season; the workers themselves decided whether to stay on or leave when there was little work to do. Moreover, the hatters were ever vigilant to preserve their skilled status. They resisted any attempt by their employers to divide up their work, for fear that the eventual result would be diminution of the skill level required of craftsmen.

The journeyman's control of his work was a central facet of the centuries-old hatting tradition, but it did not go unchallenged in the nineteenth century. Despite the fact that many Gilded Age hat manufacturers had started out as journeymen, and shared sympathy for the finishers' values, their business interests clashed with their sentiments. Manufacturers found themselves under constant pressure to keep production costs down so that they could make a profit in the exceedingly tight market. They frequently turned to their journeymen's wages as sources for potential savings. Some manufacturers, particularly those who made cheap hats which did not require fine finishing, tried to eliminate the problem altogether by hiring nonunion immigrants to work for low wages and without restrictive rules. Newark and Yonkers became centers of this sort of trade in the 1880s. Elsewhere, employers tried to speed up production, to reduce the degree of skill necessary to finish hats, and to expand the labor supply. They demanded that employees stop drinking on the job; they prohibited journeymen from leaving the shop; they sought relaxation of apprenticeship rules; and perhaps most important, they attempted to divide the task of hat finishing into separate jobs.

Since the union men resisted such challenges to their control of work, disputes over work rules often touched off strikes and became the subject of collective bargaining. Hatters retained substantial control over the production process, but it is also true that by 1890, employers had made significant inroads. For example, in order to fulfill their promises to employers, finishers had surrendered their freedom to strike whenever they were dissatisfied, to break off from work at will, and to call a shop meeting on whim. That was just the beginning. Employers forced hatters to abandon the local, informal, intimate, and spontaneous control of the workplace which they preferred. When employers developed new strategies, out of the myriad possibilities open to them the hatters chose the one they believed would allow them to hold on to as much of their accustomed way of life as possible, even at the expense of possible economic advantage.

In the early days of hatters' unionism, the journeymen responded to employers' attempts to cut wages or change work rules by striking or picketing. If resistance failed, the local unions would try to recoup their losses by convincing strikebreakers to join the union; this process was known as whitewashing. Its drawback was that each strike loss brought into the hatters' locals journeymen who were not highly skilled nor imbued with craft tradition. The finishers' culture was in danger of being seriously diluted.

Danbury hatters experienced a major defeat in 1882–83, and, two years later, Orange hatters lost again while South Norwalk journeymen narrowly averted defeat. In response, the hatters began to search for alternative strategies for preserving their traditional culture.

The finishers had had a national union since 1854, but the organization had been weak and decentralized during its first three decades. Its most significant accomplishment had been its role in coordinating the finishers' fight against prison hatting in 1878–82. While this success had bolstered the association's prestige, before 1884 the finishers relied on their shop crews and locals, rather than on their national union, to preserve their traditional way of life.

In 1885, this practice changed when the national officers undertook two initiatives to bolster the journeymen's power. First, they proposed that hat manufacturers throughout the industry organize a trade association for the purpose of ratifying a trade agreement with the finishers and allied craftsmen, known as hat makers. Under such an agreement, management and labor would establish uniform wage and work standards, thereby eliminating with one stroke both strikes and excessive competition. Outsiders would be frozen out of the industry.

Such an agreement was never fully implemented because the manufacturers could not all agree among themselves and the makers' locals could not coordinate their efforts. The finishers were more cohesive, and more willing to try out the experiment, but even they had difficulties when the union of Orange hatters antagonized its employers by holding out for higher piece rates in the winter of 1885–86.

Such problems did not mean that the trade agreement was shelved, however; the finishers' association and some of the manufacturers pursued an agreement until 1890. In the process, the HFNTA underwent substantial changes. As long as the finishers were pursuing industrial peace, they had to grant their national union power, for no agreement was viable if one local violated it. Consequently, in the years from 1885 to 1890, the

HFNTA gained substantial authority over its affiliates on such matters as when men could strike, when they could request wage increases, and when they had to submit disputes to arbitration.

At the same time, the HFNTA was earning prestige and authority by implementing a second strategy for bolstering its members' power—the union label. Boycotting had become popular among American workers in the early 1880s and had become a factor in the hatters' South Norwalk strike in 1845–85. Shortly thereafter, association President Dennis J. Hagerty suggested that the finishers and makers adopt their own union label and urged workers around the United States to buy only those hats that carried a label, specifying that the hat had been produced in a union factory. After 1884, when the HFNTA joined the Knights of Labor, the label strategy had become highly effective.

As with the trade agreement, the union label could only be effective if the HFNTA had strong control over its affiliates and members, because if a firm in one part of the country operated successfully in defiance of the label, the plan's credibility would be compromised. Consequently, the association grew more centralized, becoming much like the business unions organized and advocated by Samuel Gompers and Adolph Strasser. It was only natural that the hatters would become more conscious of themselves as part of the labor movement.

It may seem strange that hatters joined the Knights of Labor to promote a union label as an instrument to force employer compliance with craft rules at the same time the Hat Finishers' National Trade Association developed into an effective instrument for promoting labor-management cooperation, but hatters saw the two strategies as complementary, not contradictory. They needed a strong national union if they were to offer their bosses the carrot—conciliation—and they needed a strong national union to wield the stick—the union label—against recalcitrant employers. Whether hatters joined with the Knights of Labor or with the American Federation of Labor was, for them, a matter of convenience. In 1885, it was the Knights that seemed more able to help the hatters' boycotts; in 1895, it was the AF of L. Both organizations affected the HFNTA in the same way: both broadened the finishers' sense of solidarity with other workers. All this must seem puzzling to students of labor history who are used to seeing the Knights' "reform unionism" and the AF of L's "business unionism" as ideological opponents and opposites, but as Norman Ware demonstrated half a century ago, there was more that united the two organizations than divided them. The hatters' story simply highlights the validity of Ware's argument.

In 1896, the finishers went so far as to relinquish the craft autonomy on which their union was built; the new organization, the Union Hatters of North America, amalgamated all the hatting crafts into one organization. The collectivization of hatters' trade unionism did not end with the demise of the finishers' separatism. The United Hatters affiliated with the American Federation of Labor; entering the federation meant that workers in scores of crafts would join in solidarity with the hatters by respecting their union label. In six years, the hatters' boycotts forced all but twelve firms to grant union recognition. Only the Supreme Court, with its decision *Loewe v. Lawlor* (1908), was able to overcome the hatters' new strategy.

Hatters and Labor History

This book has argued that hatters' collective action in the United States was an effort to preserve age-old craft traditions that separated hatters from other craftsmen; over time, the hat manufacturers' efforts to increase output and lower costs spurred journeymen to develop a trade union strategy that was ever more collective, more deliberate, and more disciplined. The spontaneous, informal control of the workplace by autonomous artisans gave way to centralized, national unionism. Then the hatters joined with other skilled workers to promote nationwide boycotts on behalf of the union label. The hatters' practice of solidarity grew ever wider and more collective. At the beginning of their struggle, finishers recognized their commonality only with each other; under circumstances not of their own choosing, they learned how their fate was tied to the other workers in hat factories, and to skilled workers in other crafts. As the nineteenth century neared its end, hatters even began to sense they were part of a "working class" whose interest was distinct from that of the emerging industrial capitalists.

This interpretation resembles in broad outline the history of American labor sketched by John R. Commons and Selig Perlman, and elaborated by scores of scholars, but it also differs with it significantly. The differences are many: this study emphasizes the continuity in the hatters' craft culture while the Commons school emphasizes the development of economic rationality; this study emphasizes the centrality of the hatters' struggle to control the work process while conventional labor history relegates such conflicts to the margin; this study interprets the hatters' unions as expressions of the craftsmen's particular values while the Commons school details the development of "business unions"; and this study emphasizes the importance of skilled workers' solidarity expressed through union label boycotts more than the Commons school did.

Underlying these particular differences, there is a more basic divergence. The Commons model of the American economy is evolutionary; it sketches how the "expansion of the market" caused the American economy as a whole to move through sequential stages of development. Seen in this context, the hatters' success in preserving their traditions and control of work appears exceptional. In 1975, when I began researching this work, I worried that the hatters' culture of work was anachronistic. What were factory workers in the Gilded Age doing with values favoring traveling and a varied work rhythm? Why were they performing rituals of solidarity with their bosses? It all seemed preindustrial. I thought I must be stretching my evidence past all limit or hopelessly romanticizing what was there. Or could it be that my sources themselves were romanticizing a mundane reality? If all these hypotheses were wrong, the alternative seemed even worse – that hat finishers were an exceptional case, a tight-knit group of aristocrats who were able to preserve a preindustrial culture into the industrial age because their industry was oriented to high-quality consumers' goods.

The same sort of doubts arose when I began to piece together evidence about the hatters' control of work in their factories. The picture of hatters walking to and fro in the shops, leaving for a beer, or sending out for a pail when the work became hot did not square with my image of industrial America gleaned from such works as Ginger's, Cochran's, and Degler's.[1] Nor could I understand how, in a highly competitive industry, hatters could keep control of such things as hiring, firing, and distribution of work. I worried that the hat industry was so backward technologically compared to most sections of the American economy that the finishers' struggle to protect their work rules was a trivial case.

Recent historical evidence indicates that the hatters' struggles were in the mainstream of nineteenth century social development. Thus, Gregory Kealey concludes his study of the struggles of Toronto printers, moulders, and coopers to maintain control of work in their shops in the Gilded Age: "Toronto workers, who had struggled throughout the late nineteenth century for shop floor control, were about to face new, more virulent battles. The custom of workers' control, widely regarded as a right, had become deeply embedded in working class culture. The fight, initially to maintain and later to extend this control, became the major locus of class struggle in the opening decades of the twentieth century."[2]

At the same time that Gregory Kealey was reporting how skilled workers had struggled to maintain their control of work processes, David Montgomery published a sweeping analysis of "Workers' Control of Machine Production in the Nineteenth Century." Like Kealey, Montgomery argued that this battle was not confined to workers in small, highly skilled crafts still slumbering in the preindustrial age. Rather, Montgomery was concerned with "the veterans of industrial life: 'iron moulders, glass blowers, coopers, paper machine tenders, locomotive engineers, mule spinners, boiler makers, pipe fitters, typographers, jiggermen in potteries, coal miners, iron rollers, puddlers, and heaters, the operators of McKay or Goodyear stitching machines in shoe factories, and in many instances, journeymen machinists and fitters in metal works,' " all those who possessed high degrees of skill that allowed them to control their work in the years following the Civil War, and who all waged determined struggles to preserve their power thereafter.[3]

Kealey's and Montgomery's studies indicate that the hatters' struggle to control work was not atypical, but we can go beyond that. The entire question of whether the hatters' struggles were typical or not is based on the Commons and Perlman model, in which American crafts and craftsmen followed one pattern of development at approximately the same pace. That assumption is unfounded. The American textile industry developed earlier and more rapidly than did shoemaking; New England textile owners organized factories before Philadelphia manufacturers did. Manufacturing methods in the barrel-making industry followed timeworn paths until the late 1870s, when Standard Oil introduced new machines that eliminated the cooper's trade. Hat manufacturers introduced finishing machines at the same time, but they did not prove adequate for producing high-quality goods. In short, capitalist development in nineteenth-century America was fitful and uneven.[4] As David Montgomery has noted in his review article, "To Study the People,"

> The insights provided by recent studies of capitalist development in both factory and artisanal settings warn us against the analytical pitfalls inherent in such tempting dichotomies as "industrial" vs. "preindustrial" and in the notion of a "take-off" in economic growth. They also suggest that the formation of a modern working class involved a wide variety of human experiences. The working lives of canal laborers were very different from those of mid-century butchers, weavers, or seamstresses, just as the "cultural baggage" brought by migrants differed considerably from one group to another.[5]

Nor is uneven development characteristic solely of the American capitalist economy. Raphael Samuel documents in great detail how social relations, market structures, and technological development varied widely among the trades of mid-Victorian London.[6] Those variations had important consequences; for example, the workers' ability to slow down, sabotage, obstruct, or prevent the introduction of new inventions depended on the power relations between unions and employers — on the workers' solidarity and skill level, on the employers' size, organization, and market position.[7]

Uneven Development and Human Solidarity

If we follow Montgomery's and Samuel's approaches, recognizing that uneven development of capitalist society is characteristic, we will be more attentive to the particularities of struggles in the various social and industrial sectors. Thus, while all skilled workers in late nineteenth- and early twentieth-century America found their status and security threatened by the growing power of industrial capitalists, different craft groups possessed different resources for meeting the challenge, they had different values to defend, and they had different strategies for defending them. Moreover, each craft group faced a different problem, for the threat posed by business management varied depending on each industry's particular pace and pattern of development. The historical outcome — the nature of each union's development, the strike record of each trade, the degree of control over work each union preserved — depended on the interaction of both variables, what the workers brought into the situation and the particular situation they faced.

David Brody, the dean of American labor historians, has recently pointed out the danger in any approach emphasizing the particularity of workers' historical experience — it makes impossible the development of a new synthesis for labor history. What Brody calls for — that historians see "the workers they are studying in the context of job and industry, an economic approach to the history of American workers" — is not incompatible with a recognition that workers' historical experiences varied widely in the unevenly developing industrial society.[8] Professor Brody's own book, *Workers in Industrial America,* is perhaps our best example of how attention to cultural diversity may be combined with a careful analysis of economic development, with struggles over the work process constituting the arena where the two concerns intersect.[9]

If historians do not follow Montgomery's and Brody's examples, and instead focus on the general process by which American labor developed, then historians are likely to portray workers in the abstract — as "aristocrats of labor," as "autonomous craftsmen," as "economic men," as "militant proletarians," or as "class-conscious masses." All these formulations, whatever their analytic value may be, serve to blind us to the human dignity, to the unique individual and social reality of hatters, coopers, machinists, potters, and so on. As the journeymen's individual and collective characters disappear in the realm of the abstract, as the scholar becomes ever more distant from the complex detail of the historical experience, workers become pawns in ideological and academic struggles. Labor history becomes a surrogate for labor politics, and the writing of labor history becomes a form of vicarious militancy. Undoubtedly, this is likely to be the case to some extent, even in the best of circumstances. Eric Hobsbawm has pointed out that labor history has always been an intensely ideological field, but Hobsbawm went on to argue that the dissolution of the monolithic parties of the left has made it possible to write a less doctrinaire history today than it was thirty years ago.[10]

Labor history at its best is writing which makes clear who the workers were, what their previous experiences had been, what challenges they faced, and what their choices were; it is writing, in short, that allows readers to imagine themselves to be in the workers' place in an act of solidarity between the historian and the subjects of the story. It is an affirmation of human dignity and of the struggle for democracy.

The world described in these pages was a world characterized by a pervasive sense of solidarity among skilled workers, a solidarity almost unimaginable in the United States today, although Polish workers in the union named Solidarity have reminded all of us how powerful that sense of common humanity can be. When workers supported each other vis-à-vis their foremen, when they refused to cross the picket lines of craftsmen from another trade, when they refrained from smoking nonunion cigars, or wearing nonunion hats, their practice of solidarity was not a sign they liked the others, that they agreed with them, or even that they shared all their values. It was simply and powerfully a recognition that skilled craftsmen stood in a common relation to the businessmen who were changing their world. Then, solidarity rested on thousands of personal acts, private decisions to restrict output, to honor picket lines, to boycott nonlabel goods. A sense of solidarity was a human emotion, expressed in song, marches, and processions, in long, colorful speeches, in puns, jokes, stories, and legends.

At the core of this society of solidarity was the work group and the production process. Our society has changed so much in this century that it is hard for us to imagine the social meaning of work three generations ago. Now work is instrumental, a means to a living, a way to earn free time, a burden to endure. Studs Terkel's brilliant book on *Working* in contemporary America shows that those jobs which Americans find to be fulfilling and intrinsically valuable also tend to be jobs where people work on their own, as professionals or artists, so even there the sense of solidarity, based on a recognition that through collective effort people can create what is most valuable to them, is absent.

In the nineteenth century, skilled workers saw their jobs as central to their lives because their work was so different from what most employment is like today. Hatters, carpenters, machinists, printers, and many other craftsmen had to make decisions about how to do their tasks properly, had to take responsibility for their products, and had to take initiatives to solve new problems. They had to learn to get along with one another so that solidarity based on personal actions would remain effective. In their workshops and through their unions, they had to think about matters of organizational strategy, about political economy, about social change. They had a sense of themselves as respected citizens doing valuable work, and their daily experiences in the mills, plants, shops, and factories reaffirmed that sense of themselves.

Of course, it would be foolish to romanticize the skilled workers of the late nineteenth century, if for no other reason than because they failed to preserve their world. They were unable to overcome the sexual, racial, and ethnic differences that separated workers from each other, that broke their solidarity, and that brought many defeats. When hat finishers returned to work before the women trimmers had gained recognition, when skilled carpenters prevented the organization of woodworkers, when militant trade unionists lobbied to exclude the Chinese, the limitations of the craftsmen's solidarity stood out only too clearly.

With their ranks divided, workers and trade unionists were unable to defeat the industrialists' drive to "rationalize production," transform the meaning of work, and replace the invisible hand of the market with management's visible hand. Consequently, workplaces and the work force changed. As Robert Hoxie pointed out in the midst of the struggle of 1915, "While machine industry has tended, and doubtless scientific management tends, to break down the solidarity of craft groups, machine industry has been the strongest force in the creation of class consciousness and industrial as well as class solidarity among the workers."[11]

The struggles against scientific management produced general strikes during World War I and the massive steel strike of 1919. Industrial solidarity, the recognition of the common humanity of factory workers, grew during the lean years of the 1920s and startled the world in the coalfields of Pennsylvania in 1933, the depots of Minneapolis and the docks of San Francisco in 1934, the tire building shops of Akron in 1936, and the auto plants of Flint in 1937.

Today, it still takes solidarity to preserve workers' rights in American workplaces, but much has changed. Solidarity has become institutionalized and bureaucratic. Workers in an auto plant refrain from undercutting each other, but their action does not rest on a personal sense of solidarity; instead, there are seniority provisions in the union contract. Elaborate schemes of job classification prevent workers from taking each other's work away. Long-term contracts even tend to discourage the personal sense of solidarity by locking employees into their jobs regardless of what grievances may arise or what injuries may be done to others.

As employers have standardized production and workers have built bureaucratic institutions to defend their rights, workplaces have become much less effective training grounds in democracy. Routinized, deskilled, and management-directed work tends to diminish employees' sense of competence; noisy working conditions or strict disciplinary rules often hinder workers from getting to know one another; the bureaucratic organization of the company and the union tend to stifle individual initiative and discourage people from developing a sense that they can participate effectively in shaping their world.[12]

As David Brody pointed out so subtly in his recent essay, "The Uses of Power: I," while unions have not contested management control of production processes since World War II, they have created important protections for workers against arbitrary management authority. The grievance machinery established a common rule of shop law; the seniority system provided security against sudden dismissal and lessened fear of supervisors' favoritism; job classification prevented employers from eliminating jobs by shuffling workers around from one task to another.[13]

For all the organizational development of national union bureaucracies that have made it possible to protect workers in these ways, the task would have been impossible if workers had forgotten the practice of solidarity. Dominant as national unions are, local unions remain the centers of the struggle for workers' rights, the site of the thousands of daily confrontations

between employees and management. Most local unions are extremely vol-
untaristic organizations. They depend on ordinary men and women from
the shop to volunteer to be stewards, and they depend on the more group-
conscious members to take unpaid jobs as local officers and committee
members. Moreover, if workers lacked trust in each others' supportiveness,
they would accept management dictates rather than file grievances. If they
did not perceive the commonality of their position vis-à-vis the superintendants, they would flout union rules to curry favor. If union leaders did not
recognize the vulnerability of every member, they would fail to defend un-
popular or oppositional members.

The American labor movement survives today because its ranks include thousands of militant activists and tens of thousands of committed
members, all imbued with solidarity. Although the industrial world has
changed, these men and women are the heirs of the Danbury hatters and
the Pullman machinists, the Homestead puddlers and the Scranton miners.
To write of American workers in the nineteenth and early twentieth century, of their particular, diverse, and complex struggles, is to practice solidarity not only with them, but with the men and women carrying on the
struggle for freedom and equality in American workplaces today, the men
and women of the American labor movement.

NOTES

1. Thomas C. Cochran, *Social Change in Industrial Society* (London: Allen and
Unwin, 1972); Ray Ginger, *Age of Excess* (New York: Macmillan and Co., 1965);
Carl Degler, *The Age of the Economic Revolution, 1876–1900* (Glencoe, Ill.: Scott,
Foresman, 1967).

2. Gregory Kealey, "The Honest Workingman," *Labour/Le travailleur* 1 (1976):
62.

3. Montgomery, "Workers Control of Machine Production," *Labor History* 17
(Fall 1976): 487. See also Daniel Nelson, *Managers and Workers* (Madison: University
of Wisconsin Press, 1975), pp. 58–66.

4. Allan Dawley, *Class and Community* (Cambridge, Mass.: Harvard University
Press, 1976); Herbert Gutman, "La politique ouvriere de la grande entreprise
Americaine de l'age du clinquant: le cas de la Standard Oil Company," in *Le mouvement social,* n. 102 (Jan.–Mar. 1978), pp. 67–100; Irwin Yellowitz, *Industrialization
and the American Labor Movement* (Port Washington, New York: Kennikat Press,
1977), p. 64; Cynthia Shelton, "Textile Production and the Urban Laboring Class:
The Case of Early Industrialization in Philadelphia, 1787–1837," paper delivered at
the Organization of American Historians' meeting, Philadelphia, 1 Apr. 1982.

5. David Montgomery, "To Study the People: The American Working Class," *Labor History* 17 (Fall 1980): 492.

6. Raphael Samuel, "London: Workshop of the World," *History Workshop* 3 (Spring 1977): 6–72.

7. Ibid.

8. David Brody, "The Old Labor History and the New," *Labor History* 20 (Winter 1979): 125.

9. David Brody, *Workers in Industrial America* (New York: Oxford University Press, 1980). See Chapter 1 in particular.

10. Eric Hobsbawm, "Labor History and Ideology," *Journal of Social History* 7 (1974): 374–5.

11. Robert F. Hoxie, *Scientific Management and Labor* (New York: D. Appleton and Co., 1916), p. 131.

12. Richard Sennett and Jonathan Cobb, *The Hidden Injuries of Class* (New York: Alfred A. Knopf, 1973); Melvin Kohn, *Class and Conformity* (Homewood, Ill.: Dorsey Press, 1969).

13. David Brody, *Workers in Industrial America,* pp. 173–214.

Bibliography

BOOKS, ARTICLES, THESES, UNPUBLISHED PAPERS

Aitken, Hugh G. J. *Taylorism at Watertown Arsenal.* Cambridge, Mass.: Harvard University Press, 1960.

American Federationist, 1897–99.

Appleton's Cyclopedia of Applied Mechanics. New York: D. Appleton, 1893.

Aspinall, Arthur. *The Early English Trade Unions.* London: Batchford Press, 1949.

Barnett, George. *Chapters on Machinery and Labor.* Cambridge, Mass.: Harvard University Press, 1926.

_____. *The Printers.* Cambridge, Mass.: Harvard University Press, 1909.

Bemis, Edward. "The Relations of Trade Unions to Apprentices." *Quarterly Journal of Economics* 6 (October 1891): 76–93.

Bensman, David H. "Business and Culture in the Gilded Age Hatting Industry." In S. Bruchey, *Small Business in America.* New York: Columbia University Press, 1981, pp. 352–65.

_____. "The Experience of American Apprenticeship." M.A. thesis, Columbia University, 1972.

Berthoff, Rowland T. *British Immigrants in American Labor.* Cambridge, Mass.: Harvard University Press, 1953.

Birdsall, William C. "The Problem of Structure in the Knights of Labor." *Industrial and Labor Relations Review* 6 (July 1953): 532–46.

Bishop, J. L. *A History of American Manufacturing.* 3 vols. New York: Augustus M. Kelly, 1966.

Braverman, Harry. *Labor and Monopoly Capital.* New York: Monthly Review Press, 1974.

Brigham, Walter T. *Baltimore Hats, Past and Present.* Baltimore: Press of I. Friedenwald, 1890.

Broadman, Anthony E. and Michael P. Weber. "Economic Growth and Occupational Mobility in Nineteenth Century America." *Journal of Social History* 11 (1977): 52–73.

Brody, David. "The Old Labor History and the New: In Search of an American Working Class." *Labor History* 20 (Winter 1979): 111–26.

————. *Steelworkers in America.* Cambridge, Mass.: Harvard University Press, 1960.

————. *Workers in Industrial America.* New York: Oxford University Press, 1980.

Buraway, Michael. "Terrains of Contest: Factory and State under Capitalism and Socialism." *Socialist Review* 11 (1981): 83–126.

Burgess, Keith. *The Origins of British Industrial Relations.* London: Croom Helms, 1975.

Cantor, Milton, ed. *American Working Class Culture.* Westport, Conn.: Greenwood Press, 1979.

Christie, Robert A. *Empire in Wood.* Ithaca: Cornell University Press, 1956.

Cincinnati Hatters Association. *Constitution* (1827).

Clawson, Dan. *Bureaucracy and the Labor Process.* New York: Monthly Review Press, 1980.

Cochran, Thomas C. *Social Change in Industrial Society.* London: Allen and Unwin, 1972.

Commons, John R. "American Shoemakers." *Quarterly Journal of Economics* 24 (November 1909): 39–84.

————, ed. *Documentary History of Industrial Society.* Cleveland, Ohio: A. H. Clark, 1910–11.

————, et al. *History of Labor in the United States.* 4 vols. New York: The Macmillan Company, 1918–1935.

Constitution of the Danbury Hatters (1810).

Crofut and Knapp Company. *The C & K Book.* New York: Crofut and Knapp Company, 1924.

Coxe, Tench. *A Statement of the Arts and Manufactures of the United States for the Year 1810.* Elmsford, N.Y.: Maxwell Reprint Company, 1970.

Coyne, Franklin E. *The Development of the Cooperage Industry.* Chicago: Lumber Buyers Publishing Company, 1940.

Cummings, Edward. "Industrial Arbitration in the United States." *Quarterly Journal of Economics* 9 (July 1895): 353–371.

Danbury Hat Finishers' Association, *Constitution and By-laws.* In Connecticut Bureau of Labor Statistics *Annual Report* (1890).

Danenberg, Elsie Nicholas. *The Romance of Norwalk.* New York: The States History Company, 1929.

Davis, Horace. *Shoes, the Workers and the Industry.* New York: International Publishers, 1940.

Dawley, Alan. *Class and Community.* Cambridge, Mass.: Harvard University Press, 1976.

Degler, Carl. *The Age of the Economic Revolution, 1876-1900*. Glencoe, Ill.: Scott, Foresman, 1967.

Destler, Chester M. *American Radicalism, 1865-1901*. New London: Connecticut College, 1946.

Douglas, Paul H. *American Apprenticeship and Industrial Education*. New York: Columbia University Press, 1921.

Edwards, Richard. *Contested Terrain*. New York: Basic Books, Inc., 1979.

Engels, Fredrick. *Conditions of the Working Class*. Oxford: Blackwell, 1958.

Ernst, Robert. *Immigrant Life in New York City*. New York: Kings Crown Press, 1949.

Feinstein, Estelle. *Stamford in the Gilded Age*. Stamford, Conn.: The Stamford Historical Society, 1973.

Fine, Sidney. *Laissez-faire and the General Welfare State*. Ann Arbor: University of Michigan Press, 1956.

Fisher, Leonard Everett. *The Hatters*. New York: Franklin Watts, 1965.

Folsom, Joseph Fulford, ed. *The Municipalities of Essex County, New Jersey*. New York: Lewis Historical Publishing Company, 1925.

Foster, John. *Class Struggle and the Industrial Revolution*. New York: St. Martin's Press, 1974.

Francis, William H. *History of the Hatting Trade in Danbury*. Danbury: H. & L. Osborne, 1860.

Galster, Augusta. *The Labor Movement in the Shoe Industry with Special Reference to Philadelphia*. New York: The Ronald Press Company, 1924.

Genin, John N. *An Illustrated History of the Hat*. New York: J. N. Genin, 1850.

George, M. Dorothy. *London Life in the Eighteenth Century*. New York: Alfred A. Knopf, 1926.

Gilding, Bob. *The Journeymen Coopers of East London*. History Workshops Pamphlets, no. 4. Oxford: Ruskin College, 1971.

Ginger, Ray. *Age of Excess*. New York: Macmillan, 1965.

Gitelman, Howard. *Workingmen of Waltham*. Baltimore: Johns Hopkins University Press, 1974.

Gladden, Washington. "Arbitration of Labor Disputes." *Journal of Social Science,* 21 (1886): 156.

Golab, Carolyn. "The Impact of the Industrial Experience on the Immigrant Family." Paper presented at Eleutherian Mills Historical Society, 2 November 1973.

Gordon, Michael. "The Labor Boycott in New York City." *Labor History* 16 (Spring 1975): 184-229.

Green, Charles F. *The Headwear Workers*. New York: Hat, Cap and Millinery Workers Union, 1944.

Green, James. *The World of the Worker.* New York: Hill and Wang, 1980.

Grob, Gerald. *Workers and Utopia.* Chicago: Quadrangle Books, 1969.

Groneman, Carol. "She Earns as a Child: She Pays as a Man." Paper presented at Eleutherian Mills Historical Society, 2 November 1973.

Gutman, Herbert. "Class, Struggle and Community Power in Nineteenth Century American Cities." In *The Age of Industrialism in America.* Edited by Frederick C. Jaher. New York: The Free Press, 1968.

_____. "Industrial Workers Struggle for Power." In *The Gilded Age.* Edited by H. Wayne Morgan. Syracuse: Syracuse University Press, 1970.

_____. "La politique ouvriere de la grande entreprise Americaine de l'age du clinquant: le cas de la Standard Oil Company." *Le Mouvement Social,* n. 102 (Jan.-Mar. 1978), pp. 67–100.

_____. *Work, Culture and Society in Industrializing America.* New York: Alfred A. Knopf, 1976.

Habakkuk, H. J. *American and British Technology in the Nineteenth Century.* Cambridge, Mass.: Harvard University Press, 1962.

Harrington, Michael. *Socialism.* New York: Saturday Review Press, 1972.

Harvey, Katherine. *The Best Dressed Miners.* Ithaca, N.Y.: Cornell University Press, 1969.

Hasse, Adelaide R. *Index of Economic Material in Documents of the States of the United States: New Jersey, 1789-1904.* New York: Kraus Reprint Corp., 1965.

Hawkins, William E. *Life of John Hawkins.* New York: Sheldon, Blakeman and Company, 1859.

Hazard, Blanche Evans. *The Origins of the Boot and Shoe Industry.* Cambridge, Mass.: Harvard University Press, 1921.

Hiller, E. T. "The Development of the System of Control of Convict Labor in the United States." *The Journal of the American Institute of Criminal Law and Criminology* 5 (1914–15): 241–68.

_____. "Labor Unionism and Convict Labor." *Journal of the American Institute of Criminal Law and Criminology* 5 (1914–15): 851–79.

Hobsbawm, Eric. "Labor History and Ideology." *Journal of Social History* 7 (1974): 371–81.

_____. *Labouring Men.* Garden City, N.Y.: Doubleday and Company, 1967.

Hollander, Jacob H. and George E. Barnett, eds. *Studies in American Trade Unionism.* New York: H. Holt and Company, 1906.

Holmes, Robert A. *From Hare to Hair.* New York: The Crofut and Knapp Company, 1930.

Howe, Ellic, ed. *The London Compositors.* London: The Bibliographical Society, 1947.

Hoxie, Robert F. *Scientific Management and Labor.* New York: D. Appleton, 1916.

———. *Trade Unionism in the United States.* New York: D. Appleton, 1917.

Hubbard, Ethelbert. *A Little Journey to the Home of John B. Stetson.* East Aurora, N.Y.: The Roycrofters, 1916.

Hugins, Walter A. *Jacksonian Democracy and the Working Class.* Stanford, Calif.: Stanford University Press, 1970.

Isserman, Maurice. "God Bless Our American Institutions: The Labor History of John R. Commons." *Labor History* 17 (Summer 1976): 309–28.

Jones, Gareth Stedman. "Working Class Culture and Working Class Politics in London, 1870–1900." *Journal of Social History* 7 (1974): 460–508.

Johnson, David N. *Sketches of Lynn.* Westport, Conn.: Greenwood Press, 1970.

Kealey, Gregory S. "The Honest Workingman and Workers' Control." *Labour/Le travailleur* 1 (1976): 32–68.

———. "The Orange Order in Toronto: Religious Riot and the Working Class." In *Essays in Canadian Working Class History.* Edited by Gregory Kealey and Peter Warrian. Toronto: McClelland and Stewart, 1976.

Kessler-Harris, Alice. *Out to Work: A History of Wage-Earning Women in the U.S.* New York: Oxford University Press, 1982.

Knight, Edward Henry. *Knight's American Mechanical Dictionary.* Boston: Houghton, Osgood and Company, 1876.

Kohn, Melvin. *Class and Conformity.* Homewood, Ill.: Dorsey Press, 1969.

Laslett, J. H. *Labor and the Left.* New York: Basic Books, 1970.

Laslett, J. H., and S. M. Lipset, eds. *Failure of a Dream.* New York: Anchor Press, 1974.

Laurie, Bruce, Theodore Herschberg, and George Alter. "Immigrants and Social History: The Philadelphia Experience." *Journal of Social History* 9 (Winter 1976): 219–67.

Lescohier, Don. "The Knights of St. Crispin 1867–1874." *Bulletin* of the University of Wisconsin, no. 355. Madison, Wisconsin, 1910.

Lichtenstein, Irwin. "Labor Unions and the Federal Anti-Trust Law," *Chicago Federation News,* 1 Nov. 1944, pp. 2, 3, 5, 8.

McCabe, David. *The Standard Rate in American Trade Unions.* Johns Hopkins University Studies in Historical and Political Science, Series 30, no. 2. Baltimore: Johns Hopkins University Press, 1912.

McKelvey, Blake. *American Prisons.* Montclair, N.J.: Smith, Patterson Publishing Company, 1968.

McLachlan, Harry, comp. *Making a Man's Hat.* New Brunswick, N.J.: Priv. print., 1932.

McLaughlin, Virginia Yans. "Patterns of Work and Family Organization." In *The American Family in Social-Historical Perspective.* Edited by Michael Gordon. New York: St. Martin's Press, 1978.

Mandel, Bernard. "Gompers and Business Unionism, 1873-90." *Business History Review* 28 (September 1954): 264-73.

Marglin, Stephen A. "What Do Bosses Do? The Origins and Functions of Hierarchy in Capitalist Production." *The Review of Radical Political Economics* 6 (Summer 1974): 60-113.

Merritt, Walter G. *History of the League for Industrial Rights.* New York: League for Industrial Rights, 1925.

_____. *Million Against One: A Conspiracy to Crush the Open Shop.* New York: American Anti-Boycott Association, 1904.

Miller, Raymond C. "The Dockworkers Subculture and Some Problems in Cross-Cultural and Cross-Time Generalizations." *Comparative Studies in Society and History* 11 (1969): 302-14.

Mills, David. *The Twentieth Century Hat Factory.* Danbury, Conn.: The Lee-McLachlan Company, 1910-11.

Montgomery, David. *Beyond Equality.* New York: Random House, 1967.

_____. "Gutman's Nineteenth-Century America." *Labor History* 19 (Summer 1978): 416-29.

_____. "Workers' Control of Machine Production in the Nineteenth Century." *Labor History* 17 (Fall 1976): 485-509.

_____. "To Study the People." *Labor History* 21 (Fall 1980): 485-512.

_____. *Workers' Control in America.* Cambridge, Mass.: Cambridge University Press, 1979.

Musson, A. E. *British Trade Unions, 1800-1875.* London: Macmillan, 1972.

Nadworny, Milton. *Scientific Management and the Unions, 1900-1932.* Cambridge, Mass.: Harvard University Press, 1955.

Nelson, Daniel. *Managers and Workers.* Madison, Wis.: University of Wisconsin Press, 1975.

Noble, David. *America by Design.* New York: Alfred A. Knopf, 1977.

_____. "Social Choice in Machine Design." In *Case Studies on the Labor Process.* Edited by Andrew Zimbalist. New York: Monthly Review Press, 1979, pp. 18-50.

Oram, Colonel R. B. *The Dockers' Tragedy.* London: Hutchinson and Company, 1970.

Parker and Tilton. *American Hat and Fur Exhibit.* New York: Parker and Tilton, 1883.

Perlman, Selig. *A Theory of the Labor Movement.* New York: The Macmillan Company, 1958.

_____ and Philip Taft. *History of Labor in the United States,* vol. 4. Commons et al. *History of Labor in the United States.* New York: Macmillan, 1918–35.

Perry, John S. *An Analysis of the Vote on Prison Contract Labor Polled November 6, 1883.* New York: John S. Perry, 1883.

_____. "Prison Labor." Albany, N.Y., 1882–83.

Pierson, David L. *History of the Oranges to 1921.* Vols. 2, 3, and 4. New York: Lewis Historical Publishing Company, 1922.

Pinkerton, Allan. *Strikers, Communists, Tramps and Detectives.* New York: G. W. Carleton and Company, 1882.

Price, Langson L. *Industrial Peace.* London: Macmillan, 1887.

Ramirez, Bruno. *When Workers Fight.* Westport, Conn.: Greenwood Press, 1978.

Robinson, Donald B. *Spotlight on a Union.* New York: Dial Press, 1948.

Rogin, Michael Paul. "Voluntarism: The Origins of a Political Doctrine." In *The American Labor Movement.* Edited by David Brody. New York: Harper and Row, 1971.

Rosenberg, Bernard and Harry Silverstein. "Patterns of Sexual Behavior." In *Sociology.* Edited by Joseph Bensman and Bernard Rosenberg. New York: Praeger Publishers, 1975, pp. 152–64.

Rules and Regulations of the Journeymen Hat Finishers of the City and County of New York (1845).

Rules and Regulations of the New York Hat Finishers Association, 29 March 1845.

Ryan, Daniel J. *Arbitration Between Capital and Labor.* Columbus, Ohio: A. H. Smythe, 1885.

Samuel, Raphael. "London: Workshop of the World," *History Workshop 3* (Spring 1977): 6–72.

Schorestene, Salvator. *Chappellerie.* Paris, 1894.

Scott, Joan. *The Glassworkers of Carmaux.* Cambridge, Mass.: Harvard University Press, 1974.

Sennett, Richard. *Families Against the City.* Cambridge, Mass.: Harvard University Press, 1970.

_____. "Middle Class Families and Urban Violence." In *The American Family in Social-Historical Perspective.* Edited by Michael Gordon. New York: St. Martin's Press, 1973, pp. 111–35.

Sennett, Richard and Jonathan Cobb. *The Hidden Injuries of Class.* New York: Alfred A. Knopf, 1973.

Sharp, I. G. *Industrial Conciliation and Arbitration in Great Britain.* London: George Allen and Unwin Ltd., 1950.

Shaw, William H. *History of Essex and Hudson Counties.* Philadelphia: Everts and Peck, 1884.

Shelton, Cynthia. "Textile Production and the Urban Laboring Class: The Case of Early Industrialization in Philadelphia, 1787–1837." Paper delivered at the Organization of American Historians' meeting, Philadelphia, 1 April 1982.

Soffer, Benson. "The Role of Union Foremen in the Evolution of the International Typographical Union." *Labor History* 2 (Winter 1971): 62–81.

_____. "A Theory of Trade Union Development." *Labor History* 1 (Spring 1960): 141–63.

Spedden, Ernest R. *The Trade Union Label.* Baltimore: Johns Hopkins University Press, 1910.

Spon, Edward. *Spon's Encyclopedia of the Industrial Arts, Manufactures and Commercial Products.* London: E. & F. Spon, 1879–82.

Sprague, William B. "Early American Manufacture of Felt Hats." *The Chronicle of the Early American Industry Association.* (Feb.-June 1934), Feb., pp. 1, 3; Mar., pp. 2, 3; Apr., p. 6; May, p. 6; June, pp. 4, 7.

Stewart, Ethelbert. "Documentary History of the Early Organizations of Printers." U.S. Bureau of Labor, *Bulletin* 61 (November 1905): 857–1034.

Stone, Katherine. "The Origins of Job Structures in the Steel Industry." *Radical America* 7 (Nov.-Dec. 1976): 61–97.

Strassman, W. Paul. *Risk and Technological Innovation.* Ithaca, N.Y.: Cornell University Press, 1959.

Sullivan, William A. *The Industrial Worker in Pennsylvania.* Harrisburg: Pennsylvania History and Museum Commission, 1955.

Taft, Philip. *The A.F. of L. in the Time of Gompers.* New York: Harper Brothers, 1957.

Taylor, George R. *The Transportation Revolution, 1815–1860.* New York: Holt, Rinehart and Winston, 1962.

Thernstrom, Stephan. *The Other Bostonians.* Cambridge, Mass.: Harvard University Press, 1973.

_____. *Poverty and Progress.* Cambridge, Mass.: Harvard University Press, 1964.

Thompson, Edward P. *The Making of the English Working Class.* New York: Random House, 1966.

_____. "Time, Work-Discipline and Industrial Capitalism." *Past and Present* 28 (Dec. 1967): 56–97.

Thomson, John. *A Treatise on Hat-making and Felting.* Philadelphia: H. C. Baird, 1868.

Tryon, Rolla M. *Household Manufactures in the United States, 1640–1860.* Chicago: University of Chicago Press, 1917.

Ulman, Lloyd. *The Rise of the National Union.* Cambridge, Mass.: Harvard University Press, 1955.

Union Association of Journeymen Hatters of the City of Cincinnati. *Constitution and By-Laws* (1827).

Unwin, George. *Industrial Organization in the Sixteenth and Seventeenth Centuries.* Oxford: Clarendon Press, 1904.

Updegraff, Robert R. *The Story of Two Famous Hatters.* New York: Knox Hat Company, 1926.

Ure, Andrew. *A Dictionary of Arts, Manufactures and Mines.* New York: D. Appleton and Company, 1850.

Vial, Jean. *La coutume chapeliere.* Paris: F. Loviton et Cie, 1941.

Walkowitz, Daniel. "Working-Class Women in the Gilded Age." *Labor History* 12 (Summer 1972): 464–89.

Ware, Norman. *The Industrial Worker 1840–1860.* Boston: Houghton Mifflin Company, 1924.

———. *The Labor Movement in the United States 1860–1895.* New York: D. Appleton and Company, 1929.

Webb, Sidney and Beatrice Webb. *History of Trade Unionism.* London: Longmans, Green and Company, 1894.

———. *Industrial Democracy.* London: Longmans, Green and Company, 1902.

Weed, Samuel R. *Norwalk After 250 Years.* South Norwalk: C. A. Freeman, 1902.

Weiss, Harry B. and Grace N. Weiss. *The Early Hatters of New Jersey.* Trenton, N.J.: New Jersey Agricultural Society, 1961.

Wheeler, J. D. *Criminal Law Cases,* vol. 1. New York: Gould and Banks, 1823–25.

Wickes, Stephen. *History of the Oranges in Essex County, New Jersey.* Orange: Ward and Tichenor, 1892.

Willis, Frederick. *101 Jubilee Road.* London: Phoenix House, 1948.

Wilson, Lynn W. *History of Fairfield County, Connecticut,* vol. 1. Chicago: S. J. Clarke Publishing Company, 1929.

Wolfe, F. E. *Admission to American Trade Unions.* Johns Hopkins University Studies in Historical and Political Science, Series 30, no. 3. Baltimore: Johns Hopkins University Press, 1912.

Wolman, Leo. *The Boycott in American Trade Unions.* Johns Hopkins University Studies in Historical and Political Science, Series 34, no. 1. Baltimore: Johns Hopkins University Press, 1916.

Woolley, Edward. *A Century of Hats.* Danbury: The Mallory Hat Company, 1923.

Wright, Carroll D. *Industrial Conciliation and Arbitration.* Boston: Rand Avery and Company, 1881.

Wright, Thomas. *The Romance of the Shoe.* London: C. J. Farncombe and Sons, 1922.

Yearly, Clifton K., Jr. *Britons in American Labor.* Baltimore: Johns Hopkins University Press, 1957.

Yellowitz, Irwin. *Industrialization and the American Labor Movement 1850–1900.* Port Washington, N.Y.: Kennikat Press, 1977.

Yeo, Aileen and Edward P. Thompson, comp. *The Unknown Mayhew.* New York: Pantheon Books, 1971.

GOVERNMENT REPORTS

U.S. Bureau of Labor Statistics. *Annual Report,* various years.

U.S. Census Office. *Census of Manufactures of the United States,* various years.

_____. *Ninth Census of the United States, 1870,* vol. 3.

_____. *Tenth Census of the United States, 1880,* vols. 2, 3.

_____. *Compendium of the Tenth Census, 1880.*

_____. *Tenth Census: Report on the Social Statistics of Cities (1880).*

_____. *Eleventh Census* (1890), vol. 2.

U.S. Commissioner of Labor. *Report on Production by Hand and Machine Methods* (1897).

_____. *Regulation and Restriction of Output* (1904).

U.S. House of Representatives. *Hearings Before the Special Committee of the House of Representatives to Investigate the Taylor and Other Systems of Shop Management.* 3 vols. 62nd Cong., 2nd sess. Washington, D.C.: Government Printing Office, 1912.

U.S. Treasury Department, Bureau of Statistics. *Annual Report on Commerce and Navigation* (1880).

Great Britain. Parliament. *Parliamentary Papers, 1824–25.* "Report of the Select Committee on Artisans and Machinery."

Connecticut Bureau of Labor. *Annual Report* (1890); (1891).

Connecticut Special Committee on Contract Convict Labor. *Report* (1880).

Massachusetts Bureau of Statistics of Labor. *Annual Report* (1876–77); (1880–81).

Massachusetts Commission on Prison Labor. *Report* (1880).

Committee on Prison Labor of the State of New Jersey. *Report* (1879).

New Jersey Bureau of Statistics of Labor and Industries. *Annual Report* (1881); (1883); (1884); (1886); (1888).

New Jersey, Office of Inspector of Labor and Children, *First Annual Report* (1883), pp. 5–7.

Eastern Penitentiary of Pennsylvania. *Annual Report* (1875).

MANUSCRIPT COLLECTIONS

Catholic University of America. Department of Archives and Manuscripts. Powderly Collection.
Harvard University. Baker Library. Dun's Field Agent Reports.
New York University. Wagner Archives. United Hatters Collection.

NEWSPAPERS

Brooklyn Citizen. 27 Nov. 1888.
Brooklyn Eagle. Nov. 1880; Nov.-Dec. 1888.
Danbury News. Dec. 1881–Mar. 1882; Dec. 1885–Jan. 1886; Oct. 1893– Apr. 1894.
John Swinton's Paper. Nov. 1884–Apr. 1886.
National Trades' Union. 17 Jan. 1835.
Newark Centinel of Freedom. 22 Feb. 1870.
Newark Daily Advertiser. Feb. 1870; Nov. 1885–Apr. 1886; Nov. 1889.
New York Times. 3 Aug. 1895.
New York Tribune. 7 Nov. 1845.
Orange Chronicle. Feb. 1870; Oct. 1885–June 1886; Nov. 1889.
Orange Journal. 23 Nov. 1889.
Norwalk Hour. Oct. 1884–Apr. 1885.
South Norwalk Sentinel. Oct. 1884–Apr. 1885.
Young America. 29 Nov. 1884; 19 July 1845.

MAGAZINES

Bradstreet's Review. 19 Dec. 1885.
Hat, Cap and Fur Trade Review (also titled *The American Hat Review*). Jan. 1878–Nov. 1895.
Hatter and Furrier (also titled *Clothier and Hatter* and *The American Hatter*). Jan. 1878–Nov. 1895.
Hatters' Gazette (London). 1 July 1881.

Index

Note on the Author

David Bensman has long been interested in American labor history, especially in the development of artisan craft culture. His previous publications include journal articles in *Commonweal, Dissent, Working Papers,* and *The Nation.* He is currently writing a book, with Roberta Lynch, about the decline of the steel industry in southeast Chicago, for McGraw-Hill. Dr. Bensman is a faculty member of the Graduate School of Education, Rutgers University.